UNEVEN LANDSCAPES OF VIOLENCE

Studies in Critical Social Sciences Book Series

Haymarket Books is proud to be working with Brill Academic Publishers (www.brill.nl) to republish the *Studies in Critical Social Sciences* book series in paperback editions. This peer-reviewed book series offers insights into our current reality by exploring the content and consequences of power relationships under capitalism, and by considering the spaces of opposition and resistance to these changes that have been defining our new age. Our full catalog of *SCSS* volumes can be viewed at https://www.haymarketbooks .org/series_collections/4-studies-in-critical-social-sciences.

Uneven Landscapes of Violence

of Violence

Geographies of Law and
Accumulation in Mexico

Hepzibah Muñoz Martínez

Haymarket Books
Chicago, IL

First published in 2020 by Brill Academic Publishers, The Netherlands
© 2020 Koninklijke Brill NV, Leiden, The Netherlands

Published in paperback in 2021 by
Haymarket Books
P.O. Box 180165
Chicago, IL 60618
773-583-7884
www.haymarketbooks.org

ISBN: 978-1-64259-614-4

Distributed to the trade in the US through Consortium Book Sales and
Distribution (www.cbsd.com) and internationally through Ingram Publisher
Services International (www.ingramcontent.com).

This book was published with the generous support of Lannan Foundation and
Wallace Action Fund.

Special discounts are available for bulk purchases by organizations and
institutions. Please call 773-583-7884 or email info@haymarketbooks.org for more
information.

Cover design by Jamie Kerry and Ragina Johnson.

Printed in the United States.

10 9 8 7 6 5 4 3 2 1

Library of Congress Cataloging-in-Publication data is available.

To Andreas and Elena

Contents

Acknowledgements

I am intellectually indebted to Cirila Quintero Ramírez and Bob Whitney for this book. My discussions with Cirila, my friend and colleague from El Colegio de la Frontera Norte campus Matamoros, helped me to explore the continuities and changes of physical and economic violence in Mexico, particularly in the northeastern region. My conversations with Bob Whitney from the University of New Brunswick were central to my analysis of neoliberalism in its relationship to state formation as a historical, contingent and agent-driven process. I want to thank Yolanda Morán Isais as well as relatives of the disappeared in Mexico that allowed me to do accompaniment work in their struggle to find their missing ones between 2012 and 2016. This experience forced me to explore alternative ways of understanding violence as a process that connects the quotidian and the personal to larger structures of economic and political power. I am grateful to Shana Yael Shubs for her remarkable copy-editing work which allowed me to convey complex information into comprehensive and accessible language for diverse audiences. Thanks to David Fasenfest for his support and interest in the manuscript.

I also acknowledge the assistance provided by El Colegio de la Frontera Norte and El Colegio de San Luis in the research and preparation of different phases of the manuscript. I want to recognize the work of Maricruz, Ambar, Irma and Paty on issues of social reproduction. Without their support, I would not have been able to write the first draft of the manuscript.

Thanks to my parents and brother for their help in the elaboration of the manuscript, particularly their insights into the everyday experiences of violence in Tamaulipas. Lastly, I also want to thank Niko for his continuous words of encouragement and constant support of my academic endeavors.

Maps and Images

Maps

Images

CHAPTER 1

Introduction: Violent State Formation and Accumulation in Mexico

Mexico is a country with war zones. The War on Drugs—set in motion by former Mexican president Felipe Calderon Hinojosa (2006–2012)—meant the country would be militarized to combat criminal groups in the context of a market economy and increasing competition among political parties for public office (Redacción, 2007a). The result of this state policy was an escalation of human rights abuses. According to the Inter-American Commission of Human Rights (2017), the official number of disappeared people between 2007 and 2015 was 26,798, and extrajudicial killings reached an alarming 102,696 between 2006 and 2012. By the late 2000s and early 2010s, levels of violence by state and non-state forces in contemporary Mexico reached levels comparable to war-torn countries such as Syria, Afghanistan and Iraq (IISS, 2017). These war zones might not be formally acknowledged as such by the United Nations and other international agencies. The Mexican government certainly does not admit to a full extent the country's armed conflict. But for millions of average Mexicans, their daily lives are dominated by the physical and psychological realities of militarized armed conflict, sharp restrictions as to where people can go safely, fear of kidnapping, arbitrary arrest, or the keen awareness that anyone can 'disappear' for multiple reasons, or, for no apparent reason at all. The Mexican economy is so intertwined with the participants in these war zones that the business, land and labor relations, and trade and commerce of entire regions are organized around the realities of armed conflict. And, Mexican local, regional, and national politics cannot be understood without considering the fact that Mexico is a country with war zones.

The purpose of this book is to examine the processes of state formation and capital accumulation in Mexico within the context of these *de facto* war zones. The book argues that *the nexus of violence, illegality and criminality is a defining characteristic of neoliberal state formation in Mexico after 2000*. The traditional repressive state apparatus and clientelistic arrangements prevailing between the 1940s until the late 1990s under one-party rule became incompatible with political party competition and the neoliberal requirements of dispossession and the control of social dissent that emerged after 2000. For that reason, the nexus of criminality, illegality and violence became an integral aspect of neoliberal state formation in Mexico because it *is through this interplay of criminality, illegality and violence that dispossession takes place.* As the state could not dispossess people based on the older 'rules' of the political game, the rise of violence by repressive forces that are not (yet) part of the state became a form of proxy governance in order to maintain state power and facilitate accumulation. In the Mexican case, dispossesion after 2000 took the form of forced displacement, extorsion and private appropriation of public funds by criminal groups, in collaboration through direct participation or acquiescence with state authorities, while disappearances and the latent threat of violence in cities became strategies of social control. Parallel to the rise of criminality in its connection with violence and illegality, advocates of neoliberalism within and outside the state emphasized the importance of the rule of law in the neoliberal agenda from the late 1990s onwards. This emphasis *on the rule of law to protect private property and contracts reshaped the boundaries between legality and illegality, further disguising the illegal, criminal and violent origins of economic gain and providing the latter with legitimacy behind an appearance of lawfulness.* Dispossession taking place in the country illegally and violently therefore was transformed into legal economic activity through integration into global markets and the application of the neoliberal version of the rule of law.

In the book, I refer to neoliberalism as a historical phase of capitalism as well as a political class-based project characterized by the intensification of market and financial imperatives, labor discipline, and the commodification of all realms of social life for profit through state power and policy (Harvey, 2007). My focus here on everyday forms of state formation shows how the state, as the institutional materiality of the condensation of social forces, is produced and reproduced through quotidian practices of domination and shaped by conflicts and contradictions among social actors, diverse state agencies, branches of power, and concrete places (Poulantzas, 1974).

The book therefore explores the criminal, illegal and violent aspects of neoliberal state formation in Mexico through an examination of previous forms of local violence, particularly the interaction of illegality, legality and criminality in social arrangements that set compromises between subordinate and dominant social forces through local leaders under one-party ruling. This analysis therefore does not focus on the novelty of violence in Mexico after the 2000s but rather on the transformation of violence as a reflection of a larger restructuring of state and societal relations. Likewise, the book studies local and national processes of violence, criminality and illegality in connection to the global economy through its analysis of money laundering and urban development. Money laundering shows how larger and local jurisdictions in other countries allow for the transformation of illegal into legal activities, assisting global companies and the neoliberal agenda in Mexico. A focus on urban development shows how local elites, operating within the boundaries of legality and illegality, are deeply influential in urban governance in Mexico. In the process, these local elites have also helped global companies, either by opening market spaces or channeling financial proceeds from money laundering in the construction sector to global financial institutions.

The book's argument contrasts with existing analyses of Mexico's violence. The literature either depicts violence in Mexico as a result of state weakness, a consequence of the end of the control of the one-party rule over criminal groups, a deviation from proper market functioning or the outcome of neoliberalism as the latter negative effects drives marginalized populations to join criminal groups. Mainstream analyses that explain Mexico's violence as the result of state frailty overlook the collaboration between state officials and non-state armed groups (Bailey, 2014; Grayson, 2010; Lee et al., 2019). Also, the literature considers the rise in criminal violence and physical insecurity as new phenomena resulting from the end of the domination of one-party rule in the year 2000, namely *pax narcotica* (Astorga, 2007; Alonso Aranda 2015). Such view ignores that violence and illegality has continuously been part of state formation in Mexico. The challenge is to understand this transformation as the result of deeper societal changes. Studies on money laundering in Mexico consider corruption, illegality and violence as a deviation of the market economy (Buscaglia, 2013; Naim, 2006). This in turn obscures the ways in which the illegal aspects of neoliberal state formation and accumulation in Mexico in fact assist the market economy. Perspectives that consider the rise of violence as the outcome of poverty under neoliberalism potentially criminalize the poor (Watt and Zepeda, 2013), overlooking how neoliberalism has in fact privileged few powerful actors that help perpetuate violence, illegality, criminality and inequality in Mexico.

Indeed, critical analyses focus on how the rise of violence has been beneficial to state authorities and large companies and acknowledge the relationship between state officials and criminal groups (Paley, 2014; Correa-Cabrera, 2017). Yet, these perspectives assume that the categories of legality and illegality are clearly defined, when in fact they are not. The works do not recognize that law and lawlessness are constantly shifting categories and a site of contention among the various political and economic groups at play. This is an important oversight because definitions of legal order and lawlessness shape the ability of powerful economic and political actors to circumvent the law and legalize economic and physical coercion, setting the conditions for increasing violence in Mexico.

This book fills these gaps in the literature by exploring the understudied northeastern Mexico-U.S. border to understand how the shifting categories of legality and illegality are connected to local hierarchies of economic and political power, shaping the national politics of violence and the economy in Mexico. Through an approach to social space as a result of process of social interactions, the book also seeks to highlight how physical violence relies on everyday practices of state power in concrete local spaces, which are shaped by the dynamics of law, disorder and accumulation at the local, national and global level. Legal and social interactions that constitute and shape the state have a concrete spatial local character in everyday life, which impact rules of governing at larger political scales and vice versa.

The book goes beyond a limited focus on the political interaction of politicians and organized crime to examine the connections between economics, politics and local everyday practices involving multiple sets of social forces, including criminal groups, local and national politicians, the US government, international investors and labor unions and city dwellers. In this way, I show how everyday practices of power and higher-level political and economic configurations of violence mutually shape and reproduce one another. The book does not take the categories of legality and illegality for granted, but rather seeks to understand how these are produced and reproduced through social practices, including institutions and legal mechanisms, to sustain local and national state power and hierarchies of economic exclusion. Understanding legality and illegality as constructed in specific social and historical contexts is relevant for analyzing how power relations in Mexican society are reflected in the law as well as how it has enabled the use of political office for private purposes. This book also sheds light on the way people with different social-economic and political positions experience and produce concrete social spaces, and how this is conditioned by larger configurations of state and non-state violence and economic exclusion. Such an approach allows us to understand the nexus of criminality, illegality and violence not as the outcome of the absence of the state but rather as part of the re-composition of state power to exert political control to maintain neoliberal institutions and insulate the state from popular pressures.

1   Locating Criminality, Illegality, and Violence in Mexico

Processes of neoliberal state formation in Mexico need to be understood in relation to the domination of one political party and its connection to the development of national capitalism, coercion and criminality in the post-revolutionary period after 1929. The emergence of a single government party, the Institutional Revolutionary Party (Partido Revolucionario Institucional or PRI), concretized the centralization of national political power as well as the compromise reached among local bosses, some fractions of the national capitalist class and the labor and peasant movement, particularly after the 1940s. This involved the PRI's coordination of unions and peasants' organizations through its union leaders. These leaders maintained their power as long as they complied with the PRI's needs of repression and consent from Mexico's labor and peasant movement. At the same time, the PRI accommodated local forms of resistance through the party, negotiating power regionally across Mexico (Joseph and Buchenau, 2013).

The later points to the role of coercion in maintaining state power. Compliance with the ruling power of the PRI involved state violence through the military and the police as well as non-state violence, mainly through the employment of private armed forces by local bosses or *caciques* (Knight and Pansters, 2005; Davis, 2012). Illegality has also been part of Mexico's politics prior to 2000 as social and political actors navigated between legal institutions and illegal practices through repression, patronage, and clientelism (Pansters, 2018). Under the one-party rule, economic development was also tied to illegality and criminality. Indeed, illegal practices were employed by different economic and political actors to pave the way for national capitalist development, and criminal activities often were part of the creation of legal economic enterprises (Knight and Pansters, 2005; see also Chapter 2). Yet, the interaction between illegality, criminality and economic growth did not necessarily extend beyond the national economy, and the continuous presence of criminal economic activity was not central to the development of national capitalism in Mexico (see Chapter 2).

Mechanisms of political domination and consensus were therefore tied to the development of capitalism within Mexico's national borders and the reproduction of a domestic capitalist class. The emergence of large domestic holding groups was premised on state policy that supported production for the domestic market and expanding manufacturing capacity to replace imports through a range of trade and investment restrictions, government subsidies, labor regulations and planned domestic investment. Yet, such policies continued to be based on exploitative productive, political, and social relations that disproportionately benefited domestic capital, even as subordinate social forces such as the peasantry and organized labor made some relative distributional gains (Marois, 2012). This did not occur in isolation from world markets. Rather, international trade occurred and the domestic capitalist class formed ties with US and European banking syndicates (White, 1992). Yet, state authorities constrained the mobility of financial assets abroad, deeming domestic capital controls necessary for national developmental processes while welcoming some foreign capital under certain restrictions (Solís, 1997: 19).

The unfolding of a neoliberal strategy of accumulation that began in the 1980s initiated radical export-oriented structural adjustment and privatization programs and imposed tax and public service price increases on peasants, workers, and the middle classes in order to help pay for foreign public debts (Correa, 2006). At the same time, neoliberalism reconfigured the locally-embedded arrangements that allowed for the political and social tolerance of criminality, illegality and violence (Pansters, 2018). It is in this historical background that the transformation of violence, criminality and illegality needs to be located in the process of state formation in Mexico.

The book focuses on the case study of the northeastern Mexican state of Tamaulipas, part of the understudied northeastern U.S.-Mexico border, for four reasons (see Map 1). First, the northeastern Mexican state of Tamaulipas has struggled with heightened violence since 2010. Examples of this local violence include 47 clandestine mass graves found in the municipality of San Fernando in Tamaulipas between 2010 and 2011. The victims in these graves mostly came from the hijackings of passenger buses by the Los Zetas drug cartel on Mexican Federal Highway 101, which is the highway that connects Mexico City with the eastern Texan border (Red de Periodistas de a Pie, 2015). By 2014, Tamaulipas was the location of 30 percent of all kidnappings in Mexico (SESNSP, 2015). Between 2009 and 2014, Tamaulipas had one of the highest rates of internally displaced people. In 2009, 41,000 residents of Tamaulipas moved to a different location due to violence and insecurity (INEGI, 2014), and in 2014, there were 281,400 internally displaced people. Between 2010 and 2013, 93 percent of crimes were not denounced, surpassing the national rate of unreported crime (INEGI, 2013, 12). These harrowing statistics serve to illustrate the local specificity of violence, which is interwoven with other dynamics of physical insecurity (present both in Tamaulipas and elsewhere in the country) and shapes national politics, particularly after the War on Drugs was launched in 2006.

Second, starting in the 1980s, Tamaulipas became a model for free trade and markets in the country because of its proximity to the U.S., its export-processing zones (or maquiladoras) based on cheap labor, its agribusinesses, and its large petrochemical industry. Tamaulipas has more border crossings with the U.S. than any other state in Mexico, as well as two international ports in the Gulf of Mexico (Altamira and Tampico). The high levels of economic growth and foreign investment at the local level were central to the expansion of the free market economy as a development model, particularly maquiladoras, elsewhere in the country.

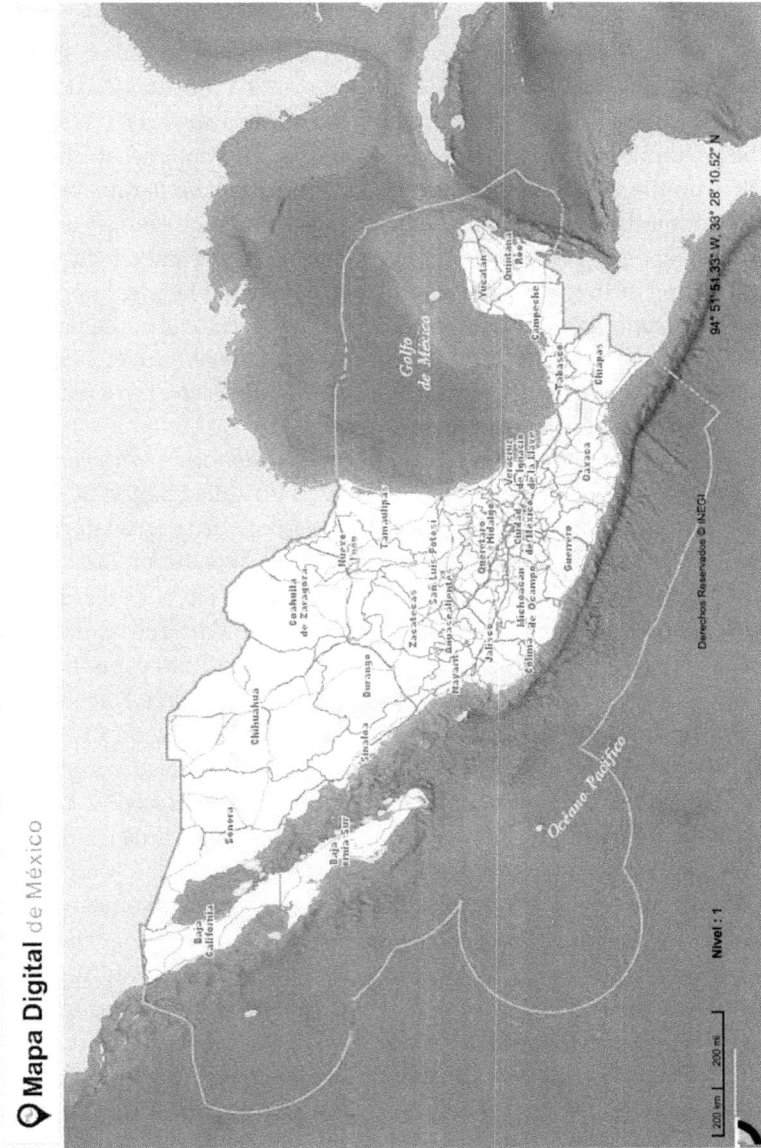

Mapa Digital de México

200 km | 200 mi | Nivel : 1

94° 5'51.33" W, 33° 28' 10.52" N

Derechos Reservados © INEGI

MAP 1   Map of Mexico and location of the state of Tamaulipas.

SOURCE: NATIONAL INSTITUTE OF STATISTICS AND GEOGRAPHY (INEGI) 2019, AGUASCALIENTES, MEXICO

Third, Tamaulipas was one of the few states where the Institutional Revolutionary Party (PRI) remained in power after the 2000 presidential elections. This year marked the decline of the PRI's 70-year control of the national Executive branch after the right-wing National Action Party (Partido Accion Nacional or PAN) won the presidential elections. For some analysts, this historical juncture signaled the beginning of Mexico's democratic transition (Castañeda, 2001; Schedler, 2005). Counter to this national tendency, however, the PRI retained the governorship in the state of Tamaulipas until 2016, when the PAN eventually won the elections for governor. During this same period, the PAN presidential administrations of Vicente Fox (2000–2006) and Felipe Calderón (2006–2012) deepened the development model based on market discipline and characterized by low wages, cheap exports, and favorable investment conditions for large companies. The implementation of this model at the national level relied heavily on the local power of the PRI in Tamaulipas to suppress, through coercion and cooptation, any form of dissent arising from disagreement with the economic model in this key region.

Fourth, innovations in the organization of non-state forms of violence by criminal groups emerged in Tamaulipas during the so-called period of democratic transition of the early 2000s. Since the 1940s, the drug cartel *Cartel del Golfo* (Gulf Cartel) had consolidated its position in the state of Tamaulipas transporting drugs from Colombia to the United States (Flores Pérez, 2014a). As the power of the Colombia cartels decreased, the Gulf Cartel created a more extensive drug trafficking network. By 1999, this cartel had hired members of the Mexican military who had quit the country's Special Mobile Force Group (Grupos Aeromóviles de Fuerzas Especiales, GAFES). This group of former military officers was known as Los Zetas and became the armed wing of the Gulf Cartel. In 2010, Los Zetas split from the Gulf Cartel, intensifying the violent struggle for control of the Tamaulipas markets, including drug trafficking, human trafficking, extortion, and kidnapping. The effects of the reorganization of violence were felt elsewhere in the country as Los Zetas expanded its operations and other drug cartels and gangs replicated its modus operandi (Grayson, 2014). The incarceration of the leaders of Los Zetas and the Gulf Cartel further fragmented these organizations into 20 gangs in the state of Tamaulipas (Nacar, 2015). Throughout this book, I refer to these cartels and gangs as criminal groups, as they have diversified their activities beyond drug trafficking to include financial fraud, money laundering, extortions, human trafficking, kidnapping, and people smuggling, among other criminal operations (Buscaglia, 2013, 26). It is important to emphasize that these criminal groups continue to operate through planned actions involving diverse actors and hierarchies, which differs from isolated and individual criminal acts

(Serrano, 2012: 143; Bailey, 2014: 87). The coordination involved in these criminal groups is key in order to understand their relationship to parallel forms of governance that in fact support the state. While there are numerous case studies on northwestern Mexico, little research has thoroughly examined the northeastern Mexico-U.S. border, where Tamaulipas is located, particularly with respect to its historical and ongoing importance in the reorganization of criminal and political violence and the rearrangement of economic relations in the country.

This book focuses on the period between 2000 and 2016 because the transformations in the economic model and the political and criminal reconfigurations mentioned above in the case study took place during this time span. This allows us to understand the changes and continuities of physical, political, criminal, and economic violence in Mexico's neoliberal state formation. The case study of Tamaulipas is therefore pivotal to addressing questions regarding the relationship between Mexico's state formation, violence and the politics of illegality and legality, the impact of socio-political and economic changes on forms of state and non-state violence, and the politics of everyday life that sustain state power and a national development model based on market discipline.

2   Violence, Criminal Groups, and the State

Mainstream analyses depict Mexico's situation of violence as if it were a new phenomenon that is the result of state institutional weakness. These analyses tend to view widespread violence and organized crime in a social, historical, and economic vacuum. Through this lens, the Mexican state is regarded as an autonomous entity, independent from organized crime, struggling to fight non-state criminal groups through legitimate state-sponsored militarization. Such interpretations have been widely held by different presidential administrations in Mexico since the mid-1990s, as well as by American security-related agencies and think tanks (Bailey, 2014: 117–118; Presidencia de la República, 2014; Lee et al., 2019; Friedman, 2008; U.S. Congress Senate Caucus on International Narcotics Control, 2010). For instance, Mexico's President Felipe Calderón (2006–2012) from the PAN party held this view when the the assassination of the PRI candidate for the gubernatorial elections in Tamaulipas ocurred in 2010. The former responded immediately to the attack: "we cannot allow crime to impose its will and its perverse rules on the decision of citizens and in elections" (Tuckman, 2010). The fact that this political assassination took place in this border state also troubled American state authorities, as they turned this political murder into an example of the increasing threat drug cartels pose to America's national security (Beittel, 2011: 1). This high-profile political assassination was thus portrayed even by Mexican state authorities themselves as a reflection of a weakening state, requiring militarization in order to maintain the Mexican state's monopoly over violence. In 2011, U.S. representatives demanded former Secretary of State Hillary Clinton's further assistance to Mexico's War on Drugs through the funding of intelligence, training, and technical assistance programs to "make sure Mexico does not become a failed state and yet another haven for terrorists" (Committee on Homeland Security, 2011). From this point of view, Mexico's violence originated from the inability of the state to maintain its monopoly over violence, therefore requiring militarization in order to control criminality and regain its monopoly over violence.

Cases of collaboration between governors and organized crime, forced disappearances, extra-judicial killings, and the control of organized crime over municipalities are seen as signs of a weak or failed state based on the assumption that state and civil society are separate entities, autonomous from one another. This separation between the state and civil society induces a reification of state power claiming a monopoly on the legitimate use of physical force within a given territory, while equating civil society with private interests (Bieler and Morton, 2006: 158). Criminal groups are thus depicted as being in opposition to the state, which ignores the existence of plural regulatory authorities and the varied connections between violence, everyday state practices and non-state actors. When the co-existence and collaboration between organized crime and state authorities is acknowledged, it is seen as the corrupting influence of drug cartels on passive state authorities (Grayson, 2010). This continuous reification of the state as holding a legitimate monopoly over violence is based on a European historical model that fails to capture the past and present processes of state formation in Latin America, which are intrinsically violent and reveal a constant articulation and re-articulation with para-state armed forces (Oszlak, 1981).

Other academic analyses, in contrast to those studies focused on Mexico as a failed or weak state, problematize assumptions regarding the passivity of the Mexican state vis-à-vis organized crime. For instance, Luis Astorga (2003, 2005, 2007) suggests that through the PRI, the Mexican state actively managed the relationship between politicians and members of criminal groups as well as the interactions among drug cartels throughout the one-party authoritarian regime that lasted more than 70 years (see also Aguilera and Castañeda, 2009). Other studies have drawn from these insights to show how this connection between the Mexican state and criminal groups in the context of electoral liberalization changed state-society relations between the 1980s and 2000s. In these analyses, the increasing poverty caused by economic liberalization as well as the Executive's lack of control over criminal groups due to the rise of opposition parties set the conditions for the increasing violence in the country and the failure of policies aimed at the prohibition of drugs (Alonso Aranda, 2015; Bailey, 2014; Grayson, 2010; Velasco, 2005). These analyses demonstrate how the militarization strategy is misguided because it leaves the relationship between political power, organized crime, and impunity intact. However, these same analyses often depict the current situation as a sudden rise of violence linked to illegality and criminality that did not exist before due to the strength of the state during the PRI's control of the presidency. In this way, these analyses underestimate coercion in the process of state-making in Mexico by over-emphasizing the control of the PRI. This control, in turn, has been understood to characterize Mexican exceptionalism in relation to the violence and repression in other places in Latin America since the 1920s (Pansters, 2012, 8, 32). Mexican exceptionalism refers to the role of the PRI in controlling politics and society, including drug-trafficking networks, without the same extreme use of force at the national level as that seen in the military dictatorships in South America and Central America (Hellman, 1994, 125-26). Under this view, the importance of the transfer of violence to local spaces to sustain Mexico's exceptionalism under the PRI is overlooked (Dominguez Ruvalcaba, 2015: 8; Knight, 1999: 107).

While the studies mentioned above focus on the politics of crime, particularly the interactions between state and non-state actors and the way these shape the legal system, policy-making, and the strategies of criminal groups, it remains important to locate these political interactions as part of the global and national economic conditions that shape these relations (Andreas and Wallman, 2009). Along these lines, political economic analyses of violence in Mexico and Latin America examine the social determinants of crime, particularly the socio-economic impact of the state withdrawal from social policy after the 1980s, during the implementation of the development model based on market discipline (Watt and Zepeda, 2013). Political economy studies also address how the global mobility of money and goods facilitates money laundering, increasing the sources of profit of criminal groups and helping them sustain funding to purchase weapons and bribe public officials. More specifically, the mobility of money and goods facilitates illegal transactions, increasing the economic power of criminal groups and turning them into transnational enterprises. While these criminal activities are facilitated by globalization, they are, at the same time, considered to be instances of corruption in Mexico and, hence, illegal (Buscaglia, 2013; Fabre, 2003; Naim, 2006; Saviano, 2013; Wainwright, 2016). Such analyses thus portray the combination of violence, criminality and illegal economic activities as detrimental to the efficient functioning of the economy as well as to the state's ability to both implement economic policy in response to neutral market forces and reproduce its monopoly over violence. This perspective fails to account for the ways in which state officials are central to the organization of formal and criminal economic activities alike, which both contribute to the creation of proxy governance mechanisms through criminal groups that enhance the market economy (Nuijten, 2003: 202).

In order to fill this gap in the literature, recent studies on Mexico's political economy of violence explore how this form of state acquiescence has become a governance mechanism to favor large national and global companies seeking to repress social discontent against private investment (Correa-Cabrera, 2017; Cruz, 2016; Desmond Arias and Goldstein, 2010; Galindo, 2005; Müller, 2016; Paley, 2014; Solís González, 2013). This literature offers important insights into the ways in which the criminal activities have become increasingly central—not just an anomaly—in national economies and the global mobility of money. Similarly, it shows how state tolerance and indifference towards violence can in fact become an effective governance mechanism to eliminate social discontent and facilitate private investment. These accounts of the politics and economics of violence in Mexico also acknowledge the role of the American economy and U.S. state policy in shaping the violence beleaguering its southern neighbor during the 1990s and the 2000s. The influence of the U.S. is particularly evident through its decisive role as the main market for drugs, its role in the militarization of the border, and the power of the arms industry and banks in the U.S. that profit from violence and money laundering in Mexico (Alfredo, 2014). This perspective emphasizes the dominance of the American state in geopolitical terms, namely the ability of the U.S. to exert control over Mexico's society and state policies via military, political, and economic influence. Such a view risks portraying the Mexican state as a passive agent responding to external stimuli, overlooking the ways in which peripheral states such as Mexico co-participate in the constitution of larger structures of power in the United States and the global economy.

Localized political economic processes are also central to understanding how economic liberalization and historical everyday practices of state formation coalesce with violent criminality at the local and national levels. There is a burgeoning literature on the everyday state practices in Mexico that become concrete in particular locations, informing the strategies and influencing the organization of criminal groups and their relations with state authorities (Bowden, 2010; Correa-Cabrera, 2017; Coyle, 2001; Duncan, 2013; Durán Martínez, 2018; Jones, 2016; Maldonado, 2010). This has led to the existence of multiple regulatory authorities with differences based on specific local influences.

This also sets the conditions for economic exploitation and state and non-state violence at the local and national levels, rendering particular populations vulnerable based on race, ethnicity, class, and gender. Gender-based vulnerability is demonstrated in the insightful contributions of gender studies on femicides in El Paso del Norte Region, particularly their focus on the intersection between violence, state power, economic restructuring, and everyday life in the killing of women (Monárrez Fragoso, 2009, 2010; Monárrez Fragoso and Bejarano, 2010; Rodríguez et al., 2007; Ruiz Marrujo, 2009; Staudt, 2009; Staudt and Robles Ortega, 2010). Such perspectives offer an examination of the historical continuity of different forms of violence and the specific ways in which legal and illegal economies connect to one another. Likewise, critical border studies focus on the relationship between space, the law, and processes of state formation in the U.S.-Mexico border regions. These analyses show how statecraft is shaped by the delimitation of border spaces produced by legal practices determining who can cross and who cannot (Alvarez, 1995, 2012; Auchter, 2013, Braticevic et al., 2017; Salter, 2006).

Most studies on the local specificity of violence in Mexico's northern border focus on the state of Chihuahua and Baja California, particularly through the lens of Ciudad Juarez and Tijuana. There are few academic studies on the politics of violence in Tamaulipas. The ones that do exist emphasize the relevance of local political elites and criminal groups in this part of Mexico. These studies focus on the particular ways in which each criminal group operates and identify members of political elites involved in criminal activities (Correa-Cabrera, 2014; Flores Pérez 2014a, 2014b; Padgett, 2016). Other analyses of Tamaulipas offer descriptive data on the levels of criminality in this state, examine the consequences of the politics of violence in Tamaulipas on vulnerable populations (such as youth and undocumented immigrants), and describe the ways in which violence has become normalized in everyday life (Arrona Palacios et al., 2011; Cantú Rivera et al., 2014; De la O and Flores, 2012; Hernández, 2017; López León, 2014; Sánchez Munguía, 2014; Zárate Ruiz, 2014).

The scarcity of academic studies on this Mexican region is largely due to the hostile political environment, which makes it difficult and dangerous to access information. Self-censorship among journalists and a lack of critical nongovernmental organizations sets Tamaulipas apart from other Mexican states with high levels of violence. For instance, in 2013, the UN Regional Office on Drugs and Crime recognized that it did not work in this state because of the lack of guarantees for the physical safety of its employees. The same is true for Amnesty International and Human Rights Watch, which in that same year expressed the difficulties in conducting research and accompaniment work in Tamaulipas, "not only because of the lack of protection of state authorities and the violence exerted by organized crime but also because of the sinister connection between the two" (De Llano, 2013). Despite these staggering barriers—and, perhaps, because of them—ongoing academic analyses of Tamaulipas and its unique characteristics that make it such an important case study are crucial for exploring this region's influence in the northern border and understanding the national politics of violence.

This book draws on the insights of the aforementioned studies, particularly their emphasis on the relationship between state and criminal groups in generating violence and the importance of the economic context in shaping inequalities that render people more vulnerable to violence. The book also acknowledges the insights in the literature on criminal violence as a form of state governance that reproduces political and economic power relations and on how these power relations become concrete in space and reflect themselves in the law. Insights related to the role of quotidian practices in sustaining unequal social relations of class, local and national political authoritarianism, and market discipline are also woven throughout the book. At the same time, however, the book departs from the analyses discussed above in two ways. First, it does not take for granted the line between legality and illegality, but rather examines the power relations behind the construction of these categories and the fetishism of the law. Jean Comaroff and John Comaroff (2006: 31-33) see the fetishism of the law as a belief in the power of the law without considering the social relations that constitute it. Indeed, critical border studies do address the power relations behind legality and illegality, but their analyses are confined to the space of the border, whereas this book explores the connections between local and national levels of the state in their articulation to the inter-state system and global accumulation. I refer to the local level of the state as the socio-political processes occurring within the jurisdiction of the state government rather than municipalities. The book uses the term politics of (il)legality when addressing the ways in which law-making and the categories of legality and illegality are connected to hierarchies of power. Privileged groups can employ the law to exert coercion while legitimizing authoritarian state practices. The book also explores how the construction of these categories is linked to processes of state formation and territoriality as well as to capitalist uneven development.

Second, the book looks at the ways in which legal and illegal economic activities—and the physical violence by state and non-state forces underpinning the latter—assist in the reproduction of capitalism and favor the interests of large companies. It shows the historical specificity and spatiality of the political and economic relations sustaining violence in Mexico before and after the year 2000, which marks the rise of the PAN after more than 70 years of PRI control over the Executive branch. This examination pays particular attention to changes in political and economic struggles within the state in relation to Mexico's uneven capitalist development and the implementation of neoliberalism in the country throughout the 1980s and 1990s.

By unpacking the concepts of legality and illegality through a geographical and political economy approach, *the book contends that criminality, illegality and violence are integral aspects of neoliberal state formation in Mexico after 2000. The rise of violence by repressive forces that are not offically (yet) part of the state became a form of proxy governance in order to maintain state power and promote dispossession in the form of forced displacement, extorsion and private appropriation of public funds. At the same time, the centrality of the legal protection of private property and contracts in Mexico's neoliberal agenda further concealed the illegal, criminal, violent origins of dispossession and financial gain. Dispossession taking place in large parts of the country illegally and violently turned into legal economic activity through market integration and the implementation of the neoliberal rule of law.*

Rather than identifying the names of economic and political elites involved with organized crime, this book focuses on the political and social conditions that have facilitated the ongoing insecurity and disempowerment of people in Mexico, particularly through local practices of political, physical, and economic coercion. It also explores the ways in which processes of state formation extend beyond one national space to influence state formation elsewhere. While the focus of the book is not how state formation and uneven development in Mexico influence the United States, it does highlight some aspects of these processes in relation to these two nation-states. The purpose is to stress the importance of understanding state-making and uneven development as connected hierarchical and overlapping socio-economic, spatial, and political arrangements. The book also emphasizes the transformation of violence in Mexico rather than its novelty, particularly the changes in the geography of violence, thereby offering an understanding of current violence in Tamaulipas as an extension of previous patterns of state violence and economic and political exclusion in everyday life.

3   Violent Spatialities of State Formation and Uneven Development

This book draws on geographical political economy to understand the interaction between the historical contingency of state territoriality and capital accumulation and the way they intertwine and overlap at different geographical scales. Such an approach conceives space as a medium and outcome of social relations rather than as a fixed container of social interactions (Lefebvre, 2001). This perspective offers an understanding of the ways in which state practices of domination, the resulting politics of (il)legality, as well as processes of uneven capitalist development and its mechanisms of exclusion are produced and reproduced in concrete spaces in everyday life. Geographical political economy focuses on how capital accumulation produces particular spatial configurations that influence the unequal distribution of wealth and power, which is shaped by pre-existing historical social relations (Sheppard, 2011).

By capital accumulation, I refer to the social and economic processes that turn labor and nature into commodities to be sold on the market and exploited for profit. This transformation takes various material forms (finance, money, production activities, and commodities) through different moments (production, circulation, realization) (Harvey, 2010). Capital accumulation also requires producers to be divorced from their means of social subsistence to turn people and nature into commodities that can be sold. This involves expropriation by force, namely primitive accumulation (Marx, 1976: 874). Primitive accumulation does not necessarily have to predate capital accumulation; rather, it is an ongoing process of expropriation that is integral to capitalist uneven development (Mandel, 1975; Harvey, 2005).

Capital accumulation involves the existence of a class that possesses nothing but the ability to work under conditions of competition. As such, social class is a social relationship that places historical beings into situations of control over the appropriation of surplus that workers produce with their labor power, which workers must sell in order to survive (Foster, 1990, 80–81). Yet, social class is not only about economic relations of production, but also positions in the political struggle (Martin, 2008, 17-18). As will be discussed in Chapter 2, an example of this is the role of union leaderships affiliated to the dominant party and classes, which could be considered part of the ruling class due to its political power as well as its influence in shaping economic relations to assist accumulation in Mexico.

Geographical political economy understands the process of neoliberalization as a historically variegated geographical process in which global parameters of market discipline are domesticated nationally according to pre-existing institutions and balances of social forces (Brenner et al., 2010). And the resulting conflicts take on spatial expressions (particularly in the nation-state) through the specific strategies of social actors that mediate institutions and political conflict inside and outside the state (Harvey, 1999: 149, 404; Albo, 2005: 68). At the same time, the state plays an important role in the production of capitalist territorial organization. It implements spatial strategies to divide, territorialize, and hierarchize social relations at—and across—different geographical scales. This is done through the state's ability to allocate tax revenues, mobilize financing based on credit for infrastructure, and control different spatial configurations through state legal regulations (Brenner, 1998: 465). Yet, the state is not considered a monolithic entity with power of its own but rather the political expression of the existing balance of forces in a given society (Poulantzas, 1974: 25). State territoriality therefore expresses the appropriation, experience, and representation of space by different classes through the nation-state to reproduce or hinder capital accumulation and particular political agendas (Brenner and Elden, 2009). Following this interpretation of the state, the book focuses on how ruling is attained through practices of state formation (Corrigan, 1994: xvii). These practices involve concrete social processes, routines, and institutions that organize people's everyday lives and give a materiality to the state, producing concrete political and economic effects (Joseph and Nugent, 1994: 20; Arexaga, 2000: 52–53).

Processes of state formation are also connected to uneven capitalist development. Unlike European states, the consolidation of Latin America's national economies occurred after nation-building and the institutionalization of the state jurisdiction over a territory (Oszlak, 1981). In other words, processes of state formation became a prerequisite for uneven development in the Western Hemisphere (Morton, 2013: 34). At the same time, uneven development at a global scale (namely the division between core and peripheral spaces in the early stages of capitalism) also shaped state sovereignty in postcolonial states (Mandel, 1975). From a geographical political economy approach, the capitalist tendency of uneven development aims to simultaneously homogenize space and produce differences. Large companies seek cheaper labor and natural resources elsewhere to suspend the obstacles they face and to assure their own future profitability, thereby redirecting financial and investment flows. This competitive struggle consists of the search for new markets, cheaper labor, and abundant and inexpensive raw materials, and it relies on the spatial deepening and expansion of capitalist social relations.

Such a competitive process relies on the production of territorial differences, particularly through the creation of fixed capital to minimize costs under conditions of inter-industrial linkages, create a social division of labor, and gain access to raw materials, labor supplies, and final consumer markets. The state then plays a central role in the process of capital territorialization, as it is through state regulations that conditions of profitability can be temporarily guaranteed within a given socio-spatial fix, producing capitalist uneven development (Brenner, 1997, 1998; Harvey, 2001: 328). The territory is then produced and reproduced by the state strategies that fragment and turn space into manageable and measurable units to both intensify market relations and deepen political domination to make the social space controllable (Ballvé, 2012; Brenner and Elden, 2009; Lefebvre, 2001). As such, processes of state formation structure conditions of capitalist uneven development, particularly though physical force and social control via the enclosure and political bordering of social relations (Ballvé, 2012; Morton, 2013: 22). Uneven development also shapes state formation. Both processes reflect tensions between contending fractions of the ruling class as well as between ruling and subordinated classes. Uneven development and state practices are shaped and mediated by local institutions alongside economic and political struggles and the participation of different social actors (Brenner, 1998).

These struggles and actors operate through and produce different hierarchical spatial arrangements, namely political scales. The territorial landscape and the capitalist social relations embedded in accumulation are not necessarily transformed by the movement of money and commodities themselves. Such a transformation requires the intervention of the state, because state institutions influence and secure socio-economic relations within a territorial fix. These interventions then take the form of the construction and reproduction of political scales, "the extent to which the regulation and command of territorially embedded social relations expand over a certain material/social space and operate over a certain distance" (Swyngedouw, 1997: 167). A political scale is socially constituted rather than a pre-given and defined natural unit of human existence, and therefore it can be transformed and contested (Swyngedouw, 2004: 33).

Such an approach to political scales shows how social space is not a fixed particular geographical extension but rather it is socially produced in everyday life. Lefebvre illustrates this through the triadic contradiction among material space, representations of space, and representational space that constitutes the production of social space under capitalism (Lefebvre, 2001). Here, material space refers to the ways in which social, economic, and political activities are shaped by physical practices and everyday routines in their interaction with material places (Lefebvre, 2001; Schmid, 2008). Representation of space is the abstract knowledge generated by dominant classes involved in the organization of space. Representational spaces involve the lived experience of space in everyday life connected to non-hegemonic creativity and resistance (Lefebvre, 2001; Schmid, 2008). This triadic dialectic is a way of approaching social space, as its dimensions are simultaneously opposing and complementary. Spatial practices are also mediated by the nation-state, and the balance of social forces condensed within the nation-state is reflected through the physical spaces of state territory, borders, and infrastructure (material space), the transformation of measurement and conceptions of space into political practice (representation of space), and the use and contestation of state territoriality (representational space) (Brenner and Elden, 2009: 365-366).

State intervention through coercion and social control also relies on the law to preserve unequal power relations. Violence and the law are, therefore, tightly connected. The state asserts legal equality in a context of a materially unequal society, preserving class-based power relations that can be violently oppressive (Corrigan and Sayer, 1985: 187; Benjamin, 1986: 296). Walter Benjamin argues that violence is closely connected to the making and the preservation of law because violence over life and death is "where the law reaffirms itself" (1986: 286). This is illustrated with Giorgio Agamben's (2005) notions of the state of exception, which is the power of state authorities to suspend laws because they are constitutive of the same power that produces the laws, determining whose lives are worth protecting and whose lives are not. This state of exception, based on the juridical framework of the state, then becomes the basis for the exercise of state sovereignty over mortality and the defining of "life as the deployment and manifestation of power" (Mbembe, 2003: 12).

The role of the law in the preservation of state sovereignty and state violence is closely linked to the construction of illegality. Interpretations that reduce issues of violence to corruption in Mexico—that is, the use of official positions within the state to carry out an illegal act—overlook how illegality is part of the legitimation of the state, particularly when state officials refer to the importance of fighting prohibited activities (Comaroff and Comaroff, 2006). In the same way, criminal violence is not in direct conflict with the law set by the state, because it needs it to organize "parallel modes of enforcement" to create the conditions for profiteering (Comaroff and Comaroff, 2006: 5). Violence and illegality, then, are not the opposite of state-organized lawfulness, but rather are constitutive of state power; they are mechanisms by which order is preserved and fear is routinized through relations of political and economic power (Green, 1996: 109). As such, the construction of legality and illegality (and state sanctioning around the latter) are governance mechanisms in the form of regulations and coercion, carried out through everyday practices of state power. These mechanisms create certain subjects and deny the existence of others (Corrigan and Sayer, 1994: 357). In the book, I refer to governance not as social systems aiming at self-discipline in isolation from the state. Rather, the state, as a site of political struggle and the outcome of the social balance of forces, organizes the conditions and the rules in which different social actors pursue their aims in lieu or parallel to traditional state policy (Jessop, 2016: 166-173).

There is also a close connection between space and the law. The law becomes concrete in space, and, in fact, organizes it, through the definition of spatial boundaries, scalar jurisdictions, and the demarcation of spaces of exception and ambiguity (von Benda-Beckmann et al., 2009, Delaney, 2010). Order is therefore reproduced through the concreteness of the law in the making of spatial divisions and spaces of exception (Aradau, 2007). Social space is always inscribed with legal meanings and produced through the law (Braverman et al., 2014). At the same time, social space shapes the ways in which the legal is politically and socially constructed and enacted. Such an understanding of the nexus between space and the legal offers an understanding that challenges notions of the law as neutral general principles (Delaney, 2010). It allows us to consider the law as a site and a process in which the politics of space become concrete, negotiated, contested, and vice versa, particularly in relation to the forms of political authority and their control over space, people, and nature (von Benda-Beckmann et al., 2009).

Yet, it is important to understand the relationship between the state, the law, disorder and space in historical context, particularly as the concept developed by Agamben is devoid of socio-historical content (Boukalas, 2014). For this reason, it is important to refer back to Nicos Poulantzas notion of the state as the condensation, reflection and institutional materiality of social relations. In this sense, the law created and sanctioned by the state is simultaneously the codification of state and class power as well as the achievements of the struggles of dominated classes (Boukalas, 2014: 121; Poulantzas, 2014: 63). Poulantzas also locates the historical context in which the socio-spatial relationship between law and exception plays out as well as the social purposes that inform this relationship (Boukalas, 2014: 113). He argues that the expansion of legal arrangements in capitalist economies is related to the increasing importance of processes of calculation for various powerful economic forces, which might also intensify class contradictions and tensions. For that reason, the legal system provides stable rules to allow for economic and political forecasting. This expansive rearrangement of the legal system allows for flexibility, namely the ability of the legal system to disregard its own rules, create states of exception, and transform them (Poulantzas, 2014: 73, 79).

This book mostly employs the term illegal and criminal, rather than the separation between illegal, illicit and informal. The use of the concept of illegality conveys the historical and social processes underlying the constructions of this category and therefore the politics of (il)legality. The classification of economic activities occurring outside of state institutions into informal, illegal, and illicit can provide insight into the actors involved in these activities. For instance, Alfonso Valenzuela Aguilera and Rafael Monroy Ortiz (2014) describe informal activities as economic practices for survival (e.g. trading legal goods outside of state regulation), whereas illicit activities refer to the transaction of illegal goods. These authors do agree, though, that the boundaries between these types of transactions, as well as the boundaries between these activities and the legal economy, are blurred and interconnected. In this sense, Carolyn Nordstrom (2000: 36) argues that the key is to understand how illegal networks are not different from the state, but rather work through state officials and institutions, extending across the separation of criminal, legal, illicit, and informal. To be clear, however, this book focuses primarily on the illegal economic activities of those in positions of power, rather than those carried out by marginalized populations as a mode of survival.

An alternative interpretation of legality and illegality, violence and criminality based on processes of state formation and critical approaches to space and the law therefore offers an understanding of the overlapping hierarchies of state power and legal authority, and their geographical expression, which suspend the law to permit experimentation with other kinds of orders and authority (Benton, 2010: 31–32). This is crucial for understanding how the selective suspension of the law in Mexico functions not only to increase the local power of criminal groups, but also to strengthen state power locally and nationally, deepen capital accumulation, and contribute to processes of state formation in the United States.

At the same time, the concepts of uneven development and state formation address the historical changes in the underlying dialectic between law and order and its geographical reflection in Mexico at the local and national levels. This allows us to identify, through the case study of Tamaulipas, the historical differences in the law, capital accumulation, and state power nexus between the period of import substitution industrialization (ISI) (1940–1981) and the neoliberal period in Mexico (1981 and onwards). Whereas political negotiations outside the law shaped power relations in the country and the politics of (il)legality during the ISI period, the logic of the market has set the parameters for the legal and institutional suspension of the law under neoliberalism. Such an approach to violence and neoliberalism in northeastern Mexico through the lens of state formation, space and the politics of (il)legality shows how subject-making and exclusion by the state is constituted and re-constituted through everyday practices in concrete spaces, and these materialized local spaces are crucial to domination as well as to social resistance in the context of Mexico's neoliberal state formation after 2000.

4   Lived Experience as Fieldwork

This book is the result of seven years of fieldwork in the state of Tamaulipas, particularly the northern city of Matamoros and the capital city, Ciudad Victoria. The study of these urban centers offers important insights into the hierarchies of power that support the intersection of direct violence, neoliberalism, and state power. They are central in driving capitalist uneven development in the country, in the local organization of a national neoliberal model through state power, and in the struggle for territory among criminal groups. Between 2009 and 2016, I documented developments in these locations connected to violence, local state practices, and neoliberalism. This period is important as it shows the intensification of tensions emanating from existing economic and political arrangements, namely the rupture of the alliance between the Gulf Cartel and its armed wing, Los Zetas, the assassination of the PRI gubernatorial candidate in Tamaulipas, and the effects of the 2007–2010 global financial crisis on export-processing zones in this region.

My interest in everyday practices of state formation and geographical political economy emanates from my experience growing up and working in the capital of Tamaulipas. When working for the state government of Tamaulipas in the early 2000s, I was asked to sign a document requesting federal government funds from a local state agency for an academic project I had not developed. The aim of the proposal was to research issues of economic competitiveness in Tamaulipas, particularly in relation to oil and gas. The project was centered around the organization of an international conference, and the presenters ranged from American diplomats and academics to Mexican state officials and large businesses, with the objective of promoting the role of the private sector in the energy industry in the northeastern region. The PRI governor at the time, Tomas Yarrington Ruvalcaba, occupied a central role in this conference. The event coincided with the governor's participation in the PRI presidential primaries for the 2006 elections. I rejected this offer and resigned shortly after this incident. The former governor was later detained by Interpol in Italy in 2017 for money laundering and connections to organized crime. In retrospect, this personal experience illustrates the nexus between legality, illegality, the economy, criminality, state power, and everyday life.

First, the incident shows how state power at the national and local level is enacted in everyday life, involving ordinary citizens in state practices with blurred boundaries between legality and illegality. Second, I was not able to denounce this incident as I could not prove it in a system where the testimony of an ordinary citizen means little vis-à-vis the power of the state at all levels. As such, the state became concrete in my daily life with the prospect of a loss of income for me and my family and the possible use of direct violence by state and non-state security forces. I feared the latter especially, as intimidation of people openly questioning local state authority by criminal groups or police was a common practice in Tamaulipas. Third, the incident is an example of how politics and the formal economy intersect with criminal activities and processes of state formation. Mcre specifically, criminal activities sustained political power at the local level, which concurrently supported the deepening of the neoliberal agenda at the national level. Large national and global private companies also had vested interest in the local neoliberal agenda in the energy sector, led by a governor with ties to criminal groups. In a way, this local agenda led by this former Tamaulipas governor was part of the cumulative state practices that assisted in the privatization of oil and gas in Mexico in 2018.

In order to understand the connections between global historical processes and national and local spatial dynamics in Mexico's political economy, I employ the incorporated comparison method and critical ethnography. Philip McMichael's incorporated comparison method (2000, 669) examines the social world as processes of social relations that are not merely external and dualistic categorizations of the global/national. Unit cases, namely nation-states, and the whole, which is the global economy, do not have internal properties that are autonomous from one another. In other words, the global economy does not exist independently of its parts (McMichael, 2000). Rather, national and global processes are mutually conditioning moments of a singular phenomenon, and they are historically specified (McMichael, 1990: 386). This historical method does not presume a social structure, but views social structure and institutions as formed through specific historical and spatial relations (McMichael, 2000: 671). From this perspective, one can understand the local and national processes of state formation in Mexico as constitutive of the international system of nation-states and global capitalism, and vice versa.

Critical ethnography is also applied in this book to understand the articulation between global and national political economy dynamics on one hand, and everyday life on the other, using participant observation in connection with the incorporated comparison method discussed above. This allows us to bridge the gap that Michael Burawoy explains: "[t]oo often Marxism is trapped in the clouds, just as ethnography can be glued to the ground" (2009: 8). Critical ethnography addresses the historical and power relations involved in participant observation (Brown and Dobrin, 2004: 4), and as I use it in this book, it offers insight into the ways class hierarchies and my social context are transferred into participant observation, and why it is necessary to reflect on this positionality in the participation of the creation of "partial, situated knowledge" (McKenzie Stevens, 2004: 170). Historically, social sciences only considered ethnographic work as work carried out in places unfamiliar to the researcher, thus it could only be done by outsiders, ignoring the views of researchers with close connections to the context of their fieldwork (Hanson, 2004: 184). Critical ethnography, on the other hand, allows for the inclusion of self-ethnography into the research process. Self-ethnography differs from autobiographical work as the former integrates self-reflexivity regarding the researcher's economic, social, and cultural position in relationship to the context under examination (Alsup, 2004: 222).

My positionality in the process of research in the making of this book was conflicting and multiple. I live in Canada, and I am able to work in both English and Spanish. As mentioned above, I was raised in the capital city of Tamaulipas, which has allowed me to understand the implications of political and economic power in everyday life in relation to Mexico's current violence. Living outside of Mexico has provided me with a position of privilege, as I am able to voice my concerns about Mexico's violence, particularly in the northeastern region, in English, protecting my personal safety against threats from both the state government and organized crime in Tamaulipas. This positionality differs greatly from the position of journalists and academics located in Tamaulipas. For this research, I used news reports by local and national journalists who lived in or traveled to Tamaulipas to collect the information, one of the most dangerous areas for this profession in the country. These journalists do not have the luxury of moving from a dangerous area of Mexico to a country like Canada. Similarly, academics working and residing in Tamaulipas and publishing in Spanish not only experience the everyday violence that is characteristic of living in this state, but they also encounter limitations on what kind of research they are able to carry out in relation to violence and how they can communicate it in Spanish. They are subject to reprisals from state authorities in the form of losing research funding or receiving threats against their physical safety from state officials and criminal groups. In this context, the work of these academics is invaluable for research on violence in Mexico. We, as academics working in the global North, do not provide sufficient recognition to and support for the work of Mexican academics working in violent zones such as Tamaulipas, even as we receive the benefits of using the information they collect and the analyses they produce.

My positionality is also affected by the fact that my family resided in this state during the period of research. This posed limits on how I conducted research on violence and my ability to raise any concerns in Spanish, as my family would be exposed to state repression or threats by organized crime. This was highly likely, given the chilling record of journalists and citizens murdered in Tamaulipas for discussing the climate of cruelty and impunity in their work and on social media.

This reflection on my position of privilege and vulnerability in researching Tamaulipas shaped the method of research I used for this project, which mostly relied on participant observation, in two ways. First, many people were afraid of speaking about their experiences with violence given the climate of fear in Tamaulipas. Second, I feared state government reprisals. I therefore decided not to conduct interviews with state authorities after they showed reluctance to share information that is supposed to be public.

Critical ethnography is particularly important in situations where the reality of terror and fear is not reflected in national data, media, or political speeches. This is the case in Tamaulipas, where local and national media do not report on violence comprehensively due to self-censorship and death threats. Politicians constantly claim that *aqui no pasa nada* (nothing is going on here). Official numbers do not accurately reveal the numbers of disappearances and killings because victims are afraid to report these crimes (Human Rights Watch, 2013). The methodologies used in this book therefore allows us to analyze how everyday life practices shape larger social and political processes and connect formal and informal structures of decision-making and power, and vice versa (Kubik, 2009: 32–33). It also raises questions about researchers' access to information and their ability to expose politically sensitive information in their own language, when the personal safety of the researchers, their families, or their interviewees might be exposed to threats by state and non-state armed forces.

5   Structure of the Book

Following this introductory chapter, Chapter 2 examines the interplay of capitalist uneven development and the politics behind the construction of legality and illegality in Mexico. This is illustrated through a study of the political and economic processes that shaped the connections of the oil sector, maquiladoras, and criminal activities in Tamaulipas to local and national states authorities between the 1950s and 2012. The political arrangements prior to the 1980s allowed for extralegal political negotiations between formal and informal local leaders to strengthen state power while deepening capitalist relations in Mexico. After the 1990s, such political negotiations outside the law were replaced by the logic of the market, which legitimized the suspension of the law in Tamaulipas to facilitate accumulation in Mexico, control popular dissent, and increase state power, giving criminal groups a more central role in these processes.

Chapter 3 shows how violence by criminal groups and the suspension of the law by the Mexican state have become governance mechanisms to enable dispossession and integrate the proceeds from criminal activities and private appropriation of public funds into global markets. This is illustrated through two cases: the first is that of exports of stolen fuel from the Mexican public oil company's operations in Tamaulipas into the American economy, and the second is the money-laundering lawsuits in a federal court in Texas against two former governors of Tamaulipas. In both of these cases, powerful actors employed neoliberal legality to lock in dispossession and integrate illegal economic activities into legal activities as part of the process of global accumulation.

Chapter 4 looks at the effects of such activities, analyzing how the proceeds of money laundering in real estate investment in the capital city of Tamaulipas intensified the politics of fear and the implosion of public life. This is illustrated through the booming construction of low-income housing, gated communities, and a new government building involving companies associated with former governors of Tamaulipas accused of money laundering in the U.S. Chapter 5 explores how the intensification of uneven development in Mexico shaped the ways in which people internalized individual competition into everyday life, setting the conditions for the increasing vulnerability of certain sectors of the population to attacks by state security forces and criminal groups such internal migrants and Central American undocumented immigrants. The chapter also shows how the use of the law assisted in the construction of the illegal status of undocumented immigrants in both Mexico and the United States, assisting the reproduction of state power as criminal groups became a form of proxy-governance to deter people from crossing national borders. Such illegal status also turned migrants into a source of income for criminal groups.

Turning to reactions and challenges to Mexico's pervasive climate of violence and exclusion, Chapter 6 examines how participatory forms of civic engagement and re-appropriation of public spaces challenge hierarchies of state power and neoliberalism in Mexico. This is illustrated through the 2014 mobilization of health workers against precarious working conditions, critical mass bike rides between 2010 and 2016, and the 2019 strike in maquiladoras in Tamaulipas. These movements emerged to counter the implosion of public life, seeking to reclaim labor rights with the language of human rights and, by occupying public space, to contest the social and economic exclusion driven by neoliberal policies and the combination of state and non-state violence. The concluding chapter shows how an understanding of the intersection of the geographies of accumulation, state power, and the law allows us to examine the ways in which violence, illegality and criminality are intrinsic to the exercise of state power at the local and national levels under neoliberalism in Mexico.

CHAPTER 2

Economies and Politics of (Il)Legality, 1950–2012

In 2001, the Industrial Workers and Laborers' Union of Matamoros (Sindicato de Jornaleros y Obreros Industriales de la Industria Maquiladora or SJOIIM) in the northern city of Matamoros in Tamaulipas published an obituary in several local newspapers for one of the alleged founders of the Gulf drug cartel, Juan N. Guerra, who passed away that year. The leader of this union, Agapito González Cavazos, also died later in 2001. A decade earlier, Don Agapito, as he was known in the border city, was imprisoned on dubious charges of tax evasion, while Juan N. Guerra was also put in jail for violating Mexican gambling law and tax evasion (Redacción, 1991). Don Agapito was released due to a lack of evidence, and the founder of the Gulf Cartel did not go to jail because of his age and poor health (Valdes Castellanos, 2013). In the same period, the leader of the national workers' union of the public oil company Petroleos Mexicanos (PEMEX), Joaquin Hernandez Galicia, also known as La Quina, was imprisoned in 1989 for illegal possession of weapons in Ciudad Madero, a city in southern Tamaulipas where the union branch became one of the union's most powerful membership sections. The historical connections between these characters are telling of the relationship between processes of state formation, uneven development, and changes in accumulation strategies in Mexico. These local leaders were part of the socio-political arrangements that had sustained the national power of the Institutional Revolutionary Party (Partido Revolucionario Institucional or PRI) and the Executive branch from the 1950s to the 1990s. And their political decline mirrored national socio-spatial transformations in Mexico throughout the 1990s as market discipline deepened, with consequences for how legality and illegality were framed in the country.

This chapter examines the political trajectory of the local leaders mentioned above to shed light on the relationship between geography, the economy, political power, violence and notions of legality and illegality in Mexico during the import substitution industrialization (ISI) period (1950s–1970s) and the deepening and consolidation of neoliberalism (1990s–2012). It focuses on the expansion of capitalist uneven development and how it has framed the relationship between law, disorder and violence, which in turn has also shaped processes of state formation in Mexico.

I argue that the interplay of capitalist uneven development in Mexico and state power during the ISI period relied on the selective institutional and juridical suspension of the law to favor political negotiations within the state among local leaders, national state authorities, and the capitalist class. These negotiations functioned within the context of a post-revolutionary authoritarian state that emerged after 1940. The so-called post-revolutionary *PRIista* system was based on a complex national hierarchy of political negotiations among new political elites from the capitalist classes, state-sponsored union and peasant organizations, and clientelistic networks of regional and local politicians. It was, however, the PRI that managed and re-negotiated national state power and political economy between the 1940s and 1980s.

The deepening of neoliberalism in Mexico during the 1990s and 2000s then replaced these political negotiations with the logic of market discipline and commodification for profit. Legal and institutional suspension of the law during this latter period facilitated accumulation in Mexico and allowed for the control of popular dissent. *The main difference in the form of institutional and legal suspension of the law between the ISI and neoliberal periods was the increasing role of criminal groups during the later period in sustaining the electoral legitimacy of local state authorities, namely winning elections as tarnished as they were, and assisting in the management of local social conflict and profitability in the absence of political negotiations with local leaders. Clearly the PRI previously governed through intimidation, blackmail, and violence. Yet, negotiations with the leaders of local unions and communities remained central to the existing economic and political arrangement, and therefore violence was not the prevalent mechanism of control. With the emergence of neoliberal state formation, violence through criminal groups in direct and indirect ways became the first option as a means to 're-discipline' the masses after decades of PRIista rule.*

First, this chapter examines how local political negotiations strengthened state power locally and nationally and deepened capital accumulation in the country between the 1950s and the 1980s. This section focuses on the parallel historical developments of the export-processing industry, the oil sector, and illegal and criminal activities in the country in order to understand the historical connections between state formation, uneven development and the construction of illegality by dominant forces within the state such as powerful national and local state officials, large companies and leaders of workers unions and criminal groups in northeastern Mexico during this period. Second, the chapter shows the rearrangement of power relations between local political leaders in Tamaulipas and national state authorities during the consolidation of neoliberalism in the 1990s as a reflection of the changing balance of forces favoring export-oriented and financially-oriented large companies. This led to the decline of political negotiations and their increasing replacement with the logic of market discipline and commodification for profit, further exposing subordinate classes to the negative effects of neoliberal spatial competition and global financial instability. Th rd, the chapter examines the rise of criminal groups as a governance mechanism for dealing with the contradictions originating from the removal of local political leaderships, the escalation of social discontent arising from the intens fication of neoliberalism, and increasing political competition in elections after the year 2000. I refer to governance as the conditions and rules organized by the state in which different social actors pursue their objectives in place or parallelly to traditional state policy (Jessop, 2016: 166–173). This section also addresses how the rise of criminal groups as a form of governance influences processes of state-making in both Mexico and the United States through the bilateral Merida Initiative and the economic benefits that accrue to Texas as a result of violence in Tamaulipas.

Through the trajectory of three local leaders in Tamaulipas—La Quina, Don Agapito, and Guerra—this chapter sheds light on how these leaders' strength and subsequent demise reflect the balance of socio-political and economic relations, the course of uneven development, and the changing configuration of power relations between the 1950s and 2012. It also shows that activities involving illicit goods and criminality are not new, particularly in relation to processes of state formation and the making of national economies. Yet, it shows the transformation of illegality and criminality as a reflection of a reconfiguration of state and society relations as the previous norms of the PRI regime were increasingly incompatible with the new model of neoliberal political economy, including the legal system. The framing and the connections between illegality and legality are therefore historically constructed, mainly by dominant forces, and connected to uneven capitalist development and processes of state formation. In this way, the chapter addresses how violence, illegality and criminality have become a defining characteristic of neoliberal state formation after 2000. As such, the fact that new processes of state formation are characterized by violence is hardly a new observation. Yet, what the Mexican case shows is that a new process of state formation is taking place *without revolution or an officially recognized war.*

1   Law, Order, and Uneven Development under ISI

The socio-historical construction of legality and illegality needs to be understood as a reflection of a particular ensemble of power relations within the state. Legality refers to state-sponsored rule, as well as state-sponsored (legal) violence while illegality implies non-state 'rule' and non-state sanctioned violence. Yet, illegal activity can take place without violence (Nuijten and Anders, 2008: 12; Ballvé, 2012). Also, those who commit criminal violence and illegal economic activities do not necessarily oppose the law, as its transgression allow these agents to profit and obtain political benefits (Comaroff and Comaroff, 2006: 2, 5, 19). The construction of legality therefore is connected to the state's suspension of the law to reproduce state power, and re-write laws in order to redefine the meanings of legality and illegality. Also, legal and institutional exception give powerful social actors the ability to circumvent the laws they promote by manipulating ambiguity. This ambiguity is related to uncertainty about who the actors are who perpetrate criminality and illegal activities as well as the mutually conditioning existence of the law and lawlessness in the context of multiple forms of violence (Harris, 1996: 8; Montoya, 2018: 92). This dialectic of lawfulness and disorder is reflected, produced, and reproduced through capitalist uneven development. This section therefore shows how the ISI period (1950s–1982) and the creation of export-processing zones or maquiladoras in the late 1960s established legal states of exception that shaped uneven development in the country. These ISI strategies also sustained processes of state-making through political arrangements based on institutional and legal exception that assisted accumulation and mediated conflict among different social classes in Mexico. Such political arrangements were characterized by the close relationship between the PRI and the Executive branch, particularly the president. More specifically, unions and informal local leaderships affiliated to the PRI supported the power of both the PRI and the Executive branch. These leaders extracted concessions from employers and state authorities to favor subordinated groups. This in turn involved the exchange of the unions' corporatist vote for the Executive and the PRI in return for concessions, favors, coercion, and bribes (Domínguez Ruvalcaba, 2015: 77; Middlebrook and Zepeda, 2003).

The ISI model was a set of policies that promoted domestic industrialization via import barriers in order to bolster domestic industry and improve the terms of trade between Mexico and its North American counterpart. The model relied on active state involvement to guide the expansion of the industrial sector while taxing imports and subsidizing domestic industry as well as agriculture. The ISI model thus made it difficult to import American goods without having to pay high tariffs (Guillén Romo, 2013). The Mexican Ministry of Industry and Commerce implemented the Border Industrialization Program in the late 1960s. Through this program, foreign manufacturers could set up and fully own maquiladoras along a 12.5-mile strip adjacent to the Mexican northern border. These plants could import machinery, raw materials, and components on a duty-free basis while using low-wage Mexican labor. They then had to guarantee that the totality of maquiladora imports and produced goods would be re-exported (Quintero Ramírez, 1997). Tamaulipas was one of the first states to carry out this development model.

These two economic strategies—ISI and maquiladoras—assisted both domestic and foreign capitalists while intensifying uneven development in Mexico, dividing the country into the export-oriented industrialized north, an industrialized center focused on domestic demand and financial speculation, and a rural south without health, education, or social services (Barkin, 1975). The juridical suspension of the laws related to the ISI model through the maquiladora program was key to mediating conflicting interests between, on one hand, the requirements of foreign capital to access cheap labor markets, and on the other, union leaders and their memberships' demand for employment in Mexico's northern border, particularly Tamaulipas. The national state, too, obtained benefits from the maquiladoras, as they provided the international currency necessary to offset the imbalances caused by international borrowing from the Mexican state and large private domestic companies (Villarreal, 2005). Maquiladoras were also part of broader changes in global uneven development, where assembly production was separated from the sites of decision-making and capital investment to take advantage of cheap labor in the Global South. This was facilitated by countries in the Global North as well. For example, changes were made to U.S. taxation law to allow American companies to relocate to Mexico's maquiladora areas without paying taxes to import Mexican goods into the United States (Quintero Ramírez, 1997).

The ISI model shaped geographical inequalities in Mexico. An example of this is the role that public companies such as PEMEX played in the economy. For instance, workers in the oil sector were better paid than their counterparts in other economic activities, creating forward economic linkages in terms of consumption in the local economies where they resided (Ruiz Durán, 1981). This enlarged the differentiation between oil and non-oil processing regions in the country. In addition, PEMEX facilitated the circulation of capital within the country as part of the ISI model. It also became part of the economic global circulation of capital when the Mexican oil company became an oil exporter in the 1970s. Not only were the exports of Mexican oil part of the global economic structure that made the increasing production of goods possible, but they also facilitated the flow of private international credit through petrodollars (Villarreal, 2005). The ISI model and the maquiladoras set the boundaries of legality and illegality, which conditioned the ability of local leaders in Tamaulipas to participate in the reproduction of capital accumulation and power relations within the Mexican nation-state.

The maquiladora program, then, established a legal state of exception within an ISI-policy framework. In other words, the rules implemented by state authorities in the economy because of the ISI model did not apply in Mexico's northern border due to maquiladoras. This context influenced the rise of the leader of the Industrial Workers and Laborers' Union of Matamoros (Industrial Workers' Union or SJOIIM from here on) as a central actor in the local management of conflict and negotiation. Prior to the maquiladoras, until the 1970s, the production and processing of agricultural goods, including cotton, had been the main activity in the border city of Matamoros, Tamaulipas. This laid the foundations of a strong local union movement through the Industrial Workers' Union. This union was affiliated to the PRI through the Mexican Confederation of Workers (Confederación de Trabajadores de Mexico or CTM), and Agapito González Cavazos, or Don Agapito, became the general secretary of this union in 1957. He remained the head of the union until his death in 2001 (SJOIIM, 2012).

When the maquiladora program was implemented in Tamaulipas, the number of assembly plants increased in Matamoros, and the workers in these maquiladoras became members of the SJOIIM (Quintero Ramírez,1997, 122-127; Quintero 2004, 295). In other parts of the country, maquiladora unions affiliated to the PRI did not offer many concessions to workers. In contrast, the maquiladora union in Matamoros achieved a forty-hour contract, extended health benefits, investment in affordable housing, and seniority rights (Quintero Ramírez, 2004: 287–88). In addition, the leader of the maquiladora union in Matamoros also became the head of the Workers' Front of Tamaulipas (Frente de Trabajadores of Tamaulipas), also affiliated to the CTM of the PRI. This gave the leader and the union, which had one of the highest number of members working in maquiladoras in the country in the 1980s, leverage in local and even national political and economic decision-making (Redacción, 1990).

In addition to accommodating the growing maquiladora sector, the ISI model maintained a favorable position towards public enterprises such as the public oil company PEMEX. The latter consolidated its role in promoting domestic industrialization through price controls and subsidized oil and gas (Boltvinik and Hernández Laos, 1981). By the late 1960s, the members of the oil workers' union reached 70,000 workers (Alonso and López, 1986: 101), grouping together an important number of workers in a strategic sector in the Mexican economy. The *de facto* leader of the oil workers' union from 1961 to 1988 was Joaquin Hernandez Galicia, or La Quina, whose power relied on the strength of the membership of the union branch he headed in southern Tamaulipas. Under his leadership, collective agreements between PEMEX and the union featured improvements in working conditions, salaries, and social benefits, and the role of the oil workers' union in the Mexican economy gave this leader and his union backers political leverage both locally and nationally (Alonso and López, 1986: 101).

The union leader of the maquiladora workers in Matamoros and the head of the public oil workers' union held positions of power in the official labor movement as a result of the juridical and institutional state of exception. For instance, the leader of the Matamoros maquiladora union mobilized members' support for the PRI, particularly during local and national elections (Lacarriere Lezama, 2010). This in turn discouraged workers' support for opposition parties or a different political regime and violated their individual right to vote. In the oil workers' union, the legal and institutional exception manifested itself through union leadership practices offering full-time job positions for sale as well as the informal power of La Quina (Alonso and López, 1986: 92-101). While this was a violation of the law, national state authorities did not disapprove of these practices outside the law or the lack of union democracy, as long as unions continued to support the regime. The corporatist vote therefore legally enabled the continuation of the political and economic power structures locally and nationally. In other words, clientelism transformed illegality into legal practices through elections (Powell, 2012: 218). As a result, the Matamoros maquiladora union and the PEMEX union's local branch in Tamaulipas were highly influential in economic and political decision-making both locally and nationally until the first half of the 1990s (see Quintero Ramírez, 2004). And mediating conflict among these interests was important to maintain the power of the PRI in Tamaulipas and nationally (Rousseau, 2017: 158), perpetuating political and economic inequalities as well as political practices supporting political and economic power.

Inevitably, these practices of state formation became concrete in people's everyday lives. In the case of Tamaulipas, the leadership of Don Agapito, and the form of labor organizing he represented, shaped local labor markets to supply cheap trained labor to maquiladoras. The union's extensive presence in the community was also key in mediating labor and social conflicts (Muñoz Martínez, 2010). It maintained labor peace in the maquiladora sector and prevented workers' discontent with the national and local state, while reproducing the uneven landscape of capitalism in the country in the form of maquiladoras (Lacarriere Lezama, 2010). Similarly, the rise of the union branch headed by La Quina in the national oil workers' union during the late 1950s followed the repression of a series of internal labor mobilizations calling for union democratization and higher salaries in 1947 and 1958 (Alonso and López, 1986: 72, 89). Constant dissent within the oil workers' union ultimately led to intervention by the national Executive power to favor the union branch headed by La Quina, who ensured membership discipline and continued political support for the PRI and the national Executive branch (González Rodarte, 2002). La Quina further extended the union's power in local communities with oil operations by including a clause in the collective agreement requiring PEMEX to channel funds into community projects administered by the union (González Rodarte, 2002). The union leadership also provided funding to different union branches depending on their loyalty (Alonso and López, 1986: 94). Both the local Tamaulipas branch of the oil workers' union and the Matamoros maquiladora union thus strongly influenced the local and national political economy, illustrating both how state-making is produced and refashioned through local spaces of everyday life, and, at the same time, how these local spaces are refashioned according to dynamics at higher political scales.

The rise of the Gulf Cartel in Tamaulipas also illustrates the intersection of uneven development and everyday processes of state formation. The delimitation of boundaries through trade restrictions were part of both economic nation-building and the configuration of state power in the early stages of capitalist development (see Morton, 2013). Such developments were accompanied by categories constructing the legality, illegality and criminality of economic transactions. This was influential, for example, in the growth of profitable contraband activities in Mexico throughout the first half of the 20th century, which later became the economic basis of the Gulf Cartel's drug-trafficking activities. The era of prohibition in the United States in the early 20th century allowed Juan N. Guerra to make profits by smuggling mezcal, a distilled agave drink made in Tamaulipas, into the United States during the late 1920s and the 1930s. His operations were located in the border city of Matamoros. The growth of his business intersected with processes of state formation in the United States, as the Volstead Act of 1919, marking the beginning of the era of prohibition in the United States, which allowed for American state intervention in everyday life (McGirr, 2016). The Volstead Act drove business linked to alcohol, gambling, and night entertainment south of the border, to places such as the New York Bar and the Crystal Palace in Reynosa, Tamaulipas (Lorey, 1999: 45-47). This led American state authorities to construct the Mexican border as a space of lawlessness, allowing them to justify the presence of the federal American state to defend 'American values' in these areas far away from Washington (Aldama, 2002; DeChaine, 2012).

After alcohol prohibition was repealed in the mid-1930s in the United States, national state authorities in Mexico established trade restrictions between 1947 and 1981 as part of the ISI model. This created a new set of profitable opportunities for Juan N. Guerra through the contraband of American goods, particularly those that were cheaper for Mexican consumers than Mexican-made products. The profits originating from the transgression of ISI policies led to other economic opportunities for the alledged founder of the Gulf Cartel, including arms contraband, control over local sex workers, and drug production and trafficking (Redacción, 1991).

These activities involved direct forms of violence to enforce compliance with the paralegality established by this criminal group in Tamaulipas, maintaining tight control over local communities. The same applies to the ways in which the Gulf Cartel organized local communities while assisting larger power structures at the national level. The leadership of the Gulf Cartel organization performed state-like practices, such as conflict mediation, while retaining its connections with the formal workings of the state (Lacarriere Lezama, 2010; Thomas, 2011: 37). For instance, people requested Juan N. Guerra's assistance to solve economic or personal disputes after state authorities ruled against them (Lacarriere Lezama, 2010). Contraband also provided cheap and durable consumption goods to a growing population of workers migrating to Tamaulipas, attracted by the maquiladoras. As such, contraband complemented the development of the maquiladoras by allowing workers to expand the purchasing power of their salaries. This could have assisted the 'apparent' success of the maquiladoras, providing further support for this program and for the leader of the maquiladora workers' union in Matamoros. The economic and political strength of the Gulf cartel and its ability to support local and national economic and political arrangements within the Mexican state thus became concrete and was produced and refashioned in localized everyday life.

As the Gulf Cartel made money out of the divide between legality and illegality, illegality then became legal through the channeling of these resources towards political activities, particularly the support of PRI candidates (Domínguez Ruvalcaba, 2015: 15). In fact, Juan N. Guerra affirmed that: "I am not a politician, but rather their friend. Indeed, I am a supporter of the PRI, I have always been, and I vote for its candidates" (Redacción, 1991). This illegality was in fact supported by the existing national and local state authorities, who received economic and/or political benefits. Customs officials, security forces, and Guerra's relatives in political positions favored these illegal transactions in exchange for economic and political support (Flores Pérez, 2014b; Padgett, 2016). This supported everyday practices of clientelism, as citizens were not able to exercise their rights through official channels or democratic state practices. Rather, they had to participate in the exchange of personal favors with both state and non-state authorities.

The connections of these three political leaders in Tamaulipas to legality and illegality need to be understood as a reflection of the relations of domination within the state at the time, rather than as corruption. As Monique Nuijten notes (2003), clientelism in Mexico was central to people's own safeguarding in a context in which the state did not provide institutional protection. The personal loyalty involved in reproducing clientelistic practices thus remained both a form of exclusion and an uncertain way of accessing resources. Members of local communities remained loyal because they did not know when community and union leaders affiliated to the PRI were going to withdraw their support. This converted rights into personal favors in everyday life, thereby transforming the legal into the illegal and further reproducing juridical and institutional exception in the country. The uneven geography of capitalism in Mexico prior to the 1980s, then, not only shaped the operations involving illegal activities, but also the ways in which they became part of the legal economy and formal politics.

In all these cases, the state suspension of the law was central to state-making at the local and national level. This created a multiple layering of overlapping legal spaces that controlled dissent by consolidating the power of the Executive and the PRI, while capitalist social relations deepened in the country through a process of proletarization. In 1950, there were 3.8 million rural and urban workers. Twenty years later, there were 8.5 million people working as wage laborers (Vidal, 1984: 29, 31). Throughout this period, the informal suspension of the law and legal experimentation was not only supported by the PRI but also by the interests of Mexican and foreign capitalist classes. While there were political differences between national and local state officials and large Mexican companies, they shared their hostility towards social mobilization against low salaries and the lack of democratic unions (Martin, 2007). And while social mobilization continued in central and southern Mexico, the concentration of plural (il)legalities in Tamaulipas, which were crucial to national state power, deterred social organizing. There were a handful of mobilizations against rising public transportation fees in the border city of Reynosa and to demand that informal urban settlements in southern Tamaulipas be formalized, yet these movements were either repressed or coopted by the multiple legal spaces that relied on the suspension of the law (Alonso Pérez, 2014: 313).

As such, the legal and/or informal suspension of the law by the state fragmented space and its constitutive social relations to ensure governability during a period of expansion of capitalist relations in the country. As Alan Knight notes referring to the PRI regime at the national level:

> But these rules, while they vetoed violence at the national level, allowed it and sometimes encouraged it at the local level [...] Indeed, it might even be argued that the successful elimination of violence at the national level involved its displacement to the provinces; local people fought and feuded so that the national elites might bask in stable civility (1999, 107).

The suspension of the law, and the class relations they reflected, were not only part of the process of uneven capitalist development within Mexico during the ISI period; these spaces were also implicated in Mexico's integration into global accumulation. More specifically, this integration was characterized by inflows of foreign investment in certain areas, particularly through maquiladoras, and the strengthening of certain powerful political and economic actors within Mexico that ensued. This in turn relied greatly on the expansion of proletarization as a reflection of the expansion of capitalist social relations worldwide (Morton, 2013: 63-86).

An analysis of the intersection between the construction (il)legality, uneven development and state formation offers an alternative interpretation of the *pax narcotica* during the PRI to understand how the post-revolutionary structures of political and economic power were based on the direct and indirect suspension of the law. As such, the economic and political oligarchy in Mexico during the corporatist period was already founded on illegality and criminality, prior to the rise of violence in the 2000s (Domínguez Ruvalcaba, 2015: 73, 81).

2 Neoliberal Prohibitions and Transgressions after 1980

The initial implementation of neoliberalism in the 1980s and its deepening during the 1990s involved the reworking of existing institutional landscapes and class configurations to set the conditions for the escalation of market discipline in the country. This entailed intensifying uneven capitalist development and changing the relationship between national and local political forces in Tamaulipas. The implementation of neoliberalism changed the relationship between legality and illegality that had characterized the ISI period, while using existing local legal and institutional exceptions to deepen neoliberalism and foster new spaces for the suspension of the law locally and nationally. Most importantly, neoliberalism framed legality along the lines of market discipline—namely profit-making, commodification, supply, and demand in Tamaulipas and across the country.

During the 1980s, the importance of the maquiladoras in Mexico's economic development model increased, as state authorities and large Mexican and global companies sought to replicate these plants' labor practices and the legal framework of tax exemptions and infrastructure incentives in other parts of the country. This was part of the initial phase of the implementation of neoliberalism, triggered by the 1982 debt crisis. Throughout the 1980s, Mexican state authorities implemented the International Monetary Fund (IMF)'s structural adjustment policies (SAPs) to access the Fund's loans to repay international investors. These SAPs included lowering wages, deregulation, and favorable conditions for large foreign and domestic capital. This trend was further intensified by the North American Free Trade Agreement (NAFTA), signed in 1994, which set the conditions for freer trade and investment as well as further safeguards for foreign investors. Both SAPs and NAFTA fostered Mexico's economic policy and development model of expanding maquiladoras (Muñoz Martínez, 2008). As a result, the value of maquiladora production increased by 334 percent between 1990 and 1995 and by 195 percent between 1995 and 2000 (INEGI, 2001: 103), and Tamaulipas represented 20.34 per cent of maquiladora production in Mexico during this period (INEGI, 2001: 121). At the same time, wages in this sector lagged behind the increase in production at a time of 25 percent average annual inflation in the 1990s (INEGI, 2001).

Mexico's increasing reliance on maquiladoras for employment and production led to an intensification of uneven capitalist development. To attract investment, localities offered more favorable investment conditions than their counterparts, such as greater infrastructure and tax incentives and cheaper labor (Hiernaux, 1991: 43). In this sense, the implementation of the neoliberal agenda in Tamaulipas was important for sustaining Mexican neoliberalism, as this local economy contained key sectors of interest for large capital, such as maquiladoras, agriculture, and the petrochemical sector. Also of importance, as discussed above, local union leaders in Tamaulipas had been highly influential in local and national economic and political decision-making prior to the 1990s. This contrasts with other Mexican northern states such as Chihuahua, where local and foreign capital shaped the political and economic agenda, while unions had only a marginal role (Quintero Ramírez, 2004). As a result, national state authorities sought to weaken local Tamaulipas leaders who opposed neoliberalism in an effort to set an example for the rest of the country.

In coordination with the federal government and the CTM, local state officials in Tamaulipas promoted lowering wages and declining labor conditions and threatened to dismantle effective collective bargaining in order to attract foreign investment in maquiladoras and other export industries. When local leaders in Tamaulipas began to resist the neoliberal agenda as it threatened the popular basis of their power position, state intervention at the local level increased, repressing insurgency within the labor movement and further fragmenting it. The local maquiladora union of Matamoros, for instance, rejected the push by the Mexican Confederation of Workers (CTM) and the state and federal government to decrease wages and social benefits in the 1990s. The union's leader, Don Agapito, was soon imprisoned under dubious charges of tax evasion in 1992. His arrest took place during collective bargaining with several maquiladoras and two weeks after he called for a strike in eight assembly plants. His arrest also occurred a few days after the local maquiladora business association met with the Mexican president to discuss its objection to the dominant maquiladora union and its leader in Matamoros (Redacción, 1992).

This weakened the power of the local labor movement and its influence in political and economic decision-making. In this context, the CTM allowed the creation of weaker, PRI-affiliated unions in this northern city and other neighboring urban centers in Tamaulipas, making unions compete with each other for maquiladoras' collective contracts through the lowering of labor demands (Quintero Ramírez, 1997). Local state officials, with the support of national state authorities, also created tripartite agreements in the 1990s through which investors committed to keeping their businesses in Tamaulipas and workers' unions agreed to relinquish their right to strike (Quintero Ramírez, 1997). These agreements further dismantled the political and economic gains achieved by the local labor movement in Tamaulipas.

This same weakening of union leadership opposing the national state and its neoliberal agenda occurred in the oil workers' union in the late 1980s and early 1990s. The head of the oil workers' union, La Quina, opposed the national Executive power's attempts to decrease the power of the union in PEMEX's decision-making and to reorganize the union by appointing leaders who supported the national state authorities' neoliberal agenda. Indirectly, national state officials further diminished the power of the union with the initial privatization of the oil company, particularly by outsourcing construction and logistics to large private companies and reducing processing activities (Rousseau, 2017: 389). The leadership of the oil workers' union responded to these measures with decreasing support for the PRI, particularly in the 1988 presidential elections. This conflict ended with the imprisonment of the *de facto* head of the oil workers' union in 1989 under charges of arms trafficking. The weakened union leadership led to a 42.6 percent drop in unionized PEMEX jobs, increased productivity through longer hours, and changes in job descriptions to turn them into non-unionized jobs (Rousseau, 2017: 384–385). In 1993, La Quina was replaced by Carlos Romero DeChamps, a supporter of the neoliberal project who remained in power in the oil workers' union for more than 25 years (Redacción, 2017a).

Around the same time, in 1991, Juan N. Guerra, the founder of the Gulf Cartel, was arrested at the age of 77 on charges of violating the gambling law in the horse races he hosted at his ranch (Redacción, 1991). The timing of his arrest coincided with NAFTA negotiations and the growing lack of legitimacy of the president at the time, Carlos Salinas de Gortari (1988–1994). This was due to suspicions of fraudulent presidential elections as well as international press attention to cases of violence and drug trafficking in Tamaulipas (Uhlig, 1991). Guerra's arrest also coincided with the rise of Guerra's nephew, Juan Garcia Abrego, in the Gulf Cartel and with the cartel's larger role in cocaine drug trafficking into the United States via Tamaulipas (Flores Pérez, 2014b).

The arrests of these local leaders were instrumental in blaming 'bad apples' for the lack of political democratization. For instance, the chief of Interpol in Mexico claimed that the detention of the founder of the Gulf Cartel was a "blunt blow against impunity" (Redacción, 1991). In response to complaints by the local business association against the leader of the maquiladora union in Matamoros in 1992, Mexican president Carlos Salinas de Gortari (1988–1994) said: "The government will act to protect the rights of workers as well as maintain the rule of law to prevent any kind of arbitrariness from those who pretend to defend workers' interests when in fact they pursue their own private interests" (Redacción, 1992). Several international newspaper editorials also considered the incarceration of the oil workers' union leader to be an important step towards democratization and the fight against corruption (Mexico's President Gets Tough, 1989; Cano, 1989). The imprisonment of local leaders in Tamaulipas thus helped to legitimate the political power of the national Executive and the national neoliberal agenda (Nuijten, 2003). This has been central to the implementation of the neoliberal agenda, particularly in the 1990s, as the new political alliance between state and capital in Mexico blamed the previous political and economic arrangements under the PRI and ISI for corruption and the lack of effectiveness of the state bureaucracy (Martin, 2007). As Nuijten puts it, "In this context the discourse of corruption deflects attention from more fundamental types of criticism of the regime and has conservative effects" (Nuijten, 2003: 173).

The decline of these local leaders resulted in the removal of the local interests they represented, which included some concessions to subordinated classes, from political and economic decision-making. This led to the partial replacement of political negotiations within the official party and in everyday life with the logic of neoliberalism, which was supported by a powerful fraction within the state as well as export and financially-oriented large national and foreign companies (Powell, 2012: 223). At the same time, undemocratic practices within PRI-affiliated unions persisted. This transformation facilitated the implementation of the neoliberal agenda, both through tripartite agreements between business, state, and unions (Martin, 2007: 52; Powell, 2012: 212), and as ongoing undemocratic practices within unions and the PRI helped to reproduce political practices constraining workers' action and sustaining economic and political inequalities. Negotiations between local interests and other factions within the PRI were largely replaced with the logic of profit-making and supply and demand promoted by large companies and a powerful fraction within the state. And social benefits, wages, community projects, and the resolution of personal disputes were not largely the result of local formal and informal political arrangements within the PRI.

Neoliberalism brought new ways to mediate social conflict and interactions in Mexico at the local and national levels. These changes also involved the redrawing of the boundaries of legality and illegality. The suspension of the law was justified in relation to the neoliberal agenda. In Tamaulipas, workers felt the effect of this redrawing of legality in the factories and in their households. For instance, local state authorities deemed maquiladoras' lack of compliance with labor law and its effects on workers' rights to be acceptable and allowed them to continue without sanction, as long as they promoted investment in the sector (for a case study on workplace risks in Tamaulipas, see Quintero Ramírez and Romo Aguilar, 2001). When a high rate of babies with birth defects were born to mothers exposed to maquiladora waste and chemicals in Matamoros, neither local or national state officials tightened enforcement of environmental law or sanctioned any companies (Red de Solidaridad de la Maquiladora, 2001: 5).

What is more, neoliberalism transformed illegal economic activities into legal ones. For instance, some contraband activities undertaken by the Gulf Cartel became legal, such as the smuggling of American beer into Tamaulipas through economic liberalization (Redacción, 1991). This activity then became less profitable, encouraging the cartel's focus on more lucrative illegal activities such as drug trafficking. Profitability and private investment thus replaced traditional forms of local and national clientelism that had shaped the construction of legality and illegality in Tamaulipas and Mexico between the 1950s and the 1980s. Similarly, state authorities deemed the undemocratic practices within unions and activities by criminal groups illegal and corrupt when they did not align with the national neoliberal agenda.

Changes in the local landscape in Tamaulipas also reflected larger transformations in the power relations within the Mexican state, which increasingly favored large financial interests, both domestic and international, as well as large Mexican business and foreign direct investment with an export-oriented focus over the concerns of local elites who were not completely supportive of neoliberalism (Morton, 2013: 113–120). As such, the Mexican state internalized the interests of both domestic and international capital to manage its own domestic economy in a manner consistent with securing international financial order. This also involved insulating the state's financial apparatus from domestic politics, exposing it instead to the influence of large international and national businesses in economic and even political decision-making (Marois, 2011: 180). Indeed, this *internationalization of the state* became part of policy trends worldwide, particularly in developing countries after the implementation of neoliberalism in the 1980s. Yet, the way in which the global parameters of neoliberalism were implemented and how they intermingled with the existing

suspension of the law were shaped by domestic institutional and informal political arrangements within Mexico. This domestication of neoliberalism created the political and economic conditions to render the ambiguity generated
by the violence of criminal groups compatible with Mexican neoliberalism,
particularly after the launching of the War on Drugs in 2006.

3   Governance, Neoliberal Consolidation and Ambiguity after 2000

During the 2000s, electoral competition increased, particularly after the rise of
the right-center National Action Party (National Action Party or PAN) to the
presidency in 2000. At the same time, the negative social effects of the implementation of the neoliberal agenda became more evident during this period.
An average of 49 percent of people were unable to afford food and social services with their income during the first decade of the 2000s (CONEVAL, 2016a).
In Tamaulipas, this percentage rose from 40.1 in 2000 to 47.8 percent in 2010
(CONEVAL, 2016b). This precariousness led to a decline in popular support for
local and national state authorities in the absence of political negotiations
with local leaders in Tamaulipas to secure concessions from subordinated
classes. Informal suspension of the law locally then became central to the preservation of state power at the national level, while the ambiguity and fear produced by criminal groups provided support for local state authorities in Tamaulipas. The latter became a central mechanism of local governance amidst
the increasing poverty produced by Mexico's economic model.

The PAN relied on the PRI at the local level in Tamaulipas to carry out the
neoliberal agenda and maintain the former's position in the presidency between 2000 and 2012. For instance, Tomás Yarrington Ruvalcaba, governor of
Tamaulipas from 1998 to 2004, helped then-president Vicente Fox to negotiate
with PRI governors during the early 2000s (Redacción, 2004). Former Tamaulipas governor Eugenio Hernández Flores (2004–2010) also collaborated with
the leader of the PRI-affiliated Teachers' Union, Elba Ester Gordillo, to support
PAN candidate Felipe Calderón Hinojosa in the 2006 presidential elections.
Calderón Hinojosa, who firmly supported the neoliberal reforms undertaken
by his predecessors, won the elections against center-left candidate Andrés
Manuel López Obrador, whose campaign had proposed a change to Mexico's
economic model (Garduno and Becerril, 2006).

The continuation of the neoliberal agenda and the existing local class configuration in Tamaulipas under a different political party in the national Executive branch led to a spatial reorganization of political power. This involved
the increased power of local political groups that favored large companies'

interests and market discipline with ad hoc national state interference. Local state officials and local capital, and the reconfiguration of the balance of forces it reflected, gained strength as long as they assisted in the deepening of neoliberalism (Powell, 2012: 228). This occurred with the proven private appropriation of public funds by Tamaulipas governors from 2000 onwards and their connections to criminal groups (see Chapter 3). Neither Fox or Calderon carried through criminal investigations on the Tamaulipas PRI governors between 2000 and 2012, as the local power of the PRI provided them with political support at the national level (Reporte Indigo, 2012). This illustrates the ability of local and dominant classes to circumvent their own regulations and laws. Rather than considering this corruption, it is crucial to understand that the law is not about eliminating transgressions, but about managing such transgressions in shifting ways depending on class interests and relations of power, in this case reflecting and shaping the rise of the neoliberal agenda in Mexico and the resulting intensification of inequalities in the country.

It was during the period of neoliberal consolidation in the late 1990s and 2000s that the power of organized criminal groups expanded nationally and even internationally. Whereas traditional forms of clientelism had previously guaranteed the triumph of the PRI in local elections, this became more difficult given the continuous economic crises and lack of concessions to peasants and workers by Tamaulipas state authorities. The intervention of criminal groups in local Tamaulipas elections then guaranteed the success of the PRI. For instance, the armed-wing of the Gulf Cartel, Los Zetas, intimidated voters to vote for the PRI candidate during the 2004 gubernatorial elections in the municipality of San Fernando, Tamaulipas (Redacción, 2004). Los Zetas replicated these practices in other municipalities, securing a PRI win of the Tamaulipas governorship in 2004. National state authorities ignored these electoral practices, as the they relied on the continuation of the local suspension of the law to deepen the national neoliberal agenda. The testimony of a resident of San Fernando during the 2004 elections reflects the obliviousness of national state authorities: "Whoever resists, dies. Local authorities collaborate with Los Pelones [Los Zetas] and the federal state does not care about us. Who can help us?" (Redacción, 2004: 25).

The symbiotic relationship between electoral competition and criminal groups was also evident in the 2010 gubernatorial elections in Tamaulipas. When people in Tamaulipas discussed candidates, they did so in terms of the candidates for the PRI primaries and their varying affiliations with criminal groups. For instance, some people argued that they favored the candidate with ties to the Gulf Cartel instead of the one connected to Los Zetas, because the latter was more violent and cruel. Because of the dominance of the PRI and its practices for winning votes, potential voters dismissed any possibility of the candidates of opposition parties winning. As a result, these voters focused on providing support to a particular candidate in the PRI primaries. This, in turn, shows how the interplay between procedural democracy, neoliberalism, and the violence of criminal groups reshaped the boundaries of the legal and the illegal. On the one hand, local state authorities encouraged the growth of illegal activities and criminal groups to sustain political power (Glendhill, 2013: 524). On the other hand, elections allowed these illegal practices to become legal as long as local economic and political powerful actors supported the national neoliberal agenda.

The case of Tamaulipas illustrates how criminal groups became a proxy agent of governance during the 2000s instead of traditional forms of clientelism, reproducing social control and maintaining the economic and political hierarchies that emerged during the 1990s at the local and national levels (Glendhill, 2013: 524). The Gulf Cartel initiated a nation-wide change in how criminal groups exerted physical violence following the rise of the opposition National Action Party to the presidency in 2000. Guadalupe Correa-Cabrera (2017) characterizes this transformation as paramilitarization, because it involved the development of armed wings of organized criminal groups and the redirection of physical violence from targeted groups and persons to the population as a whole as a consequence of widespread militarization in the country.

The fear induced by criminal groups in Tamaulipas, particularly after the transition to crueler forms of violence, became an effective instrument of social control. Economic crises since the 1990s and increasing insecurity since the late 2000s limited the range of strategies workers employ to bargain with both employers and the state and to protest against the deterioration of working conditions. For instance, the SJOIIM was unable to carry out May Day parades during the late 2000s and early 2010s as a result of violence instilled by both state and non-state armed groups (Arias, 2017; Rendón, 2016; Uresti, 2013). In 2010, workers affiliated to the maquiladora union in Matamoros also speculated that two large trucks constantly parked outside of the union building belonged to the criminal group Los Zetas, surveilling union facilities to demand extortion money and maintain control over the union leadership and membership. Maquiladora workers became targets of express kidnapping, being forcibly taken to ATMs to withdraw cash on payday or during the time of holiday bonuses (U.S. Consulate in Matamoros, 2009). This stands in contrast with the situation of the maquiladoras themselves, which did not become targets of extortion for criminal groups in Matamoros to avoid attracting the attention of U.S. state authorities, as many maquiladoras in Matamoros are part of U.S. companies (U.S. Consulate in Matamoros, 2009). This climate of fear contributed to the decline of labor dissent and therefore assisted in preserving conditions favorable to business demands for cheap labor.

Fear originating from the paramilitarization of criminal groups further suppressed dissent in Tamaulipas, as local state authorities used the existence of criminal groups to explain the murders of people challenging local state authorities. For instance, Antonio Guajardo, the candidate of the center-left PRD for the Tamaulipas municipality of Rio Bravo on the border with the U.S., was killed after he released photographs showing personal relationships between local politicians and the Gulf Cartel in a press conference in 2007 (Redacción, 2007b). Local state authorities closed the case, alleging the Gulf Cartel was the perpetrator of the crime without investigating the victim's political accusations. Miriam Elizabeth Martínez, an activist with the non-governmental organization Families of the Disappeared in Tamaulipas, was killed on Mother's Day in 2017 in San Fernando, a northern Tamaulipas municipality. Martínez became involved in the movement of relatives searching for their missing loved ones during her two-year search for her daughter, who disappeared in 2012 and was found in a clandestine grave in 2014. Her movement made evident the lack of action by state authorities and the high levels of impunity in the region. When she was murdered, the perpetrators were identified as members of Los Zetas, but state authorities did not conduct any investigation into why she had not received any state protection, despite reporting constant death threats (Juárez, 2017). This shows how criminal groups produce ambiguity, namely uncertainty about who the perpetrators are and what their motives might be. This has become increasingly central in the reproduction of state power and neoliberalism in Mexico at the local and national levels.

Criminal groups in Tamaulipas also became the main justification for the militarization of the country since the 2000s, as national and local state authorities deemed the intervention of the armed forces necessary to dismantle criminal groups and reclaim the state's monopoly over violence. Still, militarization further blurred the boundaries between legality and illegality and consolidated the state of exception as a normal condition in everyday life in Tamaulipas since the late 2000s. Through militarization, any civilian can be considered a criminal for any reason, including for participating in peaceful political activism or passing through in a public area. Clear examples of the latter are the enforced disappearance of 30 civilians by Mexican marines and the killing of a mother and two children by the same security forces in 2018. Between February and May of 2018, 30 young men were disappeared because marines deemed them suspects, without evidence, of belonging to criminal groups (Althaus, 2018). In March 2018, three victims, the mother and two daughters, were shot from a helicopter during a sustained fight with members of a criminal group in Nuevo Laredo, Tamaulipas (Reina, 2018).

Interestingly, unpopular constitutional neoliberal reforms developed between 2006 and 2014 were introduced in this context of fear and ambiguity produced by criminal groups in Tamaulipas and throughout Mexico. These reforms involved constitutional changes regarding labor and the energy sector, key sectors in Tamaulipas. The new labor law of 2012 introduced new forms of contracts to facilitate the dismissal of workers and reduce companies' contributions to social benefits. The energy reform of 2014 opened the state-owned oil to private investment, jeopardizing the labor gains of workers in the public oil company (Marois and Muñoz Martínez, 2016). These reforms had an important impact on workers in Tamaulipas, but the climate of fear and ambiguity prevented major social mobilizations against these reforms.

These emerging forms of governance in Mexico, and the ambiguity they produce, are also important in processes of state formation in the United States. The representation of the American border as a law-abiding and peaceful space legitimizes the massive state apparatus supporting strategies of border control and normalizing disciplinary and divisive practices (Alonso, 2005: 38). This form of legitimation reproduces the power structures that sustain the American state and exacerbates the politics of fear promoting the militarization of the border and the securitization of drug trafficking and addiction in both countries. The Merida Initiative, launched in 2008, further consolidated this form of legitimation as part of both Mexican and American state-making. The Merida Initiative provided U.S. $2.8 billion dollars in financial assistance between 2008 and 2017 to Mexico's state activities to combat drug trafficking and criminal groups (Ribando Seelke and Finklea, 2017: 9). Most of this Initiative's objectives are related to punitive and security issues around combating criminal groups in Mexico to guarantee political and economic conditions for the continuous flow of goods and money across borders. In contrast, the Initiative ignores the social dimensions of violence in Mexico (Wolf, 2011). For instance, the U.S. State Department withholds 15 percent of U.S. financial assistance to Mexico if it considers that Mexican state officials fail to protect human rights. Despite the high levels of forced disappearances in the country since 2008, the American Congress only retained this percentage once, in 2015 (Ribando Seelke and Finklea, 2017: 12).

U.S. federal assistance in the Merida Initiative is also directly replicated at the local level in Tamaulipas through the Safety and Prosperity Campaign (SPC), which was launched in 2018. This campaign involves direct collaboration between the state government of Tamaulipas and seven U.S. federal agencies:

Homeland Security, Air and Marine Operations, Customs and Border Protection, State Department, Border Fatrol, Drug Enforcement Agency, and U.S. Citizenship and Immigration Services. The campaign consists of intelligence collaboration and information exchange to facilitate the detection of key criminals in the fight against crime (Gcbierno del Estado de Tamaulipas, 2018). The aim of the program is to provide safety and stability to promote free trade and investment along the Tamaulipas-Texas border (Redacción, 2018); however, such an approach focuses on the criminal dimensions of violence in Tamaulipas, further fragmenting criminal groups and intensifying conflict over particular territories, exacerbating violence in this region (Asmann, 2018; Stewart, 2018). At the same time, this strategy does not address the political and economic power relations underlying the conditions leading to violence, and, in fact, it reinforces at the local level the punitive approaches already established at the national scale in Mexico. The failure of these kinds of strategies to eradicate violence proves useful for current processes of state formation in the United States because it further justifies militarization of the U.S.-Mexico border and the punitive approach to Mexico's violence. Militarization and reforms of the punitive system are centered on assisting the Mexican state to regain its full monopoly over violence, at a high human cost. The framing of drug trafficking and smuggling as an American national security issue also enforces the spatial politics of security that underlie current processes of state-making in the United States (Gallagher, 2016). At the same time, military objectives, the protection of national security in the Merida Initiative, and the criminal approach in the SPC are at the core of this mechanism of bilateral cooperation, resulting in the strengthening of state power in both countries. This shows how the suspension of the law and law-making and their concrete local manifestations become part of decisive state-making moments in both Mexico and the United States.

While the economic crises of 1995 and 2007 decreased workers' purchasing power and led to workers' discontent, the reproduction of the neoliberal agenda and the constant inflow of large private investment into the Mexican economy required the continuation of low labor standards and wages, particularly in areas of the country with a history of union strength and strong local leaderships such as Tamaulipas. Without local political leaders in Tamaulipas to mediate social conflict and provide popular support for local and national state authorities after the rise of electoral competition in 2000, national authorities relied on the informal suspension of the law to guarantee a lack of political opposition and ensure the continuation of the neoliberal agenda. This took the form of the increasing role of criminal groups as a governance mechanism. Fear and ambiguity in Tamaulipas are also constitutive of state power in both

Mexico and the United States. Processes of state formation in Mexico are, then, hierarchical and scalar processes that are interconnected to state-making in other countries. This allows us to understand how state power and capitalist accumulation are central to illegal economic transactions and the "pluralization of regulatory authority" (Roitman, 2005), casting doubt on explanations of violence in Mexico that consider criminal groups and their economic activities to be a deviation of capital accumulation and state power.

4   Conclusion

This chapter focuses on the ways in which capitalist uneven development and state formation framed the relationship between legality, illegality, criminality and violence between the 1950s and 2012, which both reflected and shaped the spatial and political dynamics of the country. It looks at the case study of three political leaders in Tamaulipas, addressing their importance not through their charismatic authority, but rather through their governance role in everyday life in local communities and their articulation to local and national structures of economic and political power.

Between the 1950s and 1980s, legal and/or informal suspension of the law intersecting with uneven development in the context of the ISI model and maquiladoras shaped the power of the head of the Matamoros maquiladora union, the strength of the leader of the national oil workers' union based in the branch in Madero, Tamaulipas, and the influence of the alleged founder of the Gulf Cartel in local and national decision-making. In the case of Tamaulipas, the maquiladora model and the demand for jobs in this sector provided the maquiladora union leader in the border city of Matamoros with great political power. The centrality of the public oil sector under ISI also set the conditions for the rising influence of the head of the oil workers' union in both Tamaulipas and national political and economic decision-making. Furthermore, the construction of legality and illegality under the ISI model set the conditions of profit-making for the Gulf Cartel in Tamaulipas, making contraband a lucrative enterprise during this period. Profits from contraband and experience with the trafficking of illegally traded merchandise ultimately branched out to arms and illegal drugs.

Uneven development in Mexico set the conditions for the political rise of these leaders in Tamaulipas, and it mutually conditioned processes of state formation and the relationship between legality and illegality. These leaders operated in the context of legal and institutional exception because their position within their organizations, their economic activities, and their negotiations

with state authorities occurred outside the law. National and local state authorities received the benefits of these leaders' interventions in local communities in everyday life, allowing them to control dissent and mediate social conflict to expand capitalist social relations in Tamaulipas and beyond and
reproduce existing hierarchical relations within the Mexican state. These hierarchical relations were characterized by the dominance of the Executive
branch and a close relationship between state institutions and the official party, the PRI, until the 1990s. Control over union membership and local communities provided the heads of the local maquiladora union, the oil workers'
union, and the Gulf Cartel with a bargaining chip that permitted the reproduction of their position within existing political and economic structures. This
strength then became an obstacle to the rise of the neoliberal agenda and its
backers, thus national state authorities weakened the power of these leaders
and their supporters in the 1990s.

As a result, local political negotiations and their politics of (il)legality were
largely replaced by the logic of neoliberalism throughout the 1990s. Without
local political leaders to mediate conflict and suppress dissent in Tamaulipas,
national state authorities from the right-center PAN came to rely on the PRI's
local undemocratic practices to sustain its state power after the rise of electoral competition in 2000. This same absence of local political forces that
could exert social control on the population by way of securing concessions for
subordinated groups, along with the context of economic instability that characterized the neoliberal global economy, set the conditions for the role of
criminal groups as a governance mechanism in Tamaulipas. In this new context of electoral competition, violence and the fear induced by criminal groups
was useful to local state authorities in Tamaulipas in their bid to win elections
and repress dissent. Transgression turned into the legal order as criminal
groups and political practices outside the law assisted in the reproduction of
formal and legal structures of state power and neoliberalism between the late
1990s and early 2010s.

The chapter shows how violence in Mexico and the geographically specific
politics of (il)legality behind it are shaped by spatially contingent processes
expressed through historically and institutionally specific regulatory frameworks and socio-economic relations. Such an approach allows us to understand the transformation of the role of violence, legality and illegality in the
country rather than addressing it as a novelty in the process of state formation.
The case study of Tamaulipas therefore reveals how criminality and illegality
became part of neoliberal state formation without a revolution or a formally
recognized war. With the emergence of neoliberal state formation, violence by
criminal groups became the prevalent mechanism to discipline the population

as previous clientelistic arrangements during the ISI period, the prevailing mechanism social control, became incompatible with both the neoliberal agenda and pluralistic electoral competition. This however was not a locally or a nationally isolated process. Rather, the case study of Tamaulipas as a border state illustrates the overlapping and multi-scalar process of state-making originating from the existence of violence and the construction of (il)legality by dominant forces.

CHAPTER 3

The (Il)Legal Space of Global Trade and Finance

In 2010, the armed wing of Los Zetas split from the Gulf Cartel, leading to an intense fight over the territory of Tamaulipas. Starting that year, the residents of Tamaulipas experienced a spike in violent crimes, shootings, kidnappings, disappearances, and militarization. By 2014, Tamaulipas had one of the highest rates of violent crimes in the country and the highest number of disappeared and kidnapped persons, numbering 5,993 between 2006 and 2018 (Senado de la República, 2015; Molina, 2019). Despite increasing violence, though, Tamaulipas continued to receive foreign investment. In 2013, the local economy received 723.8 million dollars in foreign direct investment (Macías, 2014). This was followed by 511 million dollars the following year (Redacción, 2015). Tamaulipas's annual GDP growth was 4 percent in 2014 and 5.3 percent in 2015, higher than the national GDP of 3.2 percent in 2014 and 2.2 percent in 2015 (INEGI, 2018a), and Tamaulipas was one of the Mexican states with the highest number of businesses in 2015 (104,334 businesses) (INEGI, 2018b). Nonetheless, levels of formal employment remained low, and job creation increased by only 2.2 percent, while the national average was 4.3 percent (IMSS, 2014). At the same time, the percentage of people forming the ranks of the working poor—those who work but cannot afford basic needs with their income—increased from 39.5 percent in 2013 to 44.1 percent in 2014 (CONEVAL, 2015a).

This striking incongruity between the presence of large capital investment and high levels of violence and unemployment in Tamaulipas in the early and mid 2010s was also evident in everyday life. During frequent visits to my family in Ciudad Victoria, Tamaulipas between 2010 and 2017, I witnessed the development of the expansion of national and international big retail chains. At the same time, numerous long-standing family small businesses closed down because of the increasing rate of extortions by criminal groups. If the owner of a business could not pay the extortion fee, criminal groups would begin to kill the workers of the business, continuing with each member of the owner's family until the owners paid their dues. This scenario shows how violence related to criminal activity was able to co-exist with large investment and a dynamic market economy in the context of electoral competition and a neoliberal emphasis on the rule of law.

Studies often explain this co-existence of criminality and violence with investment in the formal economy as the result of the lack of regulation over criminal economic activity and corruption (Buscaglia, 2015; Fabre, 2003; Naim, 2006;

Vulliamy, 2015; Viswanatha and Wolf, 2012). Still, these analyses render the mobility of financial flows resulting from money laundering as a deviation of capital accumulation and a result of state weakness. Consequently, these approaches continue to overlook why and how violence and criminality continues to be both functional and a central mechanism for accumulation in the context of electoral competition and neoliberalism's emphasis on the rule of law.

In order to understand the transformations of violence and criminality under neoliberalism and pluralistic elections, the chapter argues, on the one hand, that *criminal violence has become central to processes of dispossession in Mexico's neoliberal state formation.* Dispossession in Mexico after 2006 took the form of the large displacement of people from their land, property and livelihood and the closing of small-scale shops and businesses by criminal groups through extortion, kidnapping and murder. The latter form of dispossession has also implications on the employees of these small businesses. They do not only lose their jobs but also are forced to work somewhere else (maquiladoras) or forced to migrate elsewhere to find work and/or to escape violence. Criminal violence and illegality are an effective mechanism of dispossession as state officials are no longer able to carry out the latter directly due to limitations coming from electoral competition and the neoliberal rule of law. If the political party in power locally or nationally carries out dispossession directly and this causes social discontent, this might endanger the continuation of their political power in elections. The neoliberal version of the rule of law with a focus on the protection of private property and contracts constrains the ability of state officials to expropriate property and dissolve contracts as these measures might also be employed against large national and foreign companies.

On the other hand, the chapter argues *that the neoliberal agenda in Mexico turned violence and illegality into legal activities through market transactions protected by the law in and across different jurisdictions.* In this sense, the conversion of illegal dispossession into a legal activity becomes more coercive than solely illegal dispossession. It becomes more difficult for subordinated actors affected by dispossession to employ the law to defend their rights, and expose the violent origin of trade and finance, once dispossession becomes legal. In contrast, market transactions and the law protecting them, which assist the transformation of illegality/criminality/violence into a legal activity, becomes a source of profit in global trade and finance, which is legitimated behind the façade of lawfulness.

In this chapter, I address the overlapping boundaries between legality and illegality and violence by criminal groups through the politics of scale. Through this approach, economic and legal hierarchies embedded in the local, the national, and the global are considered as the extent to which state regulations and command expand over a territory at a certain distance, producing and re-producing boundaries of particular practices, policies and socio-economic re-lations (Judd, 1998; Swyngedouw, 1997, 2004; Lefebvre, 2003). Such an approach is important because it is through the movement of money and commodities across economic and legal geographical hierarchies that violent dispossession is turned into legal economic activity.

As described in the introduction of this book, capital accumulation involves contradictory processes of motion and fixity of capital, in which money moves globally to become territorially fixed in the form of real estate, production, or investment in nationally-defined currencies and interest rates to generate profits. The intervention of the national state through legislation and enforce-ment is therefore crucial in territorializing capital and mediating conflict with-in its jurisdiction (Poulantzas, 1974: 73; Tsoukalas, 1999: 67). The simultaneous motion and fixity of capital, along with the state policies that attempt to man-age this contradictory process, involve political scales in two ways. On the one hand, the fixity of capital requires relatively stable scalar arrangements such as national and local state to enable production, the appropriation of natural re-sources, and the conversion of financial assets into cash (Brenner, 1998). On the other hand, capital mobility involves an upward rescaling of the state to allow financial assets and goods to circumvent national state regulations. While the national scale is a regulatory space that secures accumulation and property relations, a greater scale of state power provides a wider territorial scope to guarantee profitable conditions for capitalist reproduction (Brenner, 1999). This makes it possible for assets to enjoy a different legal guarantee in another nation-state, thereby preserving and/or maximizing economic gains.

The first section in this chapter examines the connections between capital accumulation and the law under neoliberalism. Specifically, it identifies pro-cesses of dispossession and the transformation of the illegal and violent into the legal at multiple scales through an analysis of gas theft by criminal groups in Tamaulipas. At the international scale, this case study shows how upward scales of international trading and outsourcing transformed purportedly gas theft into a permissible activity. Similarly, at the national scale, the case study illustrates how state governance turned illegal and violent non-state disposses-sion into a legal process by enacting legislation that endorses the takeover of peasant land by non-state actors.

The second section explores cases of money laundering involving two for-mer Tamaulipas governors in a federal court in Texas. It shows how the construction of legality through the upward scale of financial flows and the downward scale of real estate investment transformed legally prohibited operations into authorized economic activities. The second section also analyzes how the intensification of uneven development in both Mexico and the United States created the conditions that enabled money laundering and the private appropriation of public funds by the two former governors. The third section focuses on how powerful economic and political actors have employed neoliberal legality—in other words, the selective use of the law to protect private property and enforce contracts—to lock in dispossession and integrate illegal activities into legal economic operations tied to global accumulation.

1   (Il)Legal Dispossession

Between 2010 and 2012, the Mexican public oil company, PEMEX, sued U.S. companies and European subsidiaries in U.S. courts for purchasing stolen fuel from criminal groups. PEMEX ultimately obtained only seventy-one million dollars in damages from five companies and one individual, when in fact, the three lawsuits together had sought three hundred million dollars in damages and involved twenty-three U.S. companies and six individuals. In court, the accused companies claimed that they were not aware it was stolen fuel. The judge in charge ruled that PEMEX had failed to present evidence that would allow jurors to estimate the amount of alleged stolen gas and that the money requested by PEMEX to compensate for damages could not be collected (Linares and Montalvo, 2016).

This case of stolen fuel has largely been depicted as another case of corruption in Mexico's state institutions and as an example of state weakness (Salazar and Velázquez, 2017; Reed, 2014). Such a view, however, does not address the connections between the local, national, and global scales. These connections are important for exposing how the multiple political scales involved in converting illegal activities into legal commodities and money serve to reinforce existing hierarchies of political and economic power at the local, national, and global levels. Indeed, the case analyzed here shows how illegal economic activities involving violence by non-state actors are not external to or an abnormality of capital accumulation. Rather, the illegal economies of criminal groups have become ever more central to capital accumulation in Mexico. This case is particularly telling because it shows how the illegality and violence of such actions are blurred and obscured by outsourcing and financial markets at a global scale.

One way criminal groups are crucial to contemporary capitalism in Mexico is in processes of dispossession that benefit from the use of fear, murder, extortion, and intimidation (Ballvé, 2012). Harvey's concept of accumulation through dispossession, based on Marx's notion of primitive accumulation, provides a lens for understanding the expropriation of physical and financial assets through violence as well as through the socioeconomic, political, and spatial processes behind dispossession (Harvey, 2005). This view implicates the illegal economy in the territorialization and deterritorialization of capital and illuminates its involvement in processes of rescaling the state for economic gain, commodifying and exploiting people as labor and as marketable objects, and circumventing regulations in the same way as legal businesses (Osorio Machado, 2013).

It was mostly the state that undertook processes of dispossession in the gas sector in Tamaulipas in the 1990s and 2000s as part of the initial privatization of the energy sector in Mexico. In the 1990s, PEMEX granted concessions only to private Mexican investors to transport, store, and distribute natural gas, while allowing foreign investors up to 49 percent in the drilling of oil and gas wells (*Ley de Inversión Extranjera,* 1993; *Ley Reglamentaria del Artículo 27 Constitucional,* 1995). In the early 2000s, Mexico further opened up the gas sector to both domestic and private companies by outsourcing multiple service contracts granted by PEMEX for the exploration and extraction of natural gas. These contracts reserved PEMEX's right to distribute and sell natural gas, yet allowed companies like Halliburton, Repsol, and Petrobras to outsource services (Rodríguez Padilla, 2010). More specifically, subsidiaries of global companies held multiple service contracts through which they subcontracted local, national, or other foreign businesses to carry out operations in the area (Pérez, 2011).

The opening up of the gas sector had a major impact on the Burgos Basin, where the gas was stolen from in the case examined here. It is the largest natural gas producing area in the country, located primarily in the state of Tamaulipas, with some areas covering the neighboring states of Coahuila, Nuevo Leon and Texas as well. The basin also has several compressor stations and the largest number of cross-border gas interconnections with the United States, via Texas. Intensified exploitation in this region required the state expropriation of peasant-owned lands and communal lands, called *ejidos,* to set up operations in the petrochemical and energy sector as well as the construction of related infrastructure such as highways and ports. Indemnity payments were low or nonexistent, as an *ejido* member in the northern municipality of San Fernando, Tamaulipas, recalls: "An engineer came to tell us that he needed to make a road in the *ejido* for the transportation of large cargo. He then met with the main authority of the *ejido,* el *comisariado ejidal,* to negotiate low payments per land lot. They proposed a payment of five thousand pesos

per lot, when a 20 x 60 m lot in this *ejido* is worth one hundred thousand pesos" (Meza, 2010).

Expropriations in the Burgos Basin brought about pollution, as PEMEX created unregulated hazardous waste landfills from the gas wells without following proper safety and environmental standards (González Arévalo, 2015). An
ejido resident in the municipality of Reynosa, Tamaulipas, recounts: "There
was a gas well that exploded a few years ago. Also, trucks come by spilling water that affects animals... We struggle to find people to help us to take care of
our animals. Families are leaving. Only us, the elderly, are staying" (Meza, 2010).
This all led to the further commodification of labor, as people deprived of their
land and other natural resources had to increasingly rely on low-paying jobs in
other parts of the country or abroad for their survival. The logic of neoliberal
capital accumulation then promoted processes of dispossession through legal
expropriations and environmental destruction in the region through the state.

The direct role of the state in dispossession was then replaced by criminal
groups in the mid-2000s. This is evident in the case of stolen hydrocarbons in
the Burgos Basin. Stolen condensed gas had been detected in U.S. markets
since 2006, and in 2007, a full 40 percent of the area's natural gas, mostly produced in Tamaulipas, was stolen (Pérez, 2012). Half of the illegal pipelines discovered in 2013 were also located in Tamaulipas (Reed, 2014: 2). Before turning
to the changes in the economic and political landscape that set these trends
in motion in the mid-2000s, it is important to describe how the illegally obtained condensed gas was actually exported. When criminal groups in Tamaulipas stole the condensed fuel through trucks and pipelines, Texas-based
import companies PetroSalum and Y Oil sent semi-truck tankers loaded with
condensate from Mexico across the border to the terminal of U.S. oil trader
Continental in the port of Brownsville, Texas. During this time, Continental's
vice president was Josh Crescenzi, former news liaison for former U.S. president George W. Bush and former vice president Dick Cheney. Continental
then sold the condensate to oil broker Murphy Energy, which in turn sold it to
oil trader Trammo (PEP v. BASF et al., S.D. Tex., 2014). Trammo eventually sold
the natural gas to global corporations such as BASF, Valero Energy Corp., and
Royal Dutch Shell (Linares and Montalvo, 2016), and these global companies,
in turn, used the illegally obtained gas as an input in their global production
processes.

This example shows how the reorganization of space under neoliberalism—
particularly the fragmentation of the production, distribution, and commercialization of gas—allowed criminal groups to accelerate the mobility of capital, increase profitability, and grant legal status to illegal fuel across national
borders through upward rescaling. It was the increasing governance role of

criminal groups in controlling dissent and mediating conflict, as explained in the previous chapter, along with high energy prices, which turned gas theft into an operation as profitable or more so than drug-trafficking, that set the conditions for the theft of condensed gas. Crucially, the profitability of these endeavors was achieved through processes of dispossession.

After 2006, dispossession in the Burgos Basin no longer took place directly via state intervention but rather through criminal groups. The intervention of these groups was a cheaper way of dispossessing small landholders, as indemnity payments could be entirely done away with. As Paley (2014) and Correa-Cabrera (2017) argue, the paramilitarization of the Gulf Cartel through Los Zetas and the increasing violence resulting from their split became a mechanism of social control that ultimately facilitated the further privatization of natural resources. The Burgos Basin area in Tamaulipas covers large extensions of rural land mostly owned by communal landholders (*ejidatarios*) and cattle ranchers. By 2016, this area was the locus of high levels of forced displacement by criminal groups and disappearances of Mexican citizens and undocumented immigrants in the country (CNDH, 2016: 83). This environment of fear and violence forced people to abandon land located in the most important gas basin in the country. The ensuing dispossession allowed criminal groups not only to obtain economic gains from agriculture and cattle ranching, but also to gain access to gas wells for commercialization (Pérez, 2011).

This climate of fear and violence also made it possible to use unfree labor in gas theft. Starting in 2009, PEMEX workers and contractors became victims of disappearance and extortion. Families of the missing workers, human rights organizations and journalists suspected that the forcibly disappeared PEMEX workers were required to provide technical assistance to criminal groups, as the theft of condensed gas is a complicated process that requires specialized knowledge (Pérez, 2011). Families of disappeared PEMEX workers denounced this crime to state authorities and sought the union's support to find their missing relatives in 2010. The state and union did not respond to the families' demands, however, as expressed by a member of one of the denouncing families: "The company [PEMEX] and the union left the families on their own." These families later received threats after pressing charges, and PEMEX and the union refused to provide pensions as there was no proof that their relatives were dead (Pérez, 2011). Both dispossession and unfree labor, then, were essential components of the cost-effectiveness of stolen condensed gas exports from Tamaulipas.

The movement of stolen condensed gas from the Burgos Basin to higher political scales in the form of trade across international borders transformed it into legal merchandise, erasing the violent dispossession and unfree labor implicated in its production and distribution. While the actual process of moving the gas from Tamaulipas into Texas did involve falsified documentation, this alone does not explain how the violence and theft ultimately dissolved through the process of outsourcing and the integration of the product into financial markets. Outsourcing allowed activities to be segregated and assets to be protected, distancing the companies from any responsibility in the political economy of violence in Mexico. In fact, this was precisely the argument BASF used to dismiss the PEMEX lawsuit; the German petrochemical company claimed that it did not know the condensate had been obtained illegally (PEP v. BASF et al., S.D. Tex., 2014). The PEMEX lawsuits against global companies thus show how the fragmentation of responsibility involved in outsourcing served to legally limit liability and distance companies from particular obligations. Law-making then allowed for this blurring of the boundaries between legality and illegality and the obscuring of the conditions of direct physical violence behind economic transactions (Birch and Siemiatycki, 2015).

Since the stolen gas was sold at below-market prices, it potentially provided each company involved in its commercialization and distribution an increase in profit margins (Pérez, 2011). For instance, Trammo made a profit in the range of 120,000 and 200,000 dollars out of 2 million dollars in stolen gas (Vaughan, 2011). Between 2006 and 2007, the sales of Continental rose, as did the value of its stock in Nasdaq (SEC, 2007). Quite tellingly, this coincides with the period when criminal groups started to sell stolen gas condensate to oil traders in the United States. This hints at the violent processes behind the exporting of illegal condensed gas that guaranteed the economic gains of U.S. companies, as they were able to buy this commodity at below-market prices and sell it at market prices. The integration of the proceeds from the purchase of stolen fuel into financial markets further erased the violent origins of the commodity, transforming illegal and criminal activities into legal operations in the global economy.

We can understand violent dispossession and repression in Tamaulipas and the legalization of stolen fuel through international trade as part of the reassertion of state power in Mexico in the context of deepening neoliberalism. The role of criminal groups in the displacement of residents in the Burgos Basin, for instance, was beneficial to state power, as the state did not have to bear the political and economic costs of dispossession through expropriation. The effects of the presence of criminal groups in Tamaulipas were not a calculated plan on the part of economic and political elites; rather, they were the cumulative outcome of the activities of social actors and strategies related to previous rounds of commodification and dispossession. Nonetheless, state complicity is evident, for example, in the fact that the PAN administration of Felipe

Calderón (2006–2012) had been aware of the stolen gas since 2006, first thanks to internal reports provided by PEMEX internal security staff headed by military officers, and since 2008 from information provided by U.S. state authorities (Pérez, 2011; Linares and Montalvo 2016). The Calderón administration did not undertake any internal investigations, and the PEMEX lawsuit was presented two years after the evidence was provided by the U.S. state authorities.

All of these developments helped lay the groundwork for the deepening of neoliberalism in the energy sector during the PRI presidential administration of Enrique Peña Nieto (2012–2018). In December 2013, the Mexican president enacted a constitutional reform that allowed the Mexican state to contract either PEMEX or private entities (previously excluded from such contracts) to explore and extract oil and other hydrocarbons through profit sharing, production sharing, services arrangements, or a combination of these options, though the hydrocarbons would continue to be national property (Presidencia de la República, 2013). This reform also allowed private investment in oil refining and in the transportation, storage, and distribution of oil, natural gas, gasoline, and diesel fuel (Presidencia de la República, 2013).

The role of criminal groups then became further established as a proxy mechanism for dispossession and theft, enabling even deeper privatization of the energy sector. First, gas theft diminished the financial gains of the public company. This became a justification for the further privatization of PEMEX, arguing that the stolen gas was indicative of the corruption inherent in PEMEX as a public company (El País, 2013). Congressmen from left-center opposition parties Revolution Democratic Party (Partido de la Revolución Democratica or PRD) and National Regeneration Movement (Movimiento de Regeneración Nacional or MORENA) noted that the Executive's delivery of documents reporting PEMEX's financial losses in April 2014 was timed to coincide with the advancement of constitutional reforms to further privatize the energy sector. It was seen as part of an informal campaign by the Executive branch and the PRI and PAN to use reports about corruption in PEMEX and the resulting financial losses as a way to justify the complete opening of Mexico's energy sector to private investment (Rosagel, 2014). This shows why it is necessary to unpack allegations of corruption, because arguments that focus only on "the abuse of public authority or trust for private benefit" (IMF, 2018) are highly compatible with and conducive to the neoliberal agenda. Such views further justify commodification—namely the transformation of goods, services, people, nature, and ideas into objects with a price for exchange—by depicting state intervention as inherently corrupt vis-à-vis orderly and 'neutral' markets.

Second, the role of criminal groups in proxy governance in the Tamaulipas Burgos Basin helped to stifle opposition to privatization among PEMEX workers as well as repress any mobilizations by small landholders fighting threats of legal or illegal dispossession of their land or environmental degradation. Forced disappearances created fear among workers in Tamaulipas and in other areas of the country and prevented them from mobilizing against the constitutional reform to further privatize PEMEX, particularly in a stronghold of PEMEX worker activism like Tamaulipas. The lack of support from the PEMEX union leadership also discouraged mobilization. Likewise, the displacement of communities and the spread of fear facilitated the *de facto* and *de jure* dispossession of small portions of communal land for gas exploitation. This was particularly important in the process of land dispossession to further the privatization of rural land, as in 2007, Tamaulipas had one of the largest numbers of *ejidos* (Morett Sánchez and Cosío Ruiz, 2017: 132).

Land dispossession and legal reforms also prepared the ground for the further exploitation of natural resources, including fracking for shale gas. Fracking leads to high levels of pollution in the environment, and the carcinogenic substances used in the process can be harmful to human health (González Arévalo, 2015). Ciudad Mier, Tamaulipas, for example, a city with one of the highest internal displacement rates caused by violence in the early 2010s, became a site of interest for fracking by global companies like Weatherford, Halliburton, and Schlumberger since 2014 (Cedillo, 2014). Dispossession by criminal groups here and in other towns allowed initial explorations for shale gas to be carried out without significant local opposition. Illegal and violent activities were thus incorporated into the legal order, as it was the abandonment of plots and the repression of residents and workers by criminal groups that paved the way for legal companies to enter into the gas extraction sector.

Several rounds of dispossession by criminal groups in the Burgos Basin in Tamaulipas were legalized over time. As Abourahme notes, dispossession is not only about depriving people of their means of production and nature, but also about the legal practices at particular scales that legalize dispossession—what he terms "law-making robbery" (2018: 108). In the case under examination here, this was achieved with the 2014 Law of Hydrocarbons. This law forces small landholders to negotiate with private companies to allow the use of their land for the exploitation, processing, or distribution of oil and gas. If there is no agreement after 180 days, the Ministry of Energy can ask a judge to grant an assignment—the legal act by which the Executive gives a private investor the right to carry out activities in the disputed area for a specific length of time (*Ley de Hidrocarburos,* 2014, Chapter 4, article 101–125). While the landholders retain ownership of the land, they cannot use it. In this way, the state does not have to bear the political and economic costs of expropriation directly, as it does not have to expropriate the land or compensate the landholders in any way (Angles Hernández, 2017: 136). This law does not contemplate cases where the owners of the land are not present in negotiations because they have abandoned their land due to violence, yet as mentioned above, the Ministry of Energy can ultimately grant the private investor the right to use the land in the owners' absence, and companies can potentially use this part of the law to access abandoned land.

Outsourcing and illegal dispossessions were also locked in by upward scalar state governance in the form of the 1994 North American Free Trade Agreement (NAFTA) between Canada, the United States, and Mexico. On the one hand, NAFTA encouraged and protected outsourcing by enabling production and trade fragmentation through tariff reductions and investment protections (see Bair and Gereffi, 2002). On the other hand, NAFTA's Chapter 11 on investor rights locked in dispossession at higher scales, especially after additional privatizing reforms in the energy sector in the early 2010s. Chapter 11 required NAFTA governments to compensate foreign investors for any direct government expropriation or other action that was 'tantamount' to an indirect expropriation. The clause was vague and it did not explicitly refer to government seizures of property. It has been interpreted by NAFTA tribunals as any domestic legislation that might be seen as discriminatory toward foreign investment (Public Citizen, 2018). As such, foreign investors could use NAFTA's Chapter 11 when the Mexican state implemented environmental measures and regulations that affected the existing or potential assets of these investors. Though the 1994 agreement exempted oil and gas from the dispute resolution mechanism of Chapter 11, changes in domestic legislation in 2013 and 2014 waived this exemption (Condon, 2016: 10).

While the new administration of Andres Manuel López Obrador from the left-center party Movement of National Regeneration (Movimiento de Regeneracion Nacional or MORENA), who assumed the presidency on December 1, 2018, announced the reversal of laws allowing for shale gas extraction and exploration and the constitutional reforms related to the energy sector in general, the new trade agreement between Canada, the United States, and Mexico signed in 2018 (USMCA) constitutes a framework that legalizes existing dispossession in the oil and gas sector. While the USMCA limits the investor-state dispute settlement mechanism contained in NAFTA's Chapter 11, USMCA's Chapter 14, particularly Annex 14-E, allows energy companies to continue to use the dispute-resolution process from the original NAFTA agreement in their already existing investment deals in Mexico (Grandoni, 2018; Whalen, 2018; Brooks, 2018; USMCA, 2018). Although USMCA's Chapter 8 allows the Mexican state to revert the constitutional reforms in the energy sector, those companies that negotiated contracts in the gas, oil, and electricity industries during the privatization of the energy sector can employ this investor-state dispute mechanism. The upward scale of investment and free trade agreements thus locks in both the implementation of the national neoliberal agenda locally and the processes of dispossession initiated by criminal groups in Tamaulipas across larger scales of governance.

The theft of hydrocarbons is not unique to the region. Hydrocarbon theft became widespread in other parts of Mexico in the late 2000s, particularly the theft of gasoline involving fuel thieves, criminal groups and high-level PEMEX employees (López Obrador, 2018). Yet, the case of large-scale hydrocarbon theft involving criminal groups in the Burgos Basin provides insights into the interconnected processes of dispossession and capital accumulation at different political scales. On the one hand, local coercive forms of dispossession by criminal groups, along with the resulting physical insecurity and fear experienced by subordinate groups on a daily basis, facilitated the opening of spaces of accumulation to large corporations in parts of Tamaulipas previously occupied by the working classes and small businesses. This in turn further deterred dissent against corporate actions and state policies. On the other hand, at the global scale of capital mobility, the legal frameworks that facilitate and protect international trading, outsourcing, and financial investments enabled the reproduction of capital accumulation and reconfigured existing political and economic hierarchies in Tamaulipas in particular and Mexico in general, helping to integrate the criminal economy into the legal one.

2   Uneven Development, Finance, and Money Laundering

In 1995, former Tamaulipas governor Emilio Martínez Manatou (1981–1987) was questioned in Switzerland as part of a lawsuit he launched against his former financial advisor. During the interrogation, he was asked why he had investments abroad, and he responded: "Because I am a politician, and in my country all politicians have their capital abroad to avoid criticism from people" (Redacción, 1995). This quote is telling of how global finance hides the origins of financial gain while protecting the holders of these assets from legal and social condemnation. In this way, finance disguises conditions of economic inequality and undemocratic practices such as the private appropriation of public funds and connections between state authorities and criminal groups, turning illegal activities into legal assets. This is not a straightforward process; it involves social and legal arrangements mediated by geography, including politics of scale. The reorganization of space under capitalist uneven development also contributes to the ways in which law and order produce and reproduce illegal practices.

This section focuses on accusations by U.S. authorities against two former governors of Tamaulipas in order to highlight two spatial processes in the nexus between criminality, illegality and violence in the process of neoliberal state formation and accumulation in Mexico. The first such process—a rescaling of funds across national and international political scales that define legality and illegality differently—made it possible for these former governors to hide the origin of funds they had obtained and protect themselves both politically and legally. This process was, of course, economically beneficial for these individual politicians and their collaborators, but it also helped to sustain the profits of global financial institutions, particularly those banks based in the United States. The second spatial process involved in these cases—money laundering—was driven by uneven development within Mexico and the United States.

The accusations against former Tamaulipas governors Tomás Yarrington Ruvalcaba (1998–2004) and Eugenio Hernández Flores (2004–2010) in a federal court in Texas are highly illustrative of rescaling, uneven development, and fetishism of the law in the process of money laundering. According to official documents in the federal court, the trail of money laundering in Yarrington Ruvalcaba's case dates back to 1998, with funds that came from both criminal groups and public money (USA v. Tomas Yarrington Ruvalcaba and Fernando Cano Martinez, S.D. Tex., 2013). According to the case files, trusted intermediaries and front companies were part of the scheme to disguise the origin of Yarrington Ruvalcaba's economic proceeds. The Gulf Cartel and Los Zetas channeled money to the former governor in exchange for local state protection, including the freedom to transport illegal drugs and carry out other criminal activities in the region (USA v. Fernando Cano Martinez, S.D. Tex., 2012). This former governor also received a share of the sale of illicit drugs (USA v. Antonio Pena-Arguelles, S.D. Tex., 2012; USA v. Tomas Yarrington Ruvalcaba and Fernando Cano Martinez, S.D. Tex., 2013; Ravelo, 2018). Meanwhile, financial activities within Mexico, the United States, and across borders masked the violence, inequality, and lack of public accountability that characterized the origin of these funds.

The 2012 case *United States of America v. Antonio Pena-Arguelles* describes Yarrington Ruvalcaba's use of a straw man, Peña Arguelles, to launder money. A straw man or *prestanombres* (name-lender) is the nominal owner or holder of title to an asset, who buys the latter on the instructions of another person using the true buyer's financial funds. Peña Arguelles collected money from criminal groups operating in Tamaulipas to bolster Yarrington Ruvalcaba's political power. Peña Arguelles and other protected witnesses declared that this money was deposited in a Mexican subsidiary of Citibank in Nuevo Laredo, Tamaulipas. In 2005, 7 million dollars were transferred from this Mexican branch to a Citigroup bank account in California. In April 2008, Peña Arguelles then transferred 4 million and 2.99 million from the California account to the Texas banks of Falcon International and Laredo National Bank (now BBVA Compass), respectively. From the Falcon International account, about 1 million dollars was deposited into the BBVA Compass account four days later. From there, Peña Arguelles moved 4.1 million dollars into the Texas bank International Bank of Commerce in 2009. Peña Arguelles used money from these accounts to buy real estate in Texas (USA v. Antonio Pena-Arguelles, S.D. Tex., 2012).

The 2012 case of *United States of America v. Fernando Cano Martinez* highlights the role of construction companies in money laundering. This forms a part of the mechanisms used for the private appropriation of public funds. The case involves Yarrington Ruvalcaba's straw man, Fernando Cano Martínez, and his company, Materiales y Construcciones Villa de Aguayo. Some work was also outsourced to front companies GMC and Janambres. The latter were construction companies focused on public works. They obtained public contracts from the Tamaulipas state government and the federal government between 2004 and 2015 as the result of a dubious bidding process (Sandoval Alarcón, 2017). The process involved unclear rules behind the allocation of public contracts to Cano Martínez's companies and the sharing of the profits from these contracts with the same state authorities awarding the contracts (Montalvo, 2017). These companies also helped to channel money from criminal groups into the formal economy (USA v. Tomás Yarrington Ruvalcaba and Fernando Cano Martinez, 2013), as money was deposited in several bank accounts in Mexico belonging to global financial institutions and then used to buy several properties in Mexico.

Cano Martínez conducted several cross-border transactions to hide the origin of the funds. He established limited liability companies (LLC) and limited partnerships (LP) in southern Texas, and the LLCs became the managing partners of the LPs. The LPs would then open bank accounts and borrow money from Texas banks to buy assets ranging from aircraft to real estate in Texas. The loans were guaranteed by public contracts and deposits made to the LP accounts from the Mexican bank accounts of front companies based in Tamaulipas, such as Materiales y Constructions Villa de Aguayo and GMC, via the Mexican-based money transmitter Monex. These and other Tamaulipas-based front companies had their Mexican bank accounts in large financial institutions such as Scotiabank, Banamex, BBV, HSBC, and Banregio. Between 2005 and 2010, these front companies carried out international transactions across the Mexico-U.S. border ranging from half a million to three million dollars (USA v. Fernando Cano Martinez, 2012). According to the accusations in the United States, Yarrington Ruvalcaba used similar schemes, with front companies receiving contracts to supply municipalities and the government of Tamaulipas and making money transfers to several banks in Texas and a Citibank branch in California (California Commerce Bank) (USA v. Real Property Known as 334 Padre Blvd., 2012; USA v. Antonio Pena-Arguelles, 2012).

The money-laundering arrangements of former governor Eugenio Hernández Flores are similar to those in the Yarrington Ruvalcaba case, as illustrated in the case of *United States of America v. Luis Carlos Castillo-Cervantes* (2017). Castillo Cervantes is a Tamaulipas-based businessman who inflated prices in his contracts to build public infrastructure and later split the gains obtained from his inflated budgets with former Tamaulipas governor Hernández Flores. Castillo Cervantes was also a shareholder of International Bank in McAllen, Texas, where three shell companies and several of Hernández Flores' straw owners of U.S. bank accounts deposited the proceeds from criminal groups and the private appropriation of public funds. For instance, a straw man named Guillermo Flores Cordero set up three front companies in the United States, which opened accounts at International Bank and then transferred money from there to the bank accounts of other straw owners and Hernández Flores himself at International Bank and Wells Fargo. These transactions amounted to thirty million dollars between 2008 and 2012 (USA v. Castillo-Cervantes, 2017). Part of this money was used to buy real estate in Texas and certificates of deposits in the United States.

It is certainly true that money laundering by Mexican state officials and politicians and the use of international financial transactions to cover up their tracks is not new. For instance, Raúl Salinas de Gortari, brother of former Mexican president Carlos Salinas de Gortari (1988–1994), was accused of money laundering in Switzerland in 1995. This case involved international bank accounts, front companies, and the participation of global banks, specifically Citigroup (GAO, 1998), but as Raúl Salinas de Gortari was a key political figure at the national scale, he was able to connect to these large financial institutions directly. What is telling in the case study of the Tamaulipas governors, though, is the increasing role of local scales in intensifying the process of uneven development, which in turn shapes constructions of legality and illegality. Analyses of how local scales of state governance in both Mexico and the United States shape process of money laundering must also look at the ways in which different political scales overlap, showing, as Lefebvre puts it, "the interpenetration and superimposition of social space" (2001: 88)

In the cases studied here, the local state level made it possible to extract economic gains and profits from criminal and illegal economic activities. Local state authorities established the context of institutional and juridical suspension of the law to allow criminal groups to operate in their jurisdiction, not only for drug-trafficking but also for extortion, kidnapping, human trafficking, and smuggling. State authorities also exempted themselves from the law to illegally access public funds for their own personal benefit. The mechanisms for accessing these public funds were, in turn, shaped by the intensification of uneven development within Mexico, particularly the need to provide competitive infrastructure for private investment, which involved the construction of roads connecting the petrochemical industry in southern Tamaulipas to main national highways as well as improvements in highways connecting Tamaulipas to the United States. Between 2003 and 2009, public works contracts granted by the government of Tamaulipas amounted to more than thirty-five million dollars (Sandoval Alarcón, 2017). These contracts featured partnerships with construction companies whose real owners were the three Tamaulipas PRI governors in power between 1998 and 2016—primarily Tomás Yarrington Ruvalcaba but also Eugenio Hernández Flores and Egidio Torres Cantú (Redacción, 2017b). While greater infrastructure investments increased the competitive position of Tamaulipas as a trade and production hub in the country (Gobierno del Estado de Tamaulipas, 2004, 2009, 2015), they also exacerbated uneven development in Mexico, as Tamaulipas competed with other northern states like Nuevo León and Chihuahua for investment.

As explained in Chapter 2, the local scale sustained the implementation of the national neoliberal agenda. For example, the terms in office of the Tamaulipas governors involved in money laundering were characterized by increasing downward pressure on workers' rights. Between 1998 and 2016, these governors allowed job precariousness in maquiladoras to persist and increase, particularly through the creation of jobs with lower wages and fewer social benefits (Quintero, 2001; Muñoz Martínez, 2010; Moctezuma, 2017). In the public sector, health care workers experienced wage repression and/or unpaid wages, job cuts, and unsafe working conditions, especially from 2010 onward (Alvarez, 2017). This coincides with a lack of oversight by national state authorities, which made it possible for the construction companies involved in money laundering—in which these governors had large economic stakes—to continue to receive federal money for infrastructure. During the Calderón administration (2006–2012), GMC obtained contracts worth approximately 40 million dollars for infrastructure projects (Redacción, 2012a). In 2014 and 2015, GMC and Materiales y Construcciones Villa de Aguayo received three federal contracts for infrastructure projects amounting to approximately 1.5 million dollars, even though national authorities knew about the criminal charges against these companies in the United States (Montalvo, 2017). National state authorities' determinations of what was legal and illegal certainly appear to have been influenced by their interests in the continuation of local neoliberalism in such a strategic economic region as Tamaulipas.

Another local scale, in this case the U.S. state of Texas, was crucial for the reterritorialization of gains and profits. The Tamaulipas governors chose Texas as the place to open bank accounts and buy assets, particularly real estate (Ravelo, 2018). On the one hand, the selection of a U.S. jurisdiction as the site for financial investment is related both to the geographical proximity of Tamaulipas to Texas and international competition between Mexico and the United States to attract capital. On the other hand, internal competition among local states within the United States to reterritorialize capital within their own jurisdictions also shaped this choice of location.

The intensification of neoliberalism in Texas can be traced back to the governorships of George W. Bush (1995–2000) and Rick Perry (2000–2015). During this period, austerity measures were imposed on health and education, while the economic environment was made more favorable to large businesses through low wages, regressive taxation (particularly low corporate and property taxes), and legal incentives to promote startup companies, limit workers' rights, and accommodate business needs (Texans for Public Justice, 2011a, 2001b; Levine, 2017). As such, the legal framework in Texas facilitated the establishment of companies and the protection of business owners and their assets, assisting Yarrington Ruvalcaba and Hernández Flores in transforming the juridical categorization of funds from illegal to legal. The choice to establish LPs and LLCs is a case in point. As the general partner, the LLC is the face of a company in all legal actions, whereas the limited partners are only subject to limited liability through the LP structure. This legal business structure protects the personal property of all investors in both LLCs and LPs and provides single taxation of profits (Bagley, 1994; Texas Secretary of State, 2018). The intensification of neoliberalism in Texas also created favorable conditions for real estate investment, particularly for out-of-state property investors, promising exemption from state income tax and low property taxes (The State of Texas Governor, 2016). The local scale of the state of Texas thus served as a fix in the process of uneven development both within the United States and between the United States and Mexico. It was key in shaping the flows of money from illegal activities from Mexico into the U.S. economy and, in doing so, transforming illegal money into legal money.

At the same time, these local scales of state governance were not unconnected to the global scale of capital mobility. Gains and profits originating from direct and structural violence in Tamaulipas became temporarily deterritorialized through the global financial system dominated by large global financial institutions as money crossed multiple borders. This in turn further transformed the legal categorization of this money in the financial sector. This global scale of capital mobility is intertwined with the national scales of both the U.S. and Mexican states. Both national states have helped global financial institutions to facilitate the deterritorialization of capital, and they have both engaged in the changing construction of legality and illegality since the 1970s with economic liberalization and the elimination of capital controls (Panitch and Konings, 2008). At the national scale, the Mexican and U.S. state authorities set the legal conditions for large banks and financial institutions to access financial resources originating from exploitation, unfree labor, and even murder. They also established the mechanisms that allow these banking institutions to legally transform the categorization of these funds from illegal to legal through their respective national financial systems. The operations of Citigroup both in Mexico and the United States are a clear example. The restructuring of the Mexican economy after the 1994 pesos crisis opened the door to foreign investment in the Mexican banking sector to boost capital adequacy. As a result, one of the largest Mexican banks, Banamex, was sold to Citigroup in 2002. By 2007, 85 percent of the banking sector was dominated by foreign investment (Marois, 2008), and the presence of subsidiaries of the same bank on both sides of the U.S.-Mexican border facilitated money laundering, as in the example of the money transfer from a Citibank subsidiary in Tamaulipas to a California account in the Yarrington Ruvalcaba case.

Similarly, the privileged position U.S. state authorities granted to financial institutions allowed these institutions to work with money originating from criminal activities with little state oversight. For instance, the documents required to open an account in Citigroup's subsidiary in California indicated that Peña Arguelles only expected to receive fifty dollars a month in his account, showing his source of income in 2005 as cattle ranching. A week later after opening the account, Peña Arguelles deposited seven million dollars into his account without raising any concerns among high-level bank executives (Katz and Campbbell, 2015). It was not until 2012, when the Federal Deposit Insurance Corporation (FDIC) and the California Department of Business Oversight (CDBO) instructed the bank to review old accounts, that a suspicious activity report was eventually filed. Later, in 2015, the FDIC fined the bank 140 million dollars for failing to comply with anti-money-laundering state regulations (Katz and Campbell, 2015). Other global financial institutions such as Wachovia and HSBC were also part of money-laundering schemes in Mexico, turning these global banks, as Ed Vulliamy (2012, 2015) suggests, into the financial services wing of criminal groups in their association with political power.

The FDIC's delay in detecting Citibank's money-laundering operations at its California branch and the relatively modest fine imposed on the bank reveal the complementarity between violence, criminal illegality, state law and global financial institutions. It is telling that money laundering in these institutions took place before and during the mortgage crisis in the United States and the 2007–2010 global financial crises. Antonio Maria Costa, former head of the UN Office on Drugs and Crime, stated in 2009 that the proceeds of crime represented "the only liquid investment capital" available to banks in danger of collapsing during the financial crisis. "Inter-bank loans were funded by money that originated from the drugs trade and other illegal activities... There were signs that some banks were rescued that way" (Syal, 2009). This describes the centrality of the nexus of criminality, illegality and violence for sustaining capital accumulation and the global financial system in a context of growing global financial instability. In this process, as we have seen, the unequal application of the law across political scales and the changing construction of legality and illegality facilitated processes of dispossession, labor exploitation, and commodification in Mexico.

In these cases, the territoriality of the state shaped the ways in which capital and money became fixed in different jurisdictions across political scales. As Lefebvre reminds us, "[o]nly the state can control flows and harmonize them within the fixed elements of the economy because the state integrates them into the dominant space it produces" (2003, 91). Under neoliberalism, the process by which the state becomes a scalar fix to territorialize capital is intensified because of increasing competition among local states and between countries. At the same time, these scalar processes shape the politics of (il)legality behind financial and real estate assets. Clearly, this is not confined to just one nation-state; rather, it involves different scalar hierarchies that intertwine and overlap (Brenner, 1998: 461, 466). In the emblematic examples discussed here, then, local and national scales of state governance and the global scale of capital are all implicated in the legalization of funds originating from direct violence in Mexico.

3 Law and Geographies of Power

The case studies of theft and dispossession in the gas basin of Tamaulipas and the accusations of money laundering against state governors reveal a considerable degree of compliance with existing legal frameworks across political scales. Why was it important for criminal groups and the accused governors in Tamaulipas to organize their illegal operations following Mexican and U.S. laws? One answer to this question is that politicians and members of criminal groups need to avoid legal problems if they are to continue their economic and political activities both inside and outside the law. However, this was not necessarily the case at the local level during the import substitution industrialization (ISI) period, when *caciques* (local bosses) openly determined the political and economic trajectories of their informal jurisdictions without significant law abidance (Flores Pérez, 2014b). An alternative interpretation that addresses the seeming compliance with the law in these cases highlights the centrality of the neoliberal rule of law as a form of legitimation and a mechanism to insulate state practices from society, including those illegal activities and non-state violence that help to sustain state power and neoliberalism.

A comparison of the political and legal processes behind dispossession and money laundering in Tamaulipas under ISI and neoliberalism reveals how the highly politicized relations mediating the connection between legal and illegal and criminal activities during ISI were partly replaced by juridical relations under neoliberalism. During the ISI period, accumulation through dispossession involved a high level of state intervention, with some assistance from paramilitary forces. In Tamaulipas, expropriations were mostly related to the exploitation of oil and gas. Dispossession involved both force and political negotiation, which often resulted in concessions to subordinated groups via PRI-affiliated unions. The state also seized land from political opponents in Tamaulipas. For example, in the 1960s, the state government seized the land of a general affiliated to a faction within the PRI opposed to the Tamaulipas governor (Flores Pérez, 2014b). Land was then redistributed among peasants and small landholders, particularly those affiliated to the PRI peasant union, in order to obtain ongoing support for the dominant local faction within the PRI. Indeed, relations of private property and between social forces were highly mediated by open political conflict and negotiation.

This was also the case in money laundering. The private appropriation of public funds involved the direct use of public money by state officials for private ends, and money laundering did not entail complex financial and legal operations across legal borders. Public officials were not investigated or punished as long as they helped to reproduce the political system, especially the dominance of the PRI and the president. In Tamaulipas, for instance, it is well-known in the city capital that the governor in power from 1975 to 1981 utilized public funds for private ends and positioned members of his family in key local political positions (Redacción, 1978). Yet the governor and his collaborators did not employ complex legal and financial instruments at multiple scales to hide the illegal origin of these funds. This was possible because the political structure in place at the time allowed public officials to enjoy the ill-gotten gains of political power in exchange for their support of the political system and the existing economic agenda (Morris, 2009: 38). Even when the law was used to legitimize money laundering and dispossession, these processes were highly mediated by political negotiations between different social forces.

During the neoliberal period, in contrast, the promise of the rule of law became one of the key features lending the neoliberal agenda in Mexico popular

appeal, given the privileged access to funds and economic opportunities en-
joyed by PRI state officials and leaders prior to neoliberalism. State authorities
advocating neoliberalism depicted the rule of law as a way to weaken the influence of clientelism in the allocation of jobs and resources. Proponents of the
rule of law in Mexico's neoliberal agenda claimed that market forces, rather
than political loyalty to the PRI, would provide equal access to labor markets
and other economic opportunities (Martin 2007). The convergence of, on
the one hand, the legitimacy of the liberal notion of the rule of law, namely the
notion of the law based on rules, reason, and rational procedures, with, on the
other hand, neoliberalism, allowed the latter to operate and legitimize state
power in ways that previous political institutions in Mexico had not—ostensibly because it offered equal opportunities to market access enforced by the law
(Brabazon, 2017). This convergence led to a neoliberal version of the rule of
law, that is the role of the state in setting rules and procedures to encourage
commodification and market discipline and guarantee contracts and property
rights (Kyeger, 2018; Biebricher, 2018). Here, the fetishism of the law disguises
how the neoliberal rule of law favors those with money and resources, as they
are the ones who are able to own property and set the terms of contracts. In
contrast, those who have nothing but their labor are not necessarily protected
under the neoliberal rule of law (Harvey, 2007, 64–66).

The intersection of the preeminence of liberal legalism and the expansion
of procedural democracy and neoliberalism in Mexico led to an expanded role
for the law in mediating relations among people as neoliberal subjects (Brabazon, 2017; Comaroff and Comaroff, 2006). Proponents of neoliberalism in Mexico promised equal opportunities in the market regardless of political affiliation (Salinas de Gortari, 1988). Politically, equality of opportunity was translated
into legislative changes to increase electoral competition among political parties in Congress during the 1990s. During this time, the Federal Electoral Institute was created and then granted independence to oversee electoral procedures. Changes in electoral law also increased public funding for elections
(Camp, 2013). The rise of the right-wing opposition National Action Party in
the 2000 presidential elections also intensified electoral competition, not only
at the national level but also in local elections (Morris, 2009: 37–40). This coincided with the deepening of neoliberal reforms in the form of privatizations
and the implementation of austerity measures.

The rule of law thus became narrowly defined as competition among political parties and the enactment of the law to protect private property and enforce
private contracts. This occurred in a social context between 1992 and 2006 in
which more than 50 percent of the population could not even afford food and
basic social services such as health and education (CONEVAL, 2015b). As such,

half of the population did not have property that could be protected by the neoliberal rule of law. Similarly, most people were not in an economic or social position to negotiate the terms of contracts with more powerful actors, particularly with respect to labor and land contracts. Nonetheless, the legal language of apparent compliance with rules and procedures became an important mechanism for the legitimation of neoliberalism in Mexico, because it offered equality of opportunity in markets. Elections, too, were depicted as another market, where 'political consumers' could make choices, and elections became the legally recognized way to access political power, which was relatively novel in Mexico (Tagle, 2008). At the same time, neoliberal legality became a way to insulate undemocratic state practices at the national and local levels. As long as electoral competition and the neoliberal agenda remained in place, state officials at the local level could carry out activities outside the law to the detriment of the population under their jurisdiction. In Tamaulipas, the state governors implicated in the money-laundering cases implemented neoliberalism locally and upheld the appearance of electoral competition, despite undemocratic practices behind securing votes for the PRI. In this way, these state officials operated, to some extent, within the boundaries of neoliberal legality.

Neoliberal legality was also crucial in the articulation between legal and illegal economies, violence, state power, and criminal groups. Under neoliberalism, juridical relations became more important than political negotiations and political conflict in cases involving dispossession, criminal activities, and the private appropriation of public funds. For instance, during the 2010s, criminal groups forced individuals to pay extortion money. If unable to pay, families would flee from their homes in Tamaulipas or were forced to sign their properties over to the criminal groups. In either case, a notary public was necessary to legalize ownership of the assets, and criminal groups relied on a network of notary publics in Tamaulipas to change ownership in title deeds (Redacción, 2017; Portugal, 2010). In some cases, notary publics were forced to perform these tasks (Flores, 2018), while in others, the notary publics were linked to political power directly through their positions as state officials in Tamaulipas or through family connections (González Antonio, 2017; Staff, 2018; Tovar, 2018). While this can be described as another example of corruption, such a description does not address the historical and socioeconomic context that shaped the need of criminal groups to legally own an asset they had obtained illegally. Indeed, as mentioned above, property grabbing by powerful groups in Tamaulipas had not necessarily relied greatly on such legal mechanisms in the past. An alternative analysis, attentive to changes in local and global political dynamics, shows how neoliberal legality shaped this imperative to legally own property, enabling criminal groups and state officials in Tamaulipas to transform illegal assets into legal assets and protect them under the law.

The neoliberal notion of the rule of law also enforces contracts and aids in the expansion of contractual relations in lieu of political negotiations and political conflict. The theft of gas in Tamaulipas and money-laundering accusations against former state governors show how this contractual shift under neoliberal legality helped transform illegal activities into legal ones. Value chains, money layering, and the establishment of shell companies involved a great number of contractual relations, which are individual agreements limited to private parties and tailored to the needs of the contract participants (Perrone, 2017). In the case of gas theft, criminal groups, PEMEX employees, and local and global companies used a variety of contracts to dissolve the administrative, political, and economic hierarchies involved into a chain of contractual relations. Money layering and the creation of shell companies included a series of contracts that ranged from bidding contracts for public works to diverse types of asset ownership and financial transactions across borders. Contractual relations therefore facilitated money laundering and the transfer of ownership involved in dispossession while the neoliberal rule of law established the framework for enforcing these contracts. Overall, the apparent compliance with rules related to property, security of contracts, and economic transactions assisted in the reproduction of neoliberal notions of the rule of law in Mexico. While neoliberal legality did not completely replace clientelism and other forms of political and economic interaction, it did become central to definitions of legality in the country.

This use of legality to hide the illegal, criminal and violent origins of economic assets is decidedly not about circumventing regulations to weaken the state. The suspension of the law depends on the state to shape the boundaries between law and disorder. As Giorgio Agamben notes, "the state of exception is thus not so much a spatiotemporal suspension as a complex topological figure in which not only the exception and the rule but also the state of nature and law, outside and inside, pass through one another" (1998: 37). The suspension of the law that allows dispossession and criminality to exist is therefore not an empty space, but rather it becomes materialized in space (Agamben, 2005: 41), and this materialization is shaped by the state-sanctioned boundaries of lawlessness and rule (Agamben, 1998: 170). Essentially, these boundaries are not fixed and completely dichotomous boundaries, because sovereign power in the form of the modern state determines this suspension of the law.

As a result, the suspension of the law that allows criminal groups and state officials to undertake processes of dispossession and money laundering can be interpreted not as a weakening but as the strengthening of state power in Mexico. For example, the narrative of criminality and corruption helped state officials legitimize violent and legal forms of state intervention after 2006 and eliminate 'bad apples' within and outside the state. Similarly, while coercive means were used to combat criminal groups in the War on Drugs strategy between 2006 and 2018, state officials also employed legal means to eliminate corruption. For instance, national state authorities have been investigating money laundering by public officials in Tamaulipas since 2000 and hydrocarbon theft in the same area since 2010, yet these cases were were ultimately thought to be isolated instances of corruption by a handful of state officials. This approach promoted the politics of exception involved in state coercion to guarantee the rule of law, while hiding the spatial hierarchies in Mexico's political economy that allowed for the selective use of the law (Muller, 2016). The articulation between criminality, violence and illegality in the process of neoliberal state formation thus remains hidden while it serves to sustain existing power relations in the country.

The nexus between (il)legality, violence and the criminal groups involved in money laundering in this chapter's case studies was also central to political power at the national scale in both Mexico and the United States during the 2010s. In Mexico, for example, the Mexican money transmitter company, Monex, simultaneously assisted in the money-laundering schemes of the Tamaulipas governors and in Peña Nieto's PRI campaign for the 2012 presidential elections. Monex distributed gift cards in exchange for votes for Peña Nieto and the PRI, and this financial support had substantial influence in securing Peña Nieto's electoral victory and a majority in Congress for his political party (Cervantes and Olmos, 2012). One of Peña Nieto's main achievements during his presidency was the constitutionalization of structural neoliberal reforms, relying both on the support of the PRI majority in Congress and on decree power. Reforms ranged from the privatization of energy and further flexibilization of labor relations in education to water privatization, all in the context of growing levels of violence in the country (Cárdenas Gracia, 2016). While elections were a legal means to access political power, then, this access was also, crucially, determined by the financial support of economic actors operating in the realms of the illegal and the criminal. The electoral outcome, ostensibly a result of competition among political parties, then helped legalize these illegal funds, as the Peña Nieto administration used its political power and the law to consolidate neoliberal reforms in the form of constitutional reforms, deepening neoliberal legality in the country.

Money laundering also provided economic gains for the U.S. national state, such as with the proceeds from asset forfeiture. These proceeds are deposited in the Department of Justice Asset Forfeiture Fund (AFF) and the Treasury Forfeiture Fund (TFF) and administered by the U.S. Treasury. The proceeds are then distributed to the Department of Justice in the case of the AFF and to the Treasury Department, the Homeland Security Department and its different agencies, the Internal Revenue Service, and the U.S. Secret Service in the case of the TFF. The Treasury also channels some of the net proceeds from forfeiture to the local law-enforcement agencies that contributed to the seizing of assets (Snyder, 2013). Between 2004 and 2009, the TFF collected an average of 361.83 million dollars a year, which increased to an annual average of 1.58 billion dollars between 2010 and 2015 (U.S. Treasury, 2004–2015). In the cases against the former governors of Tamaulipas, the Department of Justice seized several properties in Texas. Just one plane seized by the U.S. authorities was worth 4 million dollars (United States of America v. Pablo Zarate-Juarez, S.D. Tex., 2015).

While not all the assets seized by the TFF originate from criminal activities in Mexico, it is nonetheless important to note that narratives and policies related to U.S. actions to fight Mexican criminality and corruption provide economic rewards to the U.S. national state. This strengthens the state's coercive powers, as funds from the AFF and the TFF provide incentive for punitive policies rather than social policies. These punitive policies, in turn, often criminalize the poor and reproduce hierarchies of class, gender, and race (Wacquant, 2009). Criminal asset forfeiture, then, transforms illegal assets into authorized funds used to sustain state power and power hierarchies within the United States without addressing the structural conditions that increase people's vulnerability to criminality, either as individuals affected by it or as individuals forced into criminal operations indirectly at the lower level of criminal hierarchies in both Mexico and the United States.

To be clear, this use of funds from asset forfeiture is not an example of the Mexican state's weakness vis-à-vis the United States. Rather, this kind of financing from asset forfeiture has turned U.S. law-enforcement agencies into key stakeholders in decision-making in the United States, leading to greater support for the securitization strategy in Mexico (Franzblau, 2015). For instance, in a 2015 state visit by former Mexican president Peña Nieto to the United States, former U.S. president Obama remarked: "Our commitment is to be a friend and supporter of Mexico in its efforts to eliminate the scourge of violence and drug cartels that are responsible for so many tragedies inside of Mexico" (BBC, 2015). In effect, this support for securitization strengthens state power in Mexico, justifying coercive means and deflecting attention from human rights violations.

4 Conclusion

This chapter shows how violence by criminal groups, in short, became a governance mechanism to enable dispossession and how market transactions, and the law protecting them, integrated the proceeds from illegal and criminal activities into global markets. The cases of gas theft and the alleged money laundering by two Tamaulipas governors illustrate this process and how the connections between multiple overlapping scales blurred the boundaries between legality and illegality. Dispossession was carried out locally, requiring state acquiescence to enable the private appropriation of public funds. National state authorities, in collaboration with local state officials, set the conditions for the fixity of capital by supporting the local implementation of neoliberalism, privatization reforms, and favorable investment conditions for large companies. The upward scalar fixes of international trade, outsourcing, and global finance then established the conditions for shifting boundaries of legality and illegality. Here, global processes reinforced the (re)production of the suspension of the law in Mexico, both nationally and locally. It was the national scalar fix of the state, though, that established the legal framework that allowed for the movement and protection of capital in the form of money and goods.

While the cases of gas theft and money laundering in Tamaulipas are often referred to as examples of corruption and evidence of state weakness, the alternative interpretation I present here suggests that state officials shape law and disorder simultaneously, and legally protected market transactions disguise the violent, criminal and illegal origin of financial gain. This analysis therefore not only notes the blurred boundaries between state and criminal groups and shows how displacement by organized crime favors corporations; rather, it also identifies the legalistic form that money laundering has taken in the context of intensified uneven development under neoliberalism across political scales. Understood in this way, the seeming compliance with the law by criminal groups and state officials in these case studies is closely tied to the context of neoliberal legality in Mexico. The neoliberal notion of the rule of law guarantees general, formal, and clear regulations that protect private property and investment and enforce contractual arrangements. This neoliberal legality facilitated the transformation of illegal assets, obtained through direct violence, into authorized assets by integrating them into the national legal economy of the United States and the global economy, all as part of the neoliberal expansion of market rationality and profitability. Such a view thus goes beyond ideas of individualized corruption in order to tease out the blurred boundaries between legality and illegality and how these categories are framed by processes of capital accumulation under neoliberalism at multiple political scales in order to understand how the nexus of violence, illegality and criminality is integral to neoliberal state formation in Mexico.

CHAPTER 4

Urban (Dis)Orders

In December 2012, I heard multiple shots fired while staying at my family's house in Ciudad Victoria, the capital of Tamaulipas. My family and I immediately checked our social media to find out where it had been and what areas to avoid. Over the following days, I read the local newspapers looking for information and found nothing. It was not until I heard the story from a hospital staff member and read about it in a newspaper from the neighboring state of Nuevo León that I learned what had happened: three gunmen had walked into a hospital and murdered a woman.

I got another glimpse into everyday violence in Tamaulipas in the summer of 2014, when I accompanied the owner of two tortilla shops, or *tortillerías,* on her route to supervise her shops and deliver tortillas to several corner stores. Her shops and clients were located in two neighborhoods in Ciudad Victoria with high levels of poverty and violence. I learned about her strategies for avoiding violence and extortion from criminal groups, which included replacing her car with a more modest model, switching up her delivery route on a daily basis, and limiting her workday to daylight hours. Along her route, I also learned which small businesses were affected by violence and extortion, including specific details about the modus operandi of coercion, used to spread fear among small business owners not connected to criminal groups or political power.

Since 2010, these situations have become part of the daily lives of the residents of Ciudad Victoria, Tamaulipas, as is the case in several cities in Mexico. Ciudad Victoria saw particularly high levels of violence between 2010 and 2016. For example, six of the sixteen car bombs planted in Mexico by criminal groups between 2010 and 2012 exploded in Ciudad Victoria. In fact, from 2011 to 2012, the capital city of Tamaulipas was even more violent than Ciudad Juárez, a city that receives a lot of media coverage for its high levels of violence (CCSPJP, 2012: 47). Ciudad Victoria also bears the distinction of being one of the world's top ten most violent cities in countries without war every year from 2012 to 2017, according to the annual ranking of the Mexican Citizens' Council for Public Security (CCSPJP, 2012, 2013, 2014, 2015, 2016, 2017). It also makes an important case study as decision-making and negotiations processes among different powerful local, national and international groups, including criminal ones, occurred in this city.

In this context of violence, the case of Ciudad Victoria offers insights into the articulation between political power, accumulation, violence, criminality and the construction of legality and illegality in a concrete space. As we have seen, Los Zetas and the Gulf Cartel both originated in the state of Tamaulipas. The emergence of these powerful criminal groups and the ongoing serious human rights violations in this area would not have been possible without local negotiations with other political and social actors in the capital city, creating the conditions for impunity and violence at the local and national levels. This has had important consequences for the materiality of the city and its effects on residents' everyday lives.

The construction of legality and illegality in its articulation with processes of local, national, and global accumulation is not only a result of the transgression of laws to secure economic and political gain by powerful actors. This chapter examines the ways in which violence—as a force that disrupts everyday life—is built upon the quotidian practices of neoliberal state formation as they are produced and reproduced through the space of the city. My analysis, then, does not focus on criminal groups as the main cause for violence in the city but rather addresses how state practices transformed the space of the city between 2010 and 2016, creating the conditions for criminal groups to exert their strength at different political scales and rendering city residents— particularly marginalized groups—more vulnerable to direct violence. *I argue that city violence by criminal groups is in fact a form of economic and political urban governance. As economic governance, violence in the city opens up new spaces of accumulation and provides a territorial fix for the excess money originating from productive and criminal activities in order to preserve its value and obtain profits and rents. At the same time, as a form of political governance, this urban disorder becomes a way to insulate decision-making and silence dissent as part of neoliberal state formation.*

This chapter focuses on the ways in which the local fixity of money laundering altered the urban organization of the capital city of Tamaulipas with the construction of gated communities, low-quality housing for working classes, and a major government building complex. It analyzes the links between money laundering, state power, and the routinization of fear in the city using Henri Lefebvre's (2001) understanding of the contradictions of social space, with a particular focus on material space and its representation. This approach allows us to understand how the urban setting of Ciudad Victoria influences the routines of daily life (material space) and how this materiality often conforms with specific representations of space; namely, official notions of space employed in administrative control and property development (Lefebvre,

2001). Using this approach, I analyze how processes of accumulation, changing constructions of legality, state practices of control, and the fear induced by both state authorities and criminal groups are interwoven and become concrete in the city. I also show how violence and inequality in the country as well as economic and political power at higher political scales are in fact sustained in concrete spatial ways in everyday city life through the routinization of fear and the urban (re)territorialization of (il)legal money. This is central to understanding how criminal groups and the politics of (il)legality participate in capitalist urban governance. Many geographical political economy studies focus on processes of accumulation and the role of the state and formal capitalists in the design and implementation of urban planning and governance (Brenner, 2004; Pinson and Morel Journel, 2016), yet more research is needed on the role of the illegal in urban planning and city landscapes, particularly on how it changes the physical, social, and cultural dimension of urban space (Chiodelli et al., 2017).

This chapter first discusses the lived experience of residents in Ciudad Victoria, focusing on the routinization of fear in everyday life and the role of rumor in how residents experience the city. Second, it examines the relationship between state power, and money laundering in transforming the urban landscape through the construction of exclusive gated communities on one hand, and low-quality housing on the other. The third section examines the features of a new state government building complex to explore the connections between the materiality of Ciudad Victoria and representations of space. It shows how the official understanding of space and its symbolic representation reproduce undemocratic practices by distancing key public services and state-level decision-making from citizens, therefore rendering the state out of public reach, both physically and symbolically.

1   The Politics of Silence and the Routinization of Fear

Efforts to silence dissent and spread fear were part of the everyday practices of state and non-state actors in Tamaulipas during the period of study, reproducing power relations at the local level and reconfiguring state power. The quotidian practices that reproduce rumor and the politics of silence involve ordinary residents and diverse social actors in the negotiation of power in everyday encounters (Krohn-Hansen and Nustad, 2005: 10). Starting with the split between the Gulf Cartel and Los Zetas in 2010, shootings and the display of corpses became part of everyday life in the cities of Tamaulipas; people witnessed such acts of violence repeatedly. The increase of direct violence was conducive to the spread of rumor because torture, disappearances, and murder became "rumor materially enacted upon other peoples' bodies" (Feldman, 1996: 234). Rumor became the only mechanism available to urban residents in Tamaulipas for mapping the violence in the city and reducing threats to their own physical safety (Simons, 1996: 43). It became central to everyday life in Ciudad Victoria, particularly affecting residents' mobility around the city.

One of the most visible changes in everyday life was an informal curfew. This informal curfew involved average people staying off the streets and out of public space after nine o'clock at night. There were other changes, too. People lived in a constant state of alertness. Residents would constantly monitor who was outside their homes and what vehicles were driving next to them, trying to stay away from members of criminal groups and state security forces. Even in spaces considered public, such as the state university, students were afraid to discuss issues related to politics and criminal groups in their classes, fearing there could be classmates involved with criminal groups that might punish them for their comments. Alas, this suspicion was not far-fetched, as a high-ranking member of the Faculty of Law in charge of student affairs at the Autonomous University of Tamaulipas was convicted of being part of the criminal group Los Zetas in 2017 (Cedillo, 2017). Practices of fear also extended to out-of-state visitors, as residents would suggest they refrain from making comments about criminal groups or remarks regarding potentially suspicious activities. Fear, then, became a routine in people's everyday lives, "with a facade of normalcy at the same time that terror permeates and shreds the social fabric" (Green, 1996: 108).

Rumor, as unverified information in casual conversations, mobile phone calls, text messages, and social media posts, provided individuals with a map of their social context to guide their daily conduct in the city (Stewart and Strathern, 2004). People who found themselves in the middle of or close to shootings or noticed unusual activity in the streets would send messages to their friends and relatives through social media to warn others. WhatsApp groups and Facebook pages such as *Valor por Tamaulipas* (Courage for Tamaulipas) shared information about attacks, criminal groups' checkpoints, and state collusion with criminal groups in cases of disappearance and murder. One characteristic of rumor in Ciudad Victoria was the detailed descriptions of violent activities including the location, time, appearance, and possessions of both victims and victimizers. Photographs and videos were constantly uploaded to social media. Rumor thus organized life and afforded residents a sense of control over their reality. Furthermore, given the great deal of uncertainty and lack of credible information, rumor circulated not only about what had occurred but also about what might happen in relation to violence in the city (Feldman, 1996: 231).

Rumor plays a role in every community and in all social relations, and Tamaulipas is no exception. What is novel, though, is the role of rumor in transforming intangible fear into concrete violent acts that affected all residents in the city, rather than specifically targeted groups such as journalists and critics of criminal groups and local state authorities. Rumor emerged in the capital city and in the state of Tamaulipas in general because of the absence of socially credible information, largely owing to media self-censorship. Self-censorship in the media has long been central to the preservation of the politics of silence in Tamaulipas, going all the way back to the consolidation of the local power of the PRI in the 1940s. The PRI-led state government controlled the local media with so-called *chayotes* or government payments to promote the official agenda, censor social demands, and either benefit or attack particular local politicians. A system of co-optation and economic coercion was set in place that forced low-paid journalists to further the interests of their employers, who were linked, in turn, to the state at the local level. Violence, though, was seldom used against journalists in Ciudad Victoria until the late 2000s.

Indeed, border cities in Tamaulipas had been dangerous for local journalists since the 1980s (López Medellín, 2015: 17–40), but it would be decades later when this situation began to expand regionally to other parts of Tamaulipas, including Ciudad Victoria, with violence against journalists, escalating media self-censorship. In 2008, a journalist in Ciudad Victoria was found dead with signs of asphyxia. State authorities dismissed the investigation by claiming the journalist had committed suicide, though his colleagues insisted he had been killed for publishing a piece of news that Los Zetas did not want to see in the press (López Medellín, 2015). In 2010, a car bomb exploded in the Ciudad Victoria offices of the national TV broadcaster Televisa (Artículo 19, 2016, 11–12; Sandoval, 2016). Television anchors in the TV station that had been attacked later announced they would no longer be reporting on news related to criminal groups and violence (Artículo 19, 2016: 40). The result was a lack of reporting on criminal groups as well as on state involvement in violence and impunity. Between 2011 and 2015, three of Ciudad Victoria's most important local newspapers (*El Diario*, *El Mercurio*, and *Expreso*) largely restricted their reporting to the state's strategy of militarization and to accidents and crimes unrelated to criminal groups. Los Zetas also tightened its control over the flow of information in the media, sending press releases to different newspapers about what information they were allowed to release. For example, in 2011 it forced newspapers in Ciudad Victoria to publish photos of the mutilated bodies of individuals it had abducted (O'Connor, 2010).

Control over information and self-censorship in the city also intensified when bloggers and social media journalists reporting on criminal activities in

Tamaulipas became the target of attacks. In 2011, the mutilated bodies of four bloggers were placed in different areas of the city of Nuevo Laredo. The year 2014 saw the disappearance of Maria del Rosario Fuentes Rubio, a social media journalist contributing to the same Facebook page mentioned above, *Valor por Tamaulipas*, and administrator of the Twitter account and hashtag #ReynosaFollow. She was found murdered later that year. The Facebook page had a large social media following because it shared information that could not be obtained from traditional media, including information on crimes carried out by criminal groups in different parts of the state as well as photos of missing people. Understandably, the mutilation and murder of social media administrators temporarily led to increasing self-censorship by bloggers and Facebook and Twitter accounts reporting on violence in Tamaulipas (Benson, 2015).

The local state authorities also increasingly censored the national media during the 2000s. During this period, the national magazine *Revista Proceso* and the regional newspaper *El Norte* began reporting on the suspicious links between the state government and the Gulf Cartel. These newspapers could not be found in any of Tamaulipas' main cities on days when they included reporting on the relationship between local authorities and the Cartel, even though the publications were distributed to these cities. In addition to media self-censorship, then, widespread censorship of critical national printed media became the norm. The long history of self-censorship in Tamaulipas, and particularly Ciudad Victoria, sets this state apart from other violent regions in Mexico. Places like Guerrero and Veracruz, with high levels of violence, have retained independent investigative journalism despite local journalists being attacked and murdered, but Tamaulipas lacks this type of journalism, possibly due to the much longer role of self-censorship in maintaining state power in Tamaulipas. This helped enable the state to use disinformation as an attack on social witnessing amidst increasing violence (Feldman, 1996: 246).

Very specific and detailed rumors allowed city residents to create mental maps of zones to avoid at particular times to remain safe. In the initial stages of increasing violence in Ciudad Victoria, the mental maps that allowed people to make sense of the violence had profound class connotations. Upper- and middle-class residents rationalized murders and disappearances by associating poverty with criminality. As a result, residents from middle- and high-income sectors preferred to avoid poor neighbors and areas, and support for gated communities grew. The stigmatization of the poor in these rumors gave the middle and wealthy sectors of Ciudad Victoria a privileged sense of separation and safety from both violence and poverty, and as long as they could avoid certain areas of the city, circulate by car, and avoid being out at night, they felt safe and secure.

With increasingly open violence against the 'less dangerous' social classes, this sense of safety changed (Scheper-Hughes, 2003: 177). There were attacks with grenades and other explosives in areas utilized by the middle and upper classes, including shopping malls, banks, and car dealerships. Criminal groups used such attacks to pressure state actors and shape political outcomes to favor their own interests. In other words, these attacks became a violent form of lobbying—one that was not necessarily opposed to local state authorities but that implicated them through either their participation in the attacks themselves or their refusal to prevent them. Most importantly, these attacks changed the role of rumor in organizing everyday experiences in the city to avoid violence. With daytime shootings even in middle-income and wealthy areas of Ciudad Victoria and ever more people from diverse social and economic backgrounds becoming victims, the middle and wealthy classes were no longer able to distance themselves from violence.

Rumor also became a political instrument to limit access to resources and exacerbate local fears (Kirsch, 2002: 57), thereby changing the way people experienced the city. Narco-banners, are a case in point. Criminal groups used these banners in the city to communicate threats to other criminal groups, particular state officials, and the public in general. Narco-banners with images of murdered people or placed next on mutilated bodies had a particularly chilling effect. Tamaulipas state authorities also attempted to control rumor on social media by disrupting access to blogs and Twitter and Facebook accounts that were reporting on violence in Tamaulipas (Redacción, 2013). In 2014, Tamaulipas state authorities started using a software program supplied by the firm Hacking Team to infiltrate mobile phones and tablets and retrieve information anonymously (Redacción/SinEmbargo, 2015). This coincides with complaints by social media activists in Tamaulipas about anonymous harassment (Freedom House, 2015: 9). Narco-banners, state-controlled rumor and state surveillance thus intensified local fear and self-censorship.

Like in other violent cities in Mexico, the public display of corpses and dismembered and hanged bodies in Ciudad Victoria only intensified fear. Violence was directed not necessarily against a political subject but against everyday life in the city (Feldman, 1996: 247). This had profound implications for urban life, leading the population to confine its forms of political expression to private spaces where people felt more secure (Caldeira, 2000: 3). Importantly, it was not just local violence carried out by criminal groups and state authorities that had this effect. Rather, the urban landscape itself—highly influenced by the power relations between state power and capital accumulation at the national and local levels, and the politics of (il)legality—encouraged violence by criminal groups and promoted fear and distrust.

2   Spaces of (Il)Legality and Landscapes of Fear

Lived experience in the capital city of Tamaulipas is intrinsically connected to overlapping boundaries between legality and illegality produced at different political scales. This section explores how processes of money laundering in the state of Tamaulipas encouraged spatial segregation and the routinization of fear and how the suspension of the law intersected with criminality and legality in the urban space of the city. As mentioned in the previous chapter, money-laundering schemes involving local state officials and criminal groups relied on several construction companies as well as public works contracts from federal and local state agencies. The local government's direct control over the municipality of Ciudad Victoria guaranteed that laundered funds could be invested in the city with relative ease. Building on this analysis, the discussion below shows how applying these funds to new forms of spatial segregation—specifically to urban enclosures that isolate some groups into fortified spaces of political domination and private enclaves for housing, work, and recreation—shaped the routinization of fear in the city as part of the material practices of urban living (Caldeira, 2000: 3). This spatial segregation further promoted the implosion of public life and consolidated the fragmentation of society into privileged and marginalized areas, intensifying the existing disparities already caused by neoliberalism.

Urban segregation became part of the city's design during the upsurge of violence in Ciudad Victoria between 2010 and 2016. Money obtained from activities carried out in spaces of exception was rendered legal through housing policy and both state and private investment in the housing sector. The north side of the city witnessed a boom of gated communities along with retail chains and an exclusive department store (see Map 2). With just a handful of gated communities in the early 2000s, for example, Ciudad Victoria had about thirty such communities by 2017. These gated communities have private security, gardens, swimming pools, and street lights. No one is allowed inside the community unless residents authorize them as guests. Houses in these communities range from almost half a million to one million dollars (López García, 2015, 2017).

Money laundering played a direct and indirect role in the growth of these communities. While it is difficult to link all existing gated communities to construction companies involved in the U.S. money-laundering cases against the former Tamaulipas governors (Chapter 3), it is nonetheless telling that an individual linked to these cases, Farough Fatemi Corcuera, owned one of the main real estate companies participating in the gated community market. This company and another joint venture owned by the same individual received

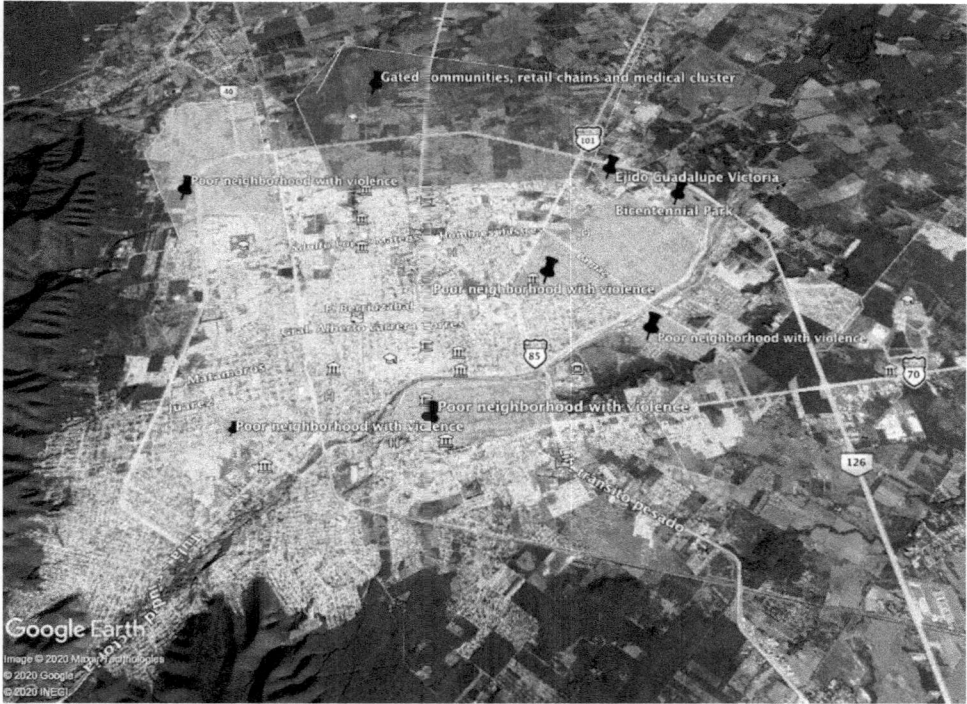

MAP 2   Urban segregation in Ciudad Victoria, Tamaulipas, Mexico.
SOURCES: GOOGLE, INEGI, ALVAREZ, 2017; GARCIA, 2015; SERNA, 2017

approximately four million dollars in the early 2000s from the very same construction company, Materiales y Construcciones Villa de Aguayo, involved in
the money-laundering accusations in the United States (Redacción, 2012b). In
effect, money laundering and the economic legality afforded by formally con-
tracting construction companies shaped the urban landscape.

During the same period, there was also an upsurge of low-income housing.
The supply of formal residential housing increased by 15 percent between 2010
and 2015 (INEGI, 2018c), and though not all of this formed a part of affordable
housing programs, the 75 percent increase in state investment in housing programs in Ciudad Victoria between 2007 and 2010 is revealing. This type of investment slowed down between 2010 and 2012, but it recovered in 2013, when
funding for housing programs rose by 225 percent (INEGI, 2018c). The most
important affordable housing program in Mexico is connected to the state
agency National Fund for Workers' Housing (Fondo Nacional de la Vivienda para los Trabajadores, or INFONAVIT). Five percent of workers' wages is

channeled into this national housing fund, and INFONAVIT administers the fund to grant mortgages to low-income workers. These mortgages in turn provide profitable opportunities for developers, supplying a ready market of prequalified customers (Soederberg, 2015). This opportunity for economic gain in the low-income housing sector was seized by several Tamaulipas state officials and individuals involved in the U.S. money-laundering cases. For instance, one of the companies of Fernando Cano, the front man of former state governor Tomás Yarrington Ruvalcaba, applied for municipal permits to build small houses, including an entire neighborhood in the south part of Ciudad Victoria (Municipio de Ciudad Victoria, 2014a). Relatives of former state governor Eugenio Hernández Flores also participated in the low-income housing market (Morales, 2017).

Low-quality construction was also characteristic of the expansion of low-income housing through INFONAVIT in Ciudad Victoria from the mid-2000s to 2016. Leaky roofs, cracked walls, and houses built on land prone to flooding, mold, and sinking streets were characteristic of the new affordable housing developments. Despite these irregularities, the houses remained on the market with the promise of INFONAVIT mortgages (Morales, 2017), and complaints by homeowners went nowhere. As a result, some homeowners decided to leave their homes (López García, 2018). This scenario was replicated in other parts of Tamaulipas; in addition to insecurity and migration, low-quality housing was one of the main causes for the growing number of abandoned houses in Tamaulipas, figuring among the states with the highest percentages of empty homes between 2010 and 2017 (Redacción, 2011; Leon, 2018).

The power obtained by state officials involved in laundering money through construction companies is indicative of the important role of financial flows in shaping the city landscape. Key individuals in the U.S. money-laundering cases were in charge of local state agencies related to urban development. One of the partners of a construction company implicated in the money-laundering accusations was the Tamaulipas minister of Public Works and Urban Development in the late 2000s (Redacción, 2007c). There were also money-laundering investigations into former directors of the Tamaulipas Institute for Housing and Urban Development (Instituto Tamaulipeco de Vivienda y Urbanismo, or ITAVU), who had been appointed by former Tamaulipas governors between 1998 and 2010. The ITAVU was responsible for helping lower-income residents to obtain INFONAVIT financing and to access other housing programs. ITAVU also covered half of the expenses incurred by municipalities for repairing the streets and building new ones. The accusations in the United States allege that one of the above-mentioned directors was a front man for companies actually owned by a previous Tamaulipas governor (U.S. Attorney's

Office, 2014) and that another director received money illegally from contractors working for the Tamaulipas state government after manipulating bids. These bribe payments were transferred into different bank accounts in Texas (USA v. All Property and Assets on Deposit or Held in the UBS Financial Services, Inc. Account Number Om 05095, S.D. Tex., 2014).

The links between the expansion of gated communities, the growth of government-supported low-income housing, and accusations of money laundering against state officials in charge of urban planning in Ciudad Victoria and Tamaulipas show how the spatial organization of the city is influenced by criminality, illegality and processes of accumulation. Criminal and illegal activities are not external but rather an important part of existing capital accumulation and its urban reproduction. This is so in three main ways. First, actions considered criminal and illegal are tied to processes of dispossession and further commodification. The land and natural resources required to mobilize capital and the larger pools of labor needed to lower production costs are secured through violent processes of dispossession which further commodify nature and people (Harvey, 2014: 53). Second, the money employed to use labor power to produce added value as profit can originate from criminal and violent activities (Harvey, 2014: 72), and the conditions of production may violate labor laws or other regulations. Third, illegal funds can reinforce the role of fictitious capital in capital accumulation, as they boost the capacity of corporations, nation-states, and banking institutions to obtain financial resources through different forms of money laundering. This additional illegal funding also allows private banking institutions to transform workers' incomes into a source of financial profit through consumption-based debt (see Lapavitsas, 2009 for an analysis of financialization under capitalism). Criminal and illegal activities clearly play a role in capital accumulation, and, as we have seen, they are also part of the process of urban capitalist development.

The involvement of political actors related to state and municipal urban development in money laundering suggests that several actors and processes, including those considered illegal and criminal, do play a role in the spatial organization of the city and its governance (Chiodelli et al., 2018). In the case of Ciudad Victoria, urban reorganization and the role of money laundering in shaping this reconfiguration helped to mobilize capital and absorb its surpluses, particularly the overaccumulation of capital as commodities, money, and/or productive capacity (Harvey, 2005). On the one hand, money laundering was important as the global financial crises of 2007–2010 led to low investment levels from existing companies in Tamaulipas and low aggregate demand from consumers. During this period, 53,970 jobs were lost in Tamaulipas, mostly in the manufacturing and the construction sectors (Díaz González and Mendoza

Sánchez, 2012), and between 2006 and 2009, foreign direct investment decreased by 20 percent (López Jiménez, 2010). In this context, proceeds channeled from the theft of public money and criminal activities like drug trafficking and extortion helped mobilize capital at the local level, particularly in the construction sector in Ciudad Victoria, resulting in urban sprawl, ever more gated communities, and the expansion of low-income housing.

On the other hand, money laundering facilitated long-term investment in capital fixity, thereby integrating and blending surpluses and rents originating from criminal and illegal activities into the legal economy. Gated communities and low-income housing, and their accompanying public works such as the construction of streets and the installation of electricity and public lighting, were part of the spatial fix that absorbed surpluses and excess rents. Given the untapped market in local real estate development, local capitalists, particularly those linked to money laundering, invested their rents and profits in land to preserve the value of their assets. Legal and illegal state assistance, both local and national, guaranteed yields for such investments. Illegal conditions in the form of overpriced, guaranteed contracts for municipal public works, secured through bribe payments, allowed local capitalists in the construction sector to make profits. Low labor and safety standards in the construction sector, contracts backed by state debt for municipal infrastructure and low-income housing allowed local contractors to make a profit legally. These operations also allowed them to blend legal funds with illegal ones to disguise the criminal origin of part of their investment.

This also points to the significant role money laundering has played in favoring financial speculation over other economic activities in the city, largely through the use of fictitious capital. Fictitious capital is based on expected future surplus value extraction, rents, and tax revenues that do not yet exist but are nonetheless convertible into money in the form of land and financial titles (Harvey, 1999: 265). Its role is particularly evident in the case of low-income housing financed through INFONAVIT. As mentioned above, INFONAVIT has access to most of Mexico's private payrolls. INFONAVIT's access to funds in Ciudad Victoria therefore ensured a market for low-income housing as well as payment for construction for local capitalists. Close political connections also guaranteed that housing developments in the city would be accredited as residences that could be purchased with INFONAVIT mortgages. INFONAVIT's mortgages are connected to its residential mortgage-backed securities (RMBS), and it is one of the largest issuers in Latin America (Soederberg, 2015). The origin of laundered money is thus further diluted through its blending into not only productive activities but also speculative finance. While there are no data available on the share of money laundering in the mortgage market in Mexico, the local case studied in this chapter suggests that money laundering is one of the mechanisms that reproduce capital accumulation and that it increases the role of financial speculation in local economic activities. Incorporating funds into the financial system is key in further disguising the source of illegal funds, once again blurring the boundaries between economic legality and illegality.

As part of the cycle of accumulation, the local real estate boom encouraged by money laundering increased the role of property as fictitious capital in the process of local accumulation. Whereas land prices in Ciudad Victoria had been stable prior to the late 2000s, the cost of property increased in the cheapest areas by more than 700 percent between 2010 and 2016 (Valadez, 2017; Gobierno del Estado de Tamaulipas, 2012: 9; 2016: 156). Similarly, gated communities and the construction of large retail chains artificially increased the cost of land and property taxes in Ciudad Victoria (De la Cruz, 2015). Ownership claims and price increases thus became part of the urban landscape of the capital city of Tamaulipas, fragmenting space and endowing it with a market price (Lefebvre, 2001: 334).

Processes of dispossession also contributed to urban sprawl. As mentioned in the introductory chapter, lawfare is the use of legal instruments to commit acts of coercion to benefit powerful political and economic groups. The northern side of Ciudad Victoria—now one of the most expensive areas in the city with numerous gated communities and large retail chains—has been a key site of development where both dispossession and lawfare have come into play. Part of this area used to belong to a rural community called Ejido Guadalupe Victoria. One of the main developers was Pedro Luis Valdés, a relative of former governor Eugenio Hernández Flores. Between 2004 and 2007, Valdés held the position of *ejido* commissioner. Legally, the *ejido* commissioner is the president of the executive committee elected by the *ejido* general assembly (García, 2016a). While the executive committee supposedly runs *ejido* affairs, the history of *ejidos* shows that in most cases the commissioner becomes the main authority, undermining the general assembly (Nuijten, 2003: 49–50). Once Valdés became the commissioner, then, he was able to obtain land from *ejido* members at below-market prices. He also promoted the construction of a large medical cluster, increasing the value of the land by 30 percent (Sánchez Treviño, 2007). As a result, his company was able to develop this area into a hub for commercial and residential services at a large profit. At the same time, in 2006, the local congress passed fast-track legislation—the State Law of Territorial Planning and Urban Development—to integrate rural land into processes of urbanization (Sánchez Treviño, 2007). This mandated the municipality to pave roads and provide water and sewage to this formerly rural area. The latter aided real estate development in the area. Ultimately, legal mechanisms were employed to carry out a process of dispossession of peasant land and community resources, with significant impacts on the spatial organization of the city.

Processes of dispossession also benefited from the threat of violence by criminal groups, which facilitated the spatial restructuring of the city and created new opportunities for accumulation. As mentioned in Chapter 3, at the same time that extortion was increasing for small and medium-sized enterprises (SMEs) in the capital city of Tamaulipas, the number of retail chains increased. In fact, the Municipal Government Report of 2013 proudly showcased the construction of foreign and national retail chains such as HEB and Walmart, with investments worth about 27 million dollars (Municipio de Ciudad Victoria, 2013a). This is indicative of how criminal violence has been influential in reconfiguring the city; SMEs shutting down because of extortion created market opportunities for large retail companies, which led to the need to secure large commercial locations for construction. The price of land thus shot up in the northern area of the city, where gated communities and a large medical cluster were built, facilitating the absorption of surpluses and rents. Through this process, the fear and violence induced by criminal groups benefited capital and facilitated its mobility by producing and reorganizing space, replacing natural landscapes with built environment (Harvey, 1989).

Not only did these developments clearly benefit capital, but the growth of gated communities, low-income housing, and large retail chains also led to urban segregation, such as that found now in Ejido Guadalupe Victoria (see map 2). The gated communities, medical cluster, and retail chains in this newly developed space in the northern part of the city received the infrastructure and public services required to live and work in the area comfortably. In contrast, the three hundred families that remained in Ejido Guadalupe Victoria did not see any benefits from this urban sprawl. In fact, the community remained without public services; the municipality did not pave the roads in the community, build a sewage network, or provide garbage collection services. The new real estate developments also blocked natural drainage, increasing the risk of flooding in the *ejido* (Mendoza, 2016a). The municipality, the state government authorities as well as local real estate developers marked the division between poor and wealthy neighborhoods with unequal public service provision and, as I discuss in the third section of this chapter, the exclusion of poor residents from city planning decisions.

Unsurprisingly, these marked spatial differences gave rise to norms of exclusion and avoidance (Caldeira, 2000: 1). Wealthy areas remained physically separated from poor neighborhoods on the city periphery, where there were high levels of violence (see map 2). Whether this was an intentional or accidental outcome of the class alliance between local state officials and local real estate developers, this segregation nonetheless became a sociospatial strategy to seemingly guarantee isolation and distance from people deemed dangerous

(Caldeira, 2000: 2). While representing the space of the city as a division be-tween dangerous and safe zones, this class alliance simultaneously produced the conditions of violence and fear in the city through its participation in money laundering. Population dispersion and subdivision came to form mech-anisms of social control as distrust and fear increased among city residents (Lefebvre, 2001: 373). This in turn helped deter large-scale mobilizing against undemocratic practices, violence, and growing evidence of the local state's col-laboration with criminal groups in the city. Segregation divided the commu-nity and made inequality and exclusion the organizing principle of the mate-rial practices of the city (Caldeira, 2000: 52).

Despite the dubious origin of the funds in some of the city's real estate in-vestments, the developments they financed were celebrated in municipal doc-uments. Municipal Development Programs from 2005 to 2016 focused on pro-moting public and private investment to develop industrial parks as well as commercial and residential real estate, and they did so by providing land be-longing to the municipality (Municipio de Ciudad Victoria, 2005, 2013b, 2017). Prior to the privatization of communal land in 1992, *ejidos* could only be incor-porated into urbanization plans when expropriated by national state authori-ties. After constitutional reforms, though, municipalities in Mexico became central to providing land for urban expansion, encouraging *ejido* members to sell their property on the real estate market in order to increase the municipal-ity's land holdings (Olivera, 2001) and facilitate the expansion of large com-mercial enterprises. In general, municipal reports and programs promoted using the land to expand the local maquiladoras as well as to extend the con-struction of gated communities and INFONAVIT housing (Municipio de Ciu-dad Victoria, 2013a).

The municipality's ability to organize space in the capital city of Tamaulipas also grew as national state authorities granted municipalities greater decision-making power for matters related to land use and the urban landscape. This process began in Mexico in the context of neoliberal restructuring in the 1990s, when national state authorities began to emphasize land use regulations in urban areas and opening up new spaces for industrialization, while marginal-izing environmental and rural concerns (Azuela, 2009). Despite this tendency, Ciudad Victoria did not have a comprehensive framework for its decision-making powers until 2012, when the Municipal Plan of Territorial Ordering and Urban Development was put in place. This coincided with the growth of con-struction projects in the city, including those linked to money laundering. The municipal plan was also a prerequisite for developing the Ejido Guadalupe Victoria, and the plan's guidelines shaped the design of the new area, including large retail chains, gated communities, and a medical cluster (García, 2016b).

Indeed, in the prevailing context of neoliberalism, decentralized city planning allowed local elites and state authorities to influence the urban organization of the economy and did little to strengthen local democratic practices. The space of the city was represented as a commodity that could be broken up into pieces to be sold on the market (Lefebvre, 2001: 319). As the case of the Ejido Guadalupe Victoria shows, space became disembedded from its social and ecological context, disrupting existing community practices. Similarly, the way municipal programs represented space reinforced the notion of the city as a locale for growth and opportunity, in line with an international pursuit of profitability. This representation of space and the decision-making powers granted to the city allowed powerful political and economic groups to shape the urban landscape while making a profit both legally and illegally.

3   Undemocratic Infrastructure

In 2010, most state government offices in Tamaulipas, dispersed throughout the capital city, were brought together into a single bureaucratic complex on the outskirts of the city (see Map 2). While the governor's office remained downtown, the local legislature, the state archives, and most of the ministries were moved to this new site. As I discuss below, the location of this new government complex reflects the balance of forces at the national and local levels, which produced a set of material spatial practices and a particular representation of space and reinforced the co-existence of violence, criminality and illegality with neoliberalism.

The site chosen for this new government complex is far from the city core and difficult to access using public transit (see Image 1). The fastest way to get

IMAGE 1   Bicentennial park. View of the civil registry in the front and skyscraper in the back.
SOURCE: HEPZIBAH MUÑOZ MARTÍNEZ, OCTOBER 2011

there is by car in preferential, faster-moving lanes, and it is not near any other streets or contiguous to any particular neighborhoods, standing isolated from its surroundings. The complex consists of four buildings and an exhibition center for the state fair. These areas are all separated by large parking lots surrounding a 130-foot monument of a flying eagle. The bureaucratic complex of buildings and the monument are called Bicentennial Park and *Bicentennial Eagle* (Image 2), respectively, thus named because the date of their inauguration in 2010 commemorated the 200th anniversary of Mexico's War of Independence.

IMAGE 2   Bicentennial eagle.
           SOURCE: HEPZIBAH MUÑCZ MARTÍNEZ, OCTOBER 2011

The building housing most of the state government offices is a 25-story sky-scraper. Another building contains the local legislature, which is not tall but larger than the civil registry building, which handles day-to-day services such as license plate payments, driver's license renewals and requests for birth certificates. The fourth building is the large convention center, called Polyforum Victoria, where the state governor presents the annual government report (Torres, 2011).

The power relations involved in the development and construction of this government complex resemble those at play in the construction of gated communities and low-income housing in Ciudad Victoria. The complex's 155 acres belonged to seven owners, all of whom had close family or work connections to high-ranking state officials at the local level between 2004 and 2016. These owners sold the land to the Institute for Housing and Urban Development, whose director at the time, Homero de la Garza Tamez, was accused of money laundering by U.S. authorities in 2014. ITAVU bought the lots for about 25,500 dollars per acre in the early 2010s (García, 2016b), yet the details and process of these purchases remain unclear. The land was eventually transferred from ITAVU to the state government five years after the building was inaugurated (Medrano Herrera, 2017). In addition to the previous owners' ties to the government, several construction companies involved in this project also had close connections with former Tamaulipas governors accused of money laundering in the United States, and in 2010, Mexico's Federal Auditor found irregularities in how federal funding was used for the construction of the complex. The audit found that the state government had both overpaid contractors and paid for construction work that did not exist (ASF, 2010). Despite these findings, though, national state authorities did not further investigate the use of federal funding in infrastructure investments in Tamaulipas, including the major public works in Bicentennial Park.

The story behind this new government complex shows how material space reflects existing political and socioeconomic power relations and reproduces them. On the one hand, the making of this built environment involved powerful political and economic groups at the local level, some of them implicated in money-laundering accusations, while national state authorities continued to support the project financially despite financial irregularities. Essentially, national state authorities did not interfere in the construction of this project as long as local state authorities in Tamaulipas continued to organize neoliberalism locally and suppress dissent, either directly or through proxy forces, including criminal groups. On the other hand, the government complex itself generated a set of exclusionary spatial and political practices. Even if criminal groups were not directly involved in the construction of this project through money laundering, the material practices engendered by this government complex further exposed people to violence. The physical isolation of the complex distances citizens from participating in local state decisions related to income distribution and public safety issues, and the resulting lack of participation then helps perpetuate impunity, undemocratic practices, and the economic and political conditions that produce violence. The government claims the concentration of government services in a single location "improves administrative efficiency and the quality of service to the population" (Gobierno del Estado de Tamaulipas, 2010a), thereby casting Bicentennial Park as an apolitical space, inconsequential for democratic participation.

In addition to the site's physical isolation, the design of the material space of the building complex itself reproduces relations of control, surveillance, and citizen disempowerment. The large, empty spaces occupied by massive parking lots and gardens and the immense size of the buildings and monument make visitors seem small and legible in relation to the state apparatus. James C. Scott defines this legibility as the administrative ordering of the nation-state to control people through categorizations and the functional segregation and hierarchization of space (1998: 88–89, 111). The vast empty spaces between hefty buildings thus make public workers and visitors feel that any actions considered inappropriate by state authorities might be noticed. As a result, people avoid the areas between empty spaces (Scott, 1998: 121). As Lefebvre reminds us, architectural design is never neutral (2001: 356). Rather, it is a social practice in which the architect interacts with other social, political, and economic actors (Stanek, 2011: 165, 250). In this case, the architecture of the government complex mobilized official representations of space, silencing the real users of this social space, particularly in their relationship with the state at the local level (Lefebvre, 2001: 356). More specifically, the structure and isolation of the complex obstructed residents' abilities to access state services, state representatives, and the state bureaucracy in an easy and democratic way. The design of the buildings and their surroundings did not take the life experiences and needs of city residents into account (Scott, 1998: 111). Instead, organizing this new center as the locus of political decision-making and power served to absorb difference and resistance (Lefebvre, 2001: 373, 378).

The relocation, concentration, and design of these government offices and their place in the city's urban landscape transformed public space, which also shaped the geography of violence in the city. In neoliberal city restructuring, public space is not eliminated, but it is transformed into a site for control and surveillance (Caldeira, 2000). Bicentennial Park eliminated the street and the square as parts of public life, and the lack of diverse commercial services and other land uses reduced the potential for sociability, furthering the implosion of public life. While this government building complex is a public space in that people can visit the areas outside the buildings without any explicit purpose, it is also a space of control and surveillance. For instance, large populations from different socioeconomic backgrounds can access the highly subsidized state fair located in Bicentennial Park but access is restricted, though, to other sites in Bicentennial Park, where the governor presents his annual report. This event can only be attended by invitation, and only those considered sufficiently important by high-ranking officials are given seats, effectively denying access to those sectors of society that might question or protest local state policies.

The government complex also reveals current processes of state formation under neoliberalism in Mexico, particularly at the local level. The discourse related to the monument, for example, shows how a fixed narrative can be imposed upon space. During the inauguration of the *Bicentennial Eagle* in the new government complex, former governor Eugenio Hernández Flores stated that the "monument symbolizes the progress of a dynamic and modern society, a society with history and with solid ideals of freedom and progress." He also spoke of the monument as an innovative, avant-garde piece that recognizes the legacy of those who "gave us a free country" (Redacción, 2010). Along the same lines, the 2010 Government State Report describes the monument as "the symbol of the independence of our nation" (Gobierno del Estado de Tamaulipas, 2010a: 136). As such, the monument transforms the country's history of struggle into one of unity and order with an emphasis on the role of modernity, especially in an economic sense, based on market discipline and the profit imperative. This is illustrative of how local processes are key to state formation in Mexico and how they are reflected in the built environment, reproducing existing power relations in society (for an insightful study of built environment and state formation in Mexico City, see Morton, 2013). It is also important to note that this notion of Mexico's history, as represented through the monument, excludes or marginalizes alternative interpretations.

The restructuring of urban space at this site and its erasure of participatory processes follow a neoliberal logic (Erdi Lelandais, 2014: 7), as the order and stability of this built environment favor local and global capital accumulation. Directly, of course, local economic and political groups received economic gains from the actual construction of the site. Gains were also obtained from the rise in local public debt between 2004 and 2016, when major infrastructure projects like Bicentennial Park were financed and low-cost housing and gated communities grew and multiplied. In 2004, local public debt was 758 million pesos. By 2010, it reached six billion pesos, a 700 percent increase. Just five years later, it had reached thirteen billion pesos, an 1806 percent increase compared to 2004 (El Mañana Staff, 2016). As local indebtedness rose, the budget of the local Ministry of Public Works grew too, by more than 2000 percent between 2011 and 2013 alone (García Fernández et al., 2017: 85). Thirty percent of indirect debt—that is, loans not obtained directly by the state governor's office—was loaned to ITAVU in 2011 (Gobierno del Estado de Tamaulipas, 2011), and in 2014, ITAVU obtained a new loan from the bank BBV Bancomer for 150 million pesos, increasing ITAVU's share of Tamaulipas' indirect public debt to 48 percent (Gobierno del Estado de Tamaulipas, 2014). It is important to keep in mind that the people in charge of these state agencies were accused of participating in a large network of money laundering in collusion with criminal groups.

Local state officials could only obtain loans with guarantees in the form of federal transfers. Federal transfers increased in 2010, and national state authorities did not place any limits on the accelerated pace of local debt growth in Tamaulipas, which was double the rate of national state indebtedness between 2006 and 2013 (García Fernández et al., 2017: 81). The loans were mostly provided by a Mexican bank, Banorte, and three international banks, Bancomer, HSBC, and Santander (El Mañana Staff, 2016). Local state authorities, with the support of national state officials, used the tax system to transfer locally produced value abroad through its indebtedness to globally connected banks. This money layering—a stage of money laundering that involved public infrastructure construction, local debt, and the transfer of local debt to global financial flows—further blurred the distinction between legal and illegal economic transactions, with the help of state power and local capital accumulation. As we have seen, these processes intersected in the physical space of the city. The explicit and implicit ties between local and global capital and local and national state authorities are not stable. Such alliances are vulnerable because the political and social strategies needed to support capital accumulation locally and those required to strengthen the economic position of people in political office with connections to criminal groups give rise to differing interests over time (Harvey, 1989: 149; 2014: 75). For instance, local construction companies that received some of the benefits of the local real estate boom but were not awarded the largest infrastructure projects because of fraudulent bidding sought an investigation into the process behind the construction of Bicentennial Park. The local legislature, in turn, supported their request (Medrano Herrera, 2017), in a context in which the PRI lost its state monopoly over political power in Tamaulipas when the PAN won the 2016 elections for governor.

The case of Bicentennial Park shows how fear, silencing, and local undemocratic practices are in fact produced, concretized, and experienced spatially. The spatial manifestation of insulating political decision-making and administration from citizens shows how material space and its official representation are intrinsic to the constitution of political and economic power. First, the material processes behind the making of this built environment reflect the power relations already in place. In this case, the ties between criminal groups, capital, and local state officials made it possible to design and build the bureaucratic complex. Capitalists, in its attempts to both command and annihilate space, required investment in and control over specific places, and the state organized and regulated social space, socializing the costs of the built environment while also strengthening the existing power relations within the state, including the position of power of senior officials in the state apparatus.

A second way that space constitutes political and economic power is evident in how the material practices embedded in the construction of Bicentennial Park reduced social space to the status of resource and force of production, ignoring social relations embedded in space. Third, this transformation of social space into abstract space reproduced forms of controlling public life and isolated citizens and residents of the city from state decision-making. As Lefebvre notes,

> abstract space...erases distinctions, as much those which derive from nature and (historical) time as those which originate in the body (age, sex, ethnicity). The dominant form of space, that of the centers of wealth and power, endeavors to mold the spaces it dominates [...]and it seeks, often by violent means to reduce the obstacles and resistance it encounters there (2001: 49).

The reproduction of spaces of control contributed to violence in Tamaulipas and its capital city. The physicality and location of the state apparatus reproduce undemocratic processes and surveillance that render people more vulnerable to abuse by state and non-state armed forces, depriving them of mechanisms to protect their human, economic, civil, and political rights. At the same time, though, the abstract space produced by a particular set of power relations is not all-controlling or consistently pervasive. As the interests driving class alliances can diverge over time, the resulting class ruptures might provide opportunities for contestation and progressive social organizing, as I discuss in Chapter 6.

4   Conclusion

This chapter uses the case study of the capital city of Tamaulipas to show how social space is produced through the nexus of illegality, criminality and violence as part of neoliberal state formation in Mexico. It examines daily fear, self-censorship, and rumor as part of the everyday practices of state power, showing how local processes are connected to structures of power at different and overlapping political scales. As rumor became the organizing mechanism of daily life in Ciudad Victoria, state authorities sought to control it, given its importance in organizing people's movements through the city and its role in intensifying fear, silencing popular dissent, and fostering distrust within communities. This control of rumor by local state authorities occurred under the auspices of national state authorities, who did not question the use of spy software or investigate attacks against local journalists and media.

Fear and self-censorship—exacerbated by rumor—are not isolated from the materiality of space. Rather, quotidian urban practices are shaped by this materiality. The construction of gated communities, low-quality housing developments, and a new government complex relied on connections between legal and illegal actors in urban planning and governance at different political scales. All three cases involved criminal groups, high-ranking state officials, and local capitalists linked to money-laundering accusations in the United States. The suspension of the law permitted under neoliberalism created blurred boundaries between legality and legality and allowed violent, criminal and illegal processes of dispossession to secure land and markets for urban sprawl. This was so for the communal land bought by a real estate developer at below-market prices and for the expanding markets available to large retail chains opened up by the closure of small and medium enterprises in the city due to extortion.

These local processes intersected at the national level, too, as state authorities provided federal funding and allowed local debt to climb to finance infrastructure projects and housing developments in the city. National state authorities did not investigate the irregularities in these public investments as long as local state officials continued to support the neoliberal security agenda at the local level. While social disenchantment with neoliberal policy and state institutions grew between 2000 and 2016, national state authorities benefited from the use of local fear to increase social control and silence dissent. Global finance, too, played a role in these processes of urban planning and governance, as securities connected to mortgages in the affordable housing sector and the indebtedness of the local state used to finance sprawl were both profitable opportunities for banks and financial investors. These same connections between local accumulation and global finance also served to further dilute the boundaries between economic legality and illegality.

The transformation of public space embodied in government services further contributed to the climate of violence and insecurity in the city in two

ways. First, the physical distancing of public services and local state representatives led to a lack of democratic participation in state decision-making. The
residents of the capital city and Tamaulipas were left without access to the
political means to advocate for non-militarized and inclusive ways to address
issues of violence and poverty. Second, the transformation of public space into
a zone of selected access, control, and surveillance eliminated the possibility
of public protests and social organizing, furthering the implosion of public life
and strengthening the power of capital, the state, and criminal groups over the
territoriality of the city. The overlapping political scales involved in urban
planning and governance ultimately also led to the implosion of public life,
urban segregation, and the spatial and symbolic isolation of city residents
from state decision-making and services. This further intensified residents' vulnerability to violence by state and non-state armed forces, obstructed their
ability to mobilize against violence and domination, and intensified impunity
and political and economic exclusion.

This chapter offered insights into how extraordinary violence is linked to
the realm of the ordinary through the city, and it highlights the connections
between quotidian practices, local spaces, and broader hierarchies of economic and political power in neoliberal state formation in Mexico. It also
shows how violence, criminality, economic illegality, and fear are not necessarily in opposition to urban economic growth at all. Rather, as Lefebvre puts it,
"economic growth and violence combine forces to produce space" (2001, 112).
In Tamaulipas, the funds originating from the direct violence of criminal
groups and the private appropriation of public funding became central to city
expansion and local, national, and international accumulation. Illegal processes also played essential roles in urban planning and governance, assisting processes of local economic growth and contributing to the implosion of public
life, urban segregation, and political exclusion. Illegality thus emerged alongside legality, establishing the spatial conditions that favored powerful companies and high-ranking state officials at the expense of the general population
(Pizzo and Altavilla 2018). Understanding these developments is central to ex-
amining urban governance in Mexico as part of neoliberal state formation, as
the practices discussed in this case study are expanding throughout the country, including, for example, the construction of ever more government com-
plexes isolated from citizens.

The state, then, is central to the organization of space. Control over space
makes political power concrete (Lefebvre, 2001: 280), and a focus on the city allows us to understand the role of the state in spatial control at this level and analyze how state authorities allow illegality to become functional to the preservation of state power and the existing neoliberal agenda. An emphasis on the role

of the city in the local, national, and global politics of (il)legality is also important to grasp neoliberal state formation in Mexico; the city is where negotiations
over illegality, criminality and violence and their social and legal construction
are shaped, determined, and reproduced to reproduce neoliberalism and state
power (Pizzo and Altavilla, 2017; Chiodelli et al., 2017). An examination of the
role of criminality and illegality in the governance of cities, in turn, is central to
questioning the power structures obstructing local processes of economic and
political democratization. Negotiations between state authorities and formal
private enterprises outside the law have historically shaped the organization of
cities in contemporary capitalism, but the role of criminal groups as a proxy
force for opening new local spaces of accumulation and enforcing state coercion is also central to urban governance in emerging capitalist economies such
as Mexico. It is essential to understand how the complex interactions of these
groups with capital accumulation and everyday life serve to thwart inclusive
participation in the life of cities.

CHAPTER 5

Uneven Development and Politics of (In)Difference

In 2007, a union leader at a seminar in the border city of Matamoros proclaimed, amid declining employment levels in export-processing zones and maquiladoras in the region, "The *Veracruzanos* [people from the Mexican state of Veracruz] are to blame for unemployment."

This othering of certain parts of the population reflects the increasing internalization of neoliberal competition in everyday life. In the case of Mexico, particularly since 2000, it has helped reproduce relations of economic and political power while exposing vulnerable populations to exclusion and violence. Migration flows, both within Mexico and across its borders, are a key component of this dynamic, which involves state authorities, juridical institutions, criminal groups, smuggling networks, international trade and employment trends, dispossessed communities, and impoverished populations.

In 2010, Mexican immigration authorities asked to see my identification card during a bus trip from the capital city of Tamaulipas to Matamoros. We were stopped at a military checkpoint in the municipality of San Fernando, and authorities requested identification cards only from selected passengers. That same year, 72 immigrants from Central and South America were murdered en masse in San Fernando, and in April 2011, 193 bodies, mostly of Central American undocumented immigrants, were found in mass graves in the same area. The victims of these massacres were traveling to Texas, which borders Tamaulipas to the north. State security forces and immigration authorities had captured the immigrants and then delivered them to the criminal group Los Zetas, who were demanding money from the families of the abducted and/or recruiting them to work for the criminal organization. When the abducted immigrants refused, the criminal group murdered them (Aguayo, 2016). The kidnapping of Central American citizens traveling without documents, with the help of immigration authorities, has been an ongoing practice since 2008, yet neither the bus companies, local residents, nor other state authorities reported these criminal events (Torres, 2012).

In these examples, workers, Mexican state authorities, and ordinary people in general see particular populations as different, as undeserving of state protection or access to jobs and wages. In Tamaulipas, this began in the early 2000s. People from central and southern regions of Mexico became targets of discrimination during an economic decline in the maquiladora sector, a key part of the local economies of Mexico's northern region. Later, the targeting

extended to Central American immigrants. This chapter examines the intersection between violence, capital accumulation, and hierarchies of power
based on socially constructed racial differences to understand the blurred
boundaries between the legal, illegal and criminal economies and how they
reproduce relations of economic and political power at the local, national, and
hemispheric levels. *This chapter argues that the intensification of uneven development in Mexico shaped how people internalized individual competition in their
everyday lives, making certain sectors of the population increasingly vulnerable
to attacks by state security forces and criminal groups.* Blaming particular populations for violence and the lack of employment diverts attention away from
the existing political and economic power structures, while the law helps construct the illegal status of undocumented immigrants in both Mexico and the
United States. *This, in turn, helps reproduce the neoliberal state, as criminal
groups become a form of proxy governance, deterring people from crossing national borders and simultaneously turning migrants into a valuable source of
profit.*

The internalization of the neoliberal logic in everyday life is often obscured
by analyses that focus on state failure or state co-optation by organized criminal groups. These discourses present a dichotomy that depicts criminal groups
as the perpetrators of violence while portraying the state as the protector of
life, disguising how the state normalizes the social structures and mechanisms
through which order is preserved and fear is routinized. As a result, these discourses fail to identify how everyday practices of state formation help classify
people in such a way that the most vulnerable groups become the main targets
of violence (Nordstrom and Rubben, 1996: 8; Green, 1996: 109). Studying violence in northeastern Mexico through the lens of everyday practices of state
formation and uneven development can overcome this shortcoming. Indeed,
critical analyses of the Mexico-U.S. border show how the construction of otherness is tied to state-making in both Mexico and the United States (Alonso,
1994, 2005; Valencia, 2016). Nonetheless, more research is needed to understand how the particular construction of otherness in a specific historical juncture is also tied to changes in capital accumulation, the balance of forces within the state at the national and local levels, and specific notions of legality and
illegality (see Sassen, 1998; Glick-Schiller, 2010, 2015). Understanding the interplay of these factors and the internalization of neoliberal subjectivity can shed
light on how illegality, criminality, and violence became central features of
Mexico's neoliberal state formation. By neoliberal subjectivity, I refer to the
ways ordinary people internalize the concept of humans as individualized and
autonomous decision-makers that employ their skills in an entrepreneurial
way in competition with others. Such notions detach people from their social

and historical contexts, placing the blame on the individual if she or he fails to obtain employment and achieve well-being rather than the existing political and economic structures of inequality (Layton, 2010; Medina-Zárate and Uchôa de Oliveira, 2019).

Practices of state formation involve concrete social processes that organize everyday life, including grouping subjects into categories, forcing subjects to fit these classifications (Scott, 1998), and processes of othering, by which certain populations are considered a deviation from the norm and therefore subordinate and inferior (Said, 1978; Spivak, 1985). Such othering can bring about the "material destruction of human bodies and populations" through state power (Mbembe, 2003: 14). Othering processes are forms of power deeply shaped by the juridical and political institutions of the territorial state (Alonso, 2005). The juridical decides what is legal and what is not and "who is disposable and who is not" (Mbembe, 2003: 27). Contemporary processes of state formation, including the state's ability to use legal practices to protect life or forsake it, are intrinsically related to the uneven development of capitalism. On the one hand, labor markets require workers to engage in individual competition, to the benefit of capital, resulting in the increasing exclusion of people based on socially constructed gender, racial, and ethnic differences (Read, 2003). On the other hand, the labor and labor potential of people considered disposable promotes the social reproduction of those whose life is deemed more valuable by state authorities and the ruling class (Rose, 2001; McIntyre and Nast, 2011). Othering, then, thanks to the individualized neoliberal logic of competition, becomes internalized in everyday life, turning the quotidian into a central element in the reproduction of capital accumulation and existing hierarchies of power within and outside Mexico.

In this chapter, I first explore how the intensification of uneven development in the 1990s and 2000s in Mexico and Central America led to increased migration to Mexico's northern border region. In this context, the intense competition for work in the declining labor market of the early 2000s led to a particular social construction of difference based on racialization, stigmatizing migrants from central and southern Mexico and people without travel documents from Central America and exposing them to economic exclusion and violence. Their resulting vulnerability to extortion and kidnapping also rendered them commodities, as criminal groups began to use them as a source of profit and economic gain. I then examine how state practices led to the internalization of neoliberal competition among workers in Mexico's northeastern region through the social and legal construction of the racialized Other. This involved constant requests for identification documents and state acquiescence to the targeting of racialized communities by criminal groups. I also discuss the role of criminal groups as a type of proxy governance, as their control of migrant flows makes them participants in both Mexican and U.S. processes of state formation.

1   Unevenness and the Production of (In)difference

As uneven development in Mexico intensified, workers already inserted in labor markets in Tamaulipas began to face precarious labor situations. Increasingly harsh competition for employment coincided with a constant influx of people from central and southern Mexico in the 1990s and early 2000s and then from Central America toward the end of the 2000s. In both cases, migrant flows were greatly influenced by previous rounds of neoliberal policies of dispossession. Legal reforms in Mexico in the early 1990s, for example, included the privatization of communal land, the removal of agricultural subsidies, the elimination of state intervention in agricultural markets, and the liberalization of agricultural trade (Otero, 2004), forcing a large number of people in the countryside to sell their land and seek employment in northern Mexico or in the United States (Gil Méndez, 2015). As a result, 30 percent of residents in the northern states were from central and southern Mexico in the 1990s. Between 1993 and 1995, 56 percent of migrants in Mexico were headed to Mexico's northern region, and 43 percent were seeking to cross into the United States (Anguiano Tellez, 1998).

Workers from regions negatively affected by these rounds of neoliberal dispossession—particularly from Veracruz, which suffered the brunt of many of these reforms—were attracted to the maquiladoras in Tamaulipas and its proximity to the United States (Anguiano Tellez, 2005). Agribusinesses in Tamaulipas also provided jobs for communities from Veracruz. In 1990, 23 percent of the population was born outside Tamaulipas, and *Veracruzanos* represented 20 percent of the out-of-state population. By 2000, the flow of people from central and southern Mexico continued to increase, and more than a third of these new residents in Tamaulipas were from Veracruz. In the state's three main border cities, 30 percent of the population came from Veracruz (INEGI, 1990, 2000), and in some localities, people from Veracruz represented 70 percent of the maquiladora labor force during the 2000s (Redacción, 2007). By 2005, 18 out of 100 people that left Veracruz went to Tamaulipas (INEGI 2007). This led to the creation of a state government office representing Veracruz in one of the border cities of Tamaulipas and to the founding of the Association of Veracruzanos in Tamaulipas (Aguilar Grimaldo, 2009; Cruz, 2009).

While flows of migrant workers from central and southern Mexico to the maquiladoras of the north continued to increase, profitability in this sector declined. And, rather than blaming the dominant structures of global production and finance, the local population began to target people from Veracruz as the main cause for the troubled employment landscape. In Tamaulipas, the number of maquiladoras decreased from 375 in 2000 to 339 in 2006 (INEGI, 2013). Maquiladoras were relocating their operations to other parts of Mexico and/or to other countries, both as a result of lower labor standards and wages in countries such as China and due to decreasing external demand for products produced in export-processing zones (De la O, 2006). As competition for increasingly precarious jobs intensified, so too did discriminatory practices by local residents, who considered themselves to be the legitimate residents of the state's northern border region. People from Veracruz were increasingly racialized as African and/or indigenous, and therefore constructed as the Other (Reyna, 2010). Those that considered themselves to be from Tamaulipas referred to migration from Veracruz as an 'invasion' (Marichel, 2015; Velazquez, 2011). And discrimination against internal migrants also intensified in rural areas during the 1990s and 2000s (Andrade Rubio, 2013: 85). Local residents in two towns in Tamaulipas with citrus production as their main economic activity expressed it as follows: "We are afraid of this population settling here. They have bad habits and they are very dirty"; and "These people might have their election card that shows their residency in Tamaulipas, but they are still *Veracruzanos*. You can tell by their physique and they speak *Jarocho* [distinct accent]" (Andrade Rubio, 2013: 86). Residents of Tamaulipas and state authorities categorized people from Veracruz based on social constructions of race that described them as inferior in relation to the 'real *Tamaulipecos*' (people from Tamaulipas), who saw themselves as White and of European descent (Herrera Ledesma, Sanchez Limon and Martinez Rocha, 2016).

In contrast, residents of the state's border cities did not see Central American immigrants as a threat in terms of competition for jobs throughout the 1980s and the 1990s. During that time, the stigmatization of and discrimination against Central American immigrants came mostly from federal and local state authorities. Central Americans without documents began migrating to Mexico to cross to the United States in the 1980s, fleeing armed conflict in their region. Their main destination in Mexico was the border cities of Tamaulipas because of their proximity to the United States (Alanis Enciso, 2000: 126). Mexican federal authorities refused to recognize their status as refugees and instead tolerated their entrance into Mexican territory without documents (Munguía, 1993: 186, 197), making Central American immigrants vulnerable to extortion by local and federal security and immigration authorities in Tamaulipas, who asked for money in exchange for allowing them to continue their journey to the border (Alanis Enciso, 2000: 126). Extortion by state authorities increased in the 1990s, when the United States strengthened its border security with Mexico and sought collaboration from Mexican authorities to stop Central Americans from entering into U.S. territory. This period also saw increased surveillance, raiding of hotels searching for people without documents, and migration check points, particularly along the U.S.-Mexico border. Mexican immigration officials argued that these new measures aimed to safeguard Mexican jobs from immigrants and protect Mexicans from the crime and disease brought by Central Americans (Munguía, 1993: 203–204).

The history of violence in Central America shaped the social and political context in which both neoliberal reforms and migrant movements took place. The region's civil wars in the 1980s, which were instigated by U.S.-trained paramilitary forces to fight guerrilla movements and leftist governments, undermined democratic participation in public life, and covert U.S. interventions in Central America established the conditions for increasing impunity and violence by both state and non-state actors in the region (Grandin, 2006; Bruneau, 2011). These conditions of violence, in turn, facilitated the implementation of neoliberal policies, including the introduction of export-processing zones, particularly in the textile sector, as well as foreign investment in natural resources, including the mining sector, without environmental, labor, or human rights protections (Maquiladora Solidarity Network, 2016; Moore and Perez Rocha, 2019). As a result, dispossession and labor precarity intensified in Central America. Minimum wages and social benefits in Central American maquiladoras remained below the poverty line; in 2018, they were 25 percent below the poverty line in El Salvador, 40 percent below in Guatemala, and 61 percent below in Honduras (Maquiladora Solidarity Network and Equipo de Investigaciones Laborales, 2018: 21). The combination of violence, precarious employment, and evictions to make way for natural resource extraction increased internal displacement and dispossession. In El Salvador, for example, 21 per cent of the country's population was forcibly displaced internally in 2012. By 2015, this percentage had doubled (Bilak, 2016: 46). And according to the UN Special Rapporteur on the Rights of Indigenous Peoples, land evictions in the region failed to consider the rights of indigenous peoples to their land (Inter-American Commission on Human Rights, 2018). Ultimately, since the late 2000s, dispossession also led to the increasing migration of people travelling without documents from Central America into Mexico and the United States, with undocumented migration from Central America to the United States up from 1.35 million people in 2005 to 1.8 million in 2015. Inevitably, of course, this mobility involved crossing the Mexican territory to reach the United States (Canales Cerón and Rojas Wiesner, 2018: 53).

The rise of undocumented migration from Central America led to two developments in Mexico's political economy of violence and capital accumulation in the case of Tamaulipas. First, undocumented migration became a lucrative business for criminal groups, which demanded payment from human smugglers to facilitate border crossings into the United States and extracted ransom from the kidnapping of undocumented migrants. Whereas in 2008 it cost 1000 U.S. dollars to cross from Central America to the United States without documents, this rose to between 9000 and 12,000 U.S. dollars by 2018 (Kulish, 2018; Borger, 2018). As we have seen in previous chapters, this was part of the reconfiguration of large criminal groups in Mexico; though previously confined to drug trafficking, their criminal activities expanded as they extended their control over human smuggling and human trafficking in collaboration with federal immigration authorities and local police (U.S. Embassy in Mexico, 2011). In this context, the life of the kidnapped or extorted person became a fictitious commodity that could be traded for a price (Valencia, 2016). In the case of kidnapping, the person is not only commodified as labor but also becomes a tradeable object that is sold in the market according to the market mechanism of supply and demand, as "cargo to smuggle, gendered bodies to sell, labor to exploit, organs to traffic, and lives to exchange for cash" (Vogt, 2013: 765). Tamaulipas is one of the most dangerous regions for Central American immigrants, especially in terms of kidnapping (Leutert, 2018: 16). The San Fernando massacre in 2010 is a gruesome illustration of this systematic trend in Mexico, in which immigrants, especially undocumented Central American immigrants, are kidnapped and killed if they refuse to work for criminal groups and/or their families do not pay ransom (CIDH, 2013: 55–56).

Second, in addition to becoming a source of economic gain for criminal groups, Central American immigrants traveling without documents became a source of cheap labor for Tamaulipas agribusinesses during the 2000s and the 2010s. Prior to the San Fernando massacre, Central American immigrants traveled through southern Mexico, particularly Chiapas and Veracruz (see map 1), to reach Tamaulipas. They then traveled along the coast of Tamaulipas (Soto La Marina and San Fernando) to work in the fisheries and the harvest of sorghum on their way to the state's border cities, Reynosa and Matamoros. In the aftermath of the massacre, this route changed and migrants began to pass through and work in the citrus agriculture center of the state, offering low-cost labor compared to workers from Tamaulipas and Veracruz (Izcara Palacios, 2014). Simón Pedro Izcara Palacios shows in his ethnographic studies how the arrival of these immigrants in the agricultural sector increased competition for jobs, which led to lower wages. Their undocumented condition also exposed Central American workers to even lower wages and precarious working conditions because, out of fear of deportation, they could not complain to state authorities. In this context of low wages and competition for employment, the mistrust of these workers and indifference about their labor conditions intensified in the host communities of Tamaulipas (2014, 2015). Simultaneously, local workers from the citrus region of Tamaulipas were emigrating to the United States in search of employment—also without documents—and similarly facing conditions of community indifference, precarious work, and low wages (Izcara Palacios and Andrade Rubio, 2012).

These dynamics of mobility within Mexico and between Central America, Mexico, and the United States are interconnected and form part of the intensification of uneven development. Undocumented migration and internal relocation and displacement are not only human right issues or aspects of human mobility but also processes connected to a historically specific juncture in global capital accumulation. Raul Delgado Wise (2013, 2014) notes that the neoliberal intensification of uneven development—in the form of economic differentiation through the lowering of wages and unequal access to natural resources to attract investment—increased environmental degradation, the flexibilization and exploitation of labor, and violence, all while facilitating capital mobility. This led to unbearable conditions in communities of origin, making migration a forced process and the dominant form of human mobility in contemporary life (Delgado Wise et al., 2013). In Mexico, neoliberal policies shaped socioeconomic conditions similar to those of Central America, also forcing migration to the United States. As a result, both Central American migration to Mexico and the United States and Mexican migration to the United States contribute to a growing reserve army of labor in the region, further cheapening the cost of labor in Mexico and the United States.

A focus on these interconnections also provides insight into how the intensification of competition facilitates discrimination and indifference. Competition establishes social hierarchies based on difference—social hierarchies that individuals internalize and that position the Other as a harmful outsider to the social and economic arrangements in place in local communities. This form of social ordering has been highly compatible with neoliberalism. First, the othering of internal and Central American migrants in Mexico has facilitated accumulation locally, nationally, and internationally by lowering production (namely labor) costs in the manufacturing and agricultural sectors. Second, those residents of Tamaulipas who remained indifferent to the conditions of internal and Central American migrants ultimately internalized and reinforced oppressive social hierarchies. Local workers channeled their resentment toward migrants because the migrants were not in a position to be able to refuse precariousness (McIntyre and Nast, 2011: 1474). Communities in Tamaulipas accused migrants of bad habits and dirtiness without questioning the power relations that kept the labor conditions of these workers precarious (Andrade Rubio, 2013: 87). The intensification of uneven development, then, also affects the production of subjectivities and creates resentment toward the Other, shifting workers' attention away from structural inequalities to the benefit of market discipline.

The third way in which othering assists neoliberalism is in considering certain portions of the human community 'socially disposable' which facilitates the social reproduction of those who are not othered by state authorities and national and local economic elites such as local, non-immigrant residents. This has become part of daily violence in Mexico—specifically the interpersonal practices and expressions that form part of the normalization of violence at a larger scale and facilitate subordination and social control (Scheper-Hughes, 1992; Scheper-Hughes and Bourgois, 2004). The neoliberal intensification of competition in conditions of uneven development has fostered self-protection and the abandonment of the Other, turning competition into a dominant form of social interaction (Springer, 2012).

2   State Power, Criminal Groups, and Accumulation through the 'Illegal' Other

State practices shape the vulnerability of undocumented migrants from Mexico and Central America. State practices generate categories that turn difference into otherness in everyday life while reinforcing market discipline at the local and national levels. These categories are reinforced by deeming the Other illegal and therefore undeserving of any state protection. It is their illegal status that forms the basis for valuing undocumented migrants as commodities, turning them into a source of profitability and/or income in both formal and criminal economies. That migrant populations are constructed as illegal and, as a result, are highly vulnerable to violence and social control is neither an undesired effect of accumulation nor an indication of state weakness. Rather, the expansion of criminal groups' control over human smuggling and trafficking and the increase in undocumented migration is entirely consistent with capital accumulation and neoliberal state formation. As Izcara Palacios (2019) notes, migrants' status as illegal in Mexico and the United States turns them into an "exploitable, subjugated and disciplined workforce" and a commodity, while the criminalization and targeting of these populations by state authorities in the two countries appeases public fears about the integrity of national borders and diverts attention from domestic sources of inequality and exclusion.

Social practices in Mexico that turned both internal and Central American migrants into the dangerous Other are related to the role of the state at the local and national levels in defining subjects in a neoliberal way—through a lens of competition while denying their social agency (Alonso, 1994: 357). Union leaders' blaming of *Veracruzanos* in the manufacturing sector for the lack of employment, for instance, complemented the state-led fragmentation of the labor movement in this border region that began in the 1990s (Quintero, 1997; see also Chapter 2). The state also produced otherness based on difference by constantly requesting identification documents from internal and Central American migrants working in the Tamaulipas agricultural sector, largely based on their skin color and appearance. These requests for documents put people's identities into question and determine their relation to violence, defining whose life is worth it and whose is not (Poole, 2004). Even Mexican nationals often lack identification documents, as those from poor communities often do not have access to government services, and if they fail to present identification when asked, they are arrested. As expressed by one worker, "you get harassed because they think you are from Central America and want to cross to the other side" (Andrade Rubio, 2013: 88).

Central American immigrants without travel documents, though, are even more vulnerable to attacks by state authorities and criminal groups; as their presence in the country is not registered, they can be allowed to live or die by state authorities and/or criminal groups without any legal repercussions. This is clear in the testimony of a local resident in the citrus producing region of Tamaulipas:

> If they [Central American immigrants] get caught, these people go missing, go missing completely. Because they do not have documents, and they are not registered anywhere, no one claims them, not even their families.... Many do not even have travel documents, so it is easier for them to be taken away, or they get killed because there is no one to claim them (Izcara Palacios, 2012a: 14).

The Inter-American Commission of Human Rights collected testimonies from Central American immigrants about witnessing mass murders, mutilations, decapitations, and the melting of bodies in barrels of acid during the late 2000s and early 2010s (CIDH, 2013). Migrants' lack of proper documentation protects state forces and criminal groups that commit acts of violence, as the migrants are considered 'outside the law' and their lives are seen as disposable.

Paradoxically, the strict controls and suspension of the law around Central American immigrants during the period of study (2000–2016) coincided with Mexican authorities' complaints about Arizona's proposed legislation to request identification documents from individuals who looked 'Hispanic' (Torre Cantalapiedra, 2017). The securitization of U.S. borders, particularly after 2001, intensified the criminalization of undocumented migrants in the United States, especially those from Mexico. Prior to 2000, the securitization of American borders involved prevention through deterrence; in practice, this meant increased enforcement and infrastructure on the U.S. southern border to heighten the risks of unauthorized entry by rerouting migration toward more dangerous areas such as the desert (Andreas, 2009). Between 2002 and 2004, state investment in border security and technologies to prevent undocumented border crossings expanded, as did the criminalization and imprisonment of undocumented immigrants in the United States, particularly those of Mexican origin (Salyer, 2009; Chavez, 2009). This disrupted the existing migrant networks in host communities in the United States and deterred previous forms of circular migration. Undocumented Mexican migrants from Tamaulipas in the United States experienced criminalization, stigma, and social isolation similar to that experienced by their Central American counterparts in Mexico (Izcara Palacio and Andrade Rubio, 2012). A focus in the United States on undocumented immigration, border control, and state practices that categorized the American Self and the Hispanic Other had the effect of defining the nature of economic and political problems in this country, particularly after the attacks on New York in September of 2001 and the financial crisis of 2007–2010. To the benefit of the neoliberal economic and existing political system, this focus diverted attention away from the class and political structures that perpetuate inequalities within the United States (Chavez, 2008; Olvera, 2016), just as othering and the focus on competition and social hierarchies did in Mexico.

The treatment of undocumented immigrants in both Mexico and the United States shows how disciplinary categorizations of people are not merely dispersed forms of power but a part of state formation processes in which state institutions and practices play a significant role (Alonso, 2005: 27–28). Processes of state formation generate subjects and identities of Self and Other along racial lines, creating hierarchies in which some identities are accepted into the territory of the state while others are forbidden (Alonso, 1994: 391). This is particularly important in territories such as the U.S.-Mexican border, where state authorities, through their different agencies, enact bordering through spatial differentiation and control, with real effects on the regulation of the mobility of people, goods, and capital that help reproduce the space of the nation-state. Both in Mexico and the United States, state practices of identification and criminalization of migrants are central to state-making. They are part of the processes of spatial homogenization that create the apparent spatial and institutional cohesion necessary to make spaces governable while (re)producing spatial differences and the Other in everyday life (van Houtum and van Naerssen, 2002).

The connection between state formation and othering is not predetermined. In this case study, the connection needs to be understood in the context of the neoliberal intensification of uneven development, which allows us to see how state formation and racialized othering are, together, compatible with neoliberalism in at least two ways. First, the neoliberal intensification of market and financial imperatives creates the inequalities that disempower and expose the many to direct violence, turning those who are excluded from state and societal protection into more exploitable labor (Springer, 2012: 139). Second, state practices that produce the Other lead to a fragmentation of the populations affected by neoliberalism. Critical assessment of neoliberal policies and critiques of the class-based hierarchies supporting the neoliberal agenda are dissuaded in everyday life. Instead, residents are encouraged to focus on securing their wealth and safety and differentiate themselves from migrants. This facilitates the reproduction of both state power and neoliberalism because inequality and lack of opportunity are blamed on migrants rather than on existing structures of political and economic power, further reifying and depersonalizing power and enabling the control of social space.

To the benefit of criminal groups, the securitization of the border and the ability of state authorities to sanction those without travel documents has increased the worthiness of migrants as a source of income. Personal relations between migrant and smuggler have thus transformed into complicated impersonal networks of smuggling and trafficking controlled by criminal groups. The porous border of the 1980s and 1990s allowed migrants to choose voluntary deportation without trial, and U.S. border authorities considered crossing the border without documents to be an administrative breach. Migrants could return to their communities of origin and resume their attempts to cross into the United States. Yet with the militarization of the U.S. border and the criminalization of undocumented migration, crossing into the United States has become costlier, creating a source of profit for criminal groups in Mexico that have the resources to help smugglers avoid U.S. border patrols (Lee, 2018: 227). Human smugglers now have to pay criminal groups an extortion fee to gain access to smuggling routes and resources (Izcara Palacios, 2012b: 2015).

Criminal groups have also sought to maximize the profitability of kidnapping, namely by kidnapping Central American citizens in large groups. The Mexican Commission of Human Rights reports that between September 2008 and February 2009, 9,857 Central American immigrants were kidnapped in 33 occurrences. The number increased to 11,333 immigrants in 214 occurrences between April and September of 2010 (CNDH, 2009, 2011), and the Inter-American Commission of Human Rights reported the abduction of 400 people in a single occurrence in 2012. According to Pedro Izcara Palacios and Karla Lorena Andrade Rubio (2019), the logic of group kidnapping is to extract small amounts of ransom from many families in Central America at a time. The small ransom payments multiplied by the large number of abductees constitute a valuable source of income for criminal groups. Moreover, the murder of some kidnapped migrants to intimidate communities at home and abroad does not represent a loss of income for criminal groups, as it helps them collect ransom from the other families. There are estimates which consider that criminal groups obtain an annual average of 20.5 million dollars from these abductions since the late 2000s (Leutert, 2018: 15).

The increasing number of deportations from the United States, particularly to the border cities of Tamaulipas, creates an additional source of revenue for criminal groups. In 2012, deportations to three border cities increased fivefold in relation to 2006, jumping from 25,376 to 124,729 deportations (CIDH, 2013: 63). Upon deportation, immigrants once again become vulnerable to extortion and violence. As a Roman Catholic priest in charge of migrant shelters in two Tamaulipas border cities says, "Deporting people here is like sending them into a trap...to be hunted down" (Marosi, 2012). In the Tamaulipas border city of Reynosa, for instance, criminal groups force migrants to pay a monthly extortion fee to stay in the city. Otherwise, they will be abducted (Saez, 2019). Migrants' legal relationship to the state thus exposes them to exploitation by criminal groups, constituting yet another effect of accumulation through dispossession; migrants' dispossession from resources in their communities of origin ultimately leads to their illegal status and, hence, their lack of physical security, rendering them commodities to be appropriated by criminal groups (Lee, 2018; Glick-Schiller, 2015).

In the process of extracting profits from the intimidation, extortion, and abduction of undocumented migrants and, more generally, racialized Others, criminal groups also become a form of proxy governance, assisting both the Mexican and U.S. states to regulate the mobility of people without documents or economic resources. In this sense, criminal groups participate in neoliberal state formation. Civil society organizations claim that records of abduction of migrants deemed illegal date back to 2008 (CNDH 2011) and continue to increase, in partnership with state authorities at local and national levels on both sides of the border (Bonello, 2016; Saez, 2019). Indeed, Mexican state authorities did not make major efforts to protect the rights of undocumented migrants from Central America, even after the San Fernando massacre of 2010 (Diaz, 2019). Instead, they allowed criminal groups to serve as a form of deterrence to regulate the flow of undocumented migrants from Central America. In effect, criminal groups both help keep migrants out of Mexican border cities and respond to U.S. pressures to prevent Central American migrants from reaching American territory (Bonello, 2016).

At the same time, security assistance from the United States continued to flow, both through the Merida Initiative and the Foreign Military Financing program, despite the human rights conditionality that stipulated that 15 percent of the funding could be withheld if U.S. authorities considered that Mexico was not making significant improvements in the area of human rights (Congressional Research Service, 2019). U.S. authorities withheld this percentage of the funding only once, in 2015, despite the pervasive lack of protection of both migrants and the population residing in Mexico in general (WOLA et al., 2018). Ultimately, criminal groups on the Mexican side help U.S. authorities to keep undocumented migrants, both Mexican and Central American, outside its national borders by means of abduction, extortion, recruitment, and murder. The policing of who remains outside the state is a function of state power, even if this policing also comes from criminal groups (Das, 2004; Mbembe, 2003). Neoliberalism provides the framework in which state-making processes and economic gain and profitability, including through criminal activities, become compatible.

3   Conclusion

This chapter examines discrimination against Mexican and Central American migrants in Tamaulipas to show how otherness is constructed in everyday state practices both within Mexico and across national borders, and it illustrates how the neoliberal intensification of uneven development shapes this process. The categories that form the basis of otherness help reproduce competition and market discipline within Mexico and promote social exclusion, with some groups less threatened than others in physical, economic, and political terms. Othering thus deters resistance, as people classified as the Self (the 'real *Tamaulipecos*' or 'real' Mexicans) direct their frustration with the unfulfilled promises of market reforms and democratization in Mexico to excluded populations instead of against political and economic elites and neoliberal policies.

The abandonment of certain portions of the population and the dividing practices of othering are intrinsic to the power of the state and the reproduction of market discipline in contemporary Mexico. Both the suspension of the law and the use of the law in constructing illegality are crucial in this process, as illegal status turns migrants into commodities and a source of profit and economic gain for both criminal groups and legal businesses. Moreover, in extracting this economic gain, criminal groups exert control over human smuggling and trafficking throughout Mexico, becoming a form of proxy governance that assists in the reproduction of border-making—an important aspect of state formation in both Mexico and the United States. Both lawfare and lawlessness contribute to neoliberal state formation through the social control of the flow of illegal mobile bodies, reproducing national borders while also facilitating an increase of exploitable and disciplined labor (Izcara Palacios, 2019).

Understanding processes of othering in everyday life is important because it allows us to see our own responsibility in creating economic and physical conditions of violence (Springer, 2012: 141). As Veena Das and Deborah Poole argue, any question of justice needs to come "not from the moral space of innocent victimhood but from the rough-and-tumble of everyday life" (2004, 251). Realizing how hierarchies of power are internalized and reproduced in quotidian life thus allows us to disrupt categories of otherness, which have become part of the nexus between criminality, illegality and violence in the process of neoliberal state formation in Mexico.

CHAPTER 6

Social Space, Law, and Everyday Forms of Resistance

The previous chapters discussed the increasing physical and economic insecurity that people face as the result of the processes of neoliberal state formation based on fieldwork conducted between 2009 and 2016 in northeastern Mexico. Contrastingly, I was also able to observe the creative ways people find to survive, organize, share information and to live with dignity in the face of such violence. The following three stories are illustrative of this. During my stay in the Mexican border city of Matamoros, I met several maquiladora workers from the main union, the Industrial Workers and Laborers' Union of Matamoros (Sindicato de Jornaleros y Obreros Industriales de la Industria Maquiladora (the Industrial Workers' Union or SJOIIM from here on)). This occurred in the aftermath of the 2007–2010 global financial crisis that affected the levels of maquiladora employment and during the escalation of violence in the city. Despite these conditions, these workers remained committed to the union because of the social benefits their labor organization was able to achieve in the collective agreement. In fact, they were very knowledgeable of the agreement's clauses and the bargaining process and they expressed their willingness to become more active in the union to defend their labor rights. These workers not only valued the role of collective organizing in their lives through the union but also recognized the importance of participating in their labor organization. In this way, they imagined the workplace as a space of respect for labor rights.

In the same period, a group of young people organized Critical Bike mass rides in the capital city of Tamaulipas on weekends. When violence in the city intensified, the bike rides started to take place on a weekday at night time. Instead of staying off the streets to avoid being physically harmed by state and non-state forces, the participants of these rides decided to take the streets at night time. People participating in the rides as well as car passengers and residents living along the bike route expressed how this weekly event offered them some respite from violence in the city. The bikers did not confront economic inequality and political violence openly. Rather, they indirectly claimed an inclusive and democratic use of public space, particularly the streets, as opposed to the use of the city for social and economic control.

In 2017, I went to the public children's hospital in the capital of Tamaulipas because of a personal emergency. The working conditions at the hospital were precarious. In the emergency room, it was obvious that doctors and nurses were overworked and that they did not have adequate medical resources available to them. One of the doctors mentioned that at some point the air conditioning of the hospital did not work in the middle of summer, when temperatures reach 40°C, and how hard it was to do their jobs under those conditions. Not only were doctors and nurses working under harsh conditions inside the hospital, but also outside it. The state prison is a few kilometers away from the children's hospital, where prison breaks and riots often occur. When this happens, medical personnel and patients are afraid of leaving the facility for fear of being caught in the middle of shootings caused by these breaks and riots. The year before, a head from a decapitated body was left in the entrance of the hospital with a message from Los Zetas threatening prison guards. Under this duress, doctors and nurses treated all their patients, mostly from a poor background, with dignity while offering the best care they could provide given the limited resources. In this case, these health care workers did not internalize the neoliberal logic of profit-seeking individualism as they continued to provide adequate medical attention to their patients despite low financial incentive.

While these experiences did not encompass a larger political movement that directly confronted the state and the neoliberal agenda, they show the stories of people improving human life in the here-and-now. These stories cannot be dismissed as merely survival strategies that do not make a difference. The actions of maquiladora workers, bike riders and health care workers involved vast efforts from these actors, facing real threats to their employment and lives by participating in the union, biking in the streets and providing dignified health care to the poor. The day-to-day struggle represents not only the most enduring site of resistance but also the only option available given the high levels of physical and economic insecurity and repression in this northeastern region. As this chapter illustrates, these actors have been able to affect policy through this quotidian resistance. They have also shown people living in conditions of economic and physical insecurity the realm of possibilities for democratic and inclusive social change through everyday resistance, setting the groundwork for more radical challenges to the neoliberal agenda. For this reason, the chapter employs James C. Scott's (1985, 1990) focus on everyday forms of resistance, namely the quotidian forms of defiance and non-cooperation that subordinate forces employ over time with little coordination or planning, and are used by both individuals and groups to resist without directly confronting dominant actors.

This chapter focuses on three different forms of resistance in Tamaulipas to examine how progressive social organizing takes place in the context of violent neoliberalism at the local level: Critical Mass bike rides reclaiming of public space, the struggles of health-care workers in Tamaulipas to improve their working conditions, and the strikes in the border city of Matamoros, Tamaulipas that won increased purchasing power for workers in maquiladoras. These three case studies are instructive for two reasons. First, the urban setting of all three cases reflects the increasing role of cities in articulating political and economic power and shaping resistance. In Mexico, 80 percent of the population lived in cities by 2018 (World Bank, 2019). Also, inequality and exclusion in Mexico are constantly reproduced in the city. Seven out of ten people living in poverty resided in urban centers between 2010 and 2016 (Alejo Vazquez 2018). For this reason, the city has become an important site of struggle, particularly in contexts where high levels of inequality and violence co-exist with the façade of liberal democracy. On the one hand, cities are key in the organization of global capitalism because they serve as nodes for local and national political decision-making, transnational economic management, consumption, and communication (Sassen, 2011). The city is also an important site of state legitimation, and urban political action therefore has repercussions for the legitimacy of state institutions. On the other hand, cities bring together populations from different socioeconomic backgrounds, making urban locales key sites of progressive resistance as different citizens must negotiate the terms of their interactions (Harvey, 1989: 303). These negotiations provide room to shape social, economic, legal, and political relations in the experience of everyday life in a way that challenges the spatial practices and representations of space imposed by law (Lefebvre 1991). Lefebvre (2001) describes this dialectically in his conception of space as a social process that is experienced, perceived, and imagined.

The second way in which these case studies are instructive derives from how the movements use the law to mobilize public transcripts to gain legitimacy and prevent repression. James C. Scott characterizes the public transcript as the established ways in which ruling classes define how subordinate actors and groups have to behave and speak in particular social settings (1990: 45,105, 111). More specifically, the public transcript says what is legitimate, what is admissible, what is the right way to go about things—all, of course, from the perspective of dominant groups (Scott, 1990: 52-54). The examples studied here show how the law is a form of public transcript that establishes what is allowed and prohibited according to dominant social forces. At the same time, these case studies show how the public transcript is challenged by making use of the law's prescribed roles and language to resist the abuse of power.

In this chapter, then, *I argue that everyday forms of resistance occur when subordinate groups use the public transcript strategically to change how people use and imagine their workplaces and the public space, even in highly repressive*

and violent contexts of economic and political domination such as Tamaulipas.
The labor movement actions in the maquiladora and health sector and Critical
Mass bike rides do not openly confront militarization, economic restructuring,
the private appropriation of public funds, or the domination of public space by
criminal groups, but these movements do reimagine workplaces and public
space in democratic and socially inclusive ways, which ultimately challenges
the everyday formation of state power and neoliberalism.

1   Streets of Hope

Development in the capital city of Tamaulipas, Ciudad Victoria, favors urban
sprawl, large commercial buildings, and wide streets for cars and cargo trucks
over affordable housing in dense neighborhoods and other forms of public and
active transportation. Official communications represent the space of the city
as a hub where commercial and governmental operations converge across the
state of Tamaulipas. The city is also planned according to potential points for
urban sprawl and the building of large commercial zones and government
buildings and roads (see Chapter 4). The city is thus imagined as a source of
profit for state authorities who work closely with construction companies in
the private appropriation of public funds. This urban landscape features few
citizen-led initiatives to occupy public space to call for social and political
change. Yet, Critical Mass bike rides began when violence escalated in 2010. I
base my analysis of Critical Mass bike rides on participant observation between 2010 and 2014 in Ciudad Victoria, Tamaulipas. The nighttime Critical
Mass bike rides in Ciudad Victoria are organized by the informal group Victoria
en Bici (Victoria on Bikes). The movement began in 2010 when young, middle-
class residents decided to recreate biking experiences they had had in cities in
developed countries in their own urban environment. The movement started
with monthly nighttime rides that then became weekly—all in a context of
high levels of violence and a tacit 9 pm curfew. There are no restrictions to
participating in the rides; organizers share information about the rides on social media, and all are invited to participate. Victoria en Bici has never been
established as a not-for-profit organization with clear leadership. Rather, it has
remained a flexible, volunteer-run movement with a continually changing
leadership.

The Critical Mass bike rides drew between one hundred and three hundred
participants during the period of study. The group departed from the square in
front of the governor's office building at 8:30 pm on Thursdays and cycled
through the main commercial and residential streets of the city, including the

governor's neighborhood. Victoria en Bici did not secure a permit or request police protection to cycle in the streets. Instead, to prevent any municipal involvement, the cyclists occupied just one lane, as if they are each riding individually. This tactic was a safety measure, as the local police were widely suspected to be involved with criminal groups, and the public transcript of the law makes it possible to take over the streets without a permit and without proclaiming a political or social goal: article 11 of the Mexican Constitution provides citizens and residents with freedom of movement within the country. This right is further supported by ambiguous statements in the Tamaulipas State Constitution about state authorities' duties to respect people's freedoms and the human rights included in the Mexican Constitution (article 16). Bike riders were therefore free to exercise their individual rights to freedom of movement.

Their compliance with the public transcript also made it possible for the Critical Mass rides to avoid openly confronting authorities while still pressuring local state authorities to follow their own rules. Local state officials frequently asserted that the city was a safe space for its residents (despite occurrences that proved otherwise (see Chapter 4)), thus they were forced to provide protection at a distance in order to not contradict their own affirmations regarding safety. The bike rides, in effect, pressured state authorities to comply with their own rhetoric. Victoria en Bici further complied with the public transcript by claiming that the group was merely promoting health, leisure, and more environmentally friendly forms of transportation—goals entirely compatible with the development plans put forward by the municipality and the state government (Municipio de Ciudad Victoria, 2013a, 2014b; Gobierno de Tamaulipas, 2010b).

As the rides became more popular, local state authorities approached the cyclists to ask if the rides had political goals. These inquiries came directly from the governor's office. Members would respond that the aim of the bike rides was "to have healthy fun with friends." Thereafter, local state authorities did not object openly to Victoria en Bici as the group complied with the public transcript.

There is a clear class component in the Critical Mass rides that also fits the public transcript. The movement began with middle-class young people. As middle-class residents of the city were among the strongest supporters of the Institutional Revolutionary Party (Partido Revolucionario Institucional, or PRI) in Tamaulipas—the party in power at the state level until 2016—local state authorities did not perceive the rides as threatening. One of the organizers was even the grandchild of a former PRI state governor from the 1980s. The organizers matched what the public transcript described as 'acceptable' citizens (those who can use public space), in contrast to the 'dangerous work-ing poor', characterized as threats to the status quo. Over time, the movement's loose structure and leadership allowed it to adapt to changing circumstances. The movement continued to be run by volunteers and had no political or eco-nomic affiliations and no membership requirements. This spontaneity and anonymity contributed to its strength, as no individual in Victoria en Bici could be the target of political or physical threats, and changes in partisan politics or the economic context did not jeopardize the movement's continuity.

While they complied with the public transcript to gain legitimacy, the Criti-cal Mass rides brought about change in the city by mobilizing a hidden tran-script that encouraged class solidarity in a period of high economic inequality and violence in the city. People from working-class backgrounds eventually took over much of the organizing under the period studied here, and partici-pants from varied economic upbringings followed their instructions. The Criti-cal Mass rides also helped destigmatize biking as an inferior activity exclusive to the working classes. Disrespect for cyclists was widespread in the capital city, reflected in the number of car accidents involving bicycles, and local newspaper reports about these accidents depicted cyclists as members of the working poor whose only means of affordable transportation was a bicycle. The working poor often joined the ride when it was part of their route toward work or home. The rides effectively showed that everyone can benefit from biking and urged city residents to respect cyclists regardless of their class. Fur-thermore, as the state did not provide protection for the Critical Mass rides, participants were responsible for taking care of each other to prevent acci-dents, which promoted solidarity among strangers from different social and economic backgrounds. This solidarity expanded beyond the Critical Mass rides, as participants also collaborated in food banks, distributed toys in poor neighborhoods, and collected donations to support low-income athletes hop-ing to compete overseas. The bike rides also provided young people with a safe space to socialize, as nightlife in the city became dangerous. Citizens occupied the streets at least once a week for these rides, reversing the escalating implo-sion of public life caused by state and criminal groups.

The bike rides gradually changed how public space in the city was lived, represented, and imagined. Through the Critical Mass movement, people tem-porarily experienced the streets as part of their daily urban routine, linking work, private life, and leisure. This stands in contrast to experiences of the streets as the exclusive space of automobiles, exclusionary real estate develop-ment, state security forces, and criminal groups. Children, many of whom had only witnessed fear and violence on the streets, looked up to the cyclists during the rides. They and others discovered new ways of imagining the streets as public spaces of solidarity, leisure, and social expression. Such imaginings defied representations of the space of the city as commodified land, markets for profit, and subversive or violent locales that needed to be controlled by the state. This shift in the conception of the streets both reversed the implosion of public life and democratized public space.

The Critical Mass rides in Ciudad Victoria ruled out open confrontations with political power. Instead, participants assumed the role assigned to them by the public transcript and performed deference and dissimulation as a strategy of resistance. The participants' claim that they were advocating a venue for healthy leisure activities was compatible with politicians' assertion that sports help youth stay away from drugs and criminal gangs. Similarly, cyclists stated that their participation was merely exercising their individual freedom of movement in the city, which is consistent with Mexican laws. By complying with the official transcript, then, the Critical Mass rides disguised their message of resistance while protecting participants' physical integrity (Scott 1990, 68–69, 94). This strategy served to reclaim public space in a highly violent context, and the movement expanded to other violent cities in Tamaulipas such as Reynosa and Tampico. At the same time, the bike rides subtly questioned existing material practices and representations of space and the dominant role of the state, criminal groups, and private capital in the daily experience of the city. By using the streets as public space, the bike rides offered an alternative notion of space. The presence of crowds in the streets made the movement highly visible, with a powerful political impact, while it also offered a sense of anonymity, lowering the risk of targeted physical attacks against any participants in particular (Scott 1990, 65–66). These bike rides used space as a political instrument of creative expression, opposing the control of public space by state, private capital, and criminal groups while creating a shared space of collaboration to strengthen the sense of community (Lefebvre, 1996)

2   Places of Terror and Human Rights as Labor Rights

Health-care workers in Tamaulipas mobilized between 2014 and 2016 to demand better working conditions. Using the language of human rights, their demands intersected with urban demands for physical safety from violence and contested the power structures that both sustained violence and promoted the privatization of the health-care sector in Tamaulipas. At the same time, the movement used public space to express its demands, indirectly confronting economic restructuring, the private appropriation of public funds, and the domination of public space by the state and criminal groups.

For the discussion that follows, it is important to locate the health-care workers' mobilization in the intersection of neoliberalism and violence in this part of the country. The escalation of violence in Tamaulipas after 2010 affected health-care workers in particular ways. Doctors and nurses were raped and kidnapped, forced to provide medical care to injured members of criminal groups. Health-care workers also faced danger in the emergency room when treating members of criminal groups, the police, or military personnel, as the threat of reprisal from a rival criminal group was always latent (Figueroa, 2018; Cedillo, 2015). This violence affected not only doctors but whole communities, as fewer doctors wanted to practice in rural and urban zones with high rates of violence. Health-care workers' experiences with violence exacerbated their already precarious working conditions. In the 1990s, neoliberal decentralization led to health-care administration and funding being downloaded to local state authorities, which further strengthened the power of local elites. They, in turn, helped to replicate neoliberalism at the local level. In Tamaulipas, decentralization allowed local political elites affiliated to the PRI to appropriate public resources for private use through bidding processes, and the federal state refrained from intervening as long as the neoliberal agenda continued to prevail (Muñoz Martínez, 2013). The health-care sector, under the control of local political elites, thus became a source of public resources ripe for private appropriation (Homedes and Ugalde, 2011).

In 2015 and 2016, for example, health-care workers in Tamaulipas complained about the lack of air conditioning during the spring and summer in health care facilities and emphasized how this put their patients' safety at risk. The absence of air conditioning was due to the state government's purchase of defective air conditioning systems at high prices through a dubious bidding process connected to a company belonging to a high-ranking local state official. Prescription drugs also proved lucrative. While government contracts showed that medicines were purchased, the local health-care system did not have sufficient medicine to carry out even basic tasks, and in some cases, the existing stock of medicines had passed their expiration dates (Gómez, 2017). Money laundering was also involved. Between 2010 and 2016, the company that won 80 percent of procurement bids to supply medicines to hospitals and clinics in Tamaulipas was owned by a Tamaulipas businessman accused in the United States of being a front-man for the money-laundering activities of two former state governors (see Chapter 3 for a more in-depth discussion of these money-laundering accusations). Neoliberal decentralization and the public appropriation of public funds in the health sector thus became complementary processes. The quality of public services declined alongside increasing irregularities in the use of funds in the health sector, while private clinics and hospitals replaced their public counterparts for the middle and upper classes. This further decreased support for the local public health-care sector in Tamaulipas, creating a two-tier health-care system that left the poorly equipped public health-care facilities for the working poor.

Working conditions for physicians and nurses in the public health sector became increasingly precarious. Most doctors and nurses did not have full-time positions in the public health-care system and, hence, had no benefits. In 2017, a physician with a limited-term contract earned 5700 pesos (285 U.S. dollars) a month, whereas the cost of living was 9172 pesos (458 U.S. dollars) (Brussolo, 2017). A nurse on contract earned 3200 pesos (160 U.S. dollars) a month. For both doctors and nurses, the workday extended to twelve hours a day (HT Agencia 2017). Health-care workers' working conditions were not only precarious because of low wages and the lack of infrastructure but also because of violence. In addition to violence at the hands of criminal groups, health-care workers also faced harassment by state authorities who accused them of being complicit with criminal groups (Gallardo Cabiedes, 2015; Soto, 2016).

Public health-care workers did not immediately complain collectively about their working conditions. The reasons were twofold. First, the leadership of their union, the Union of Public Sector Workers of Tamaulipas, had been collaborating with local state authorities since 1996 to suppress discontent among health-care workers (García, 2016; de la Rosa Castillo, 2017). Second, public health-care workers feared losing their jobs. As a result, doctors and nurses employed strategies to avoid violence such as changing their work clothes before leaving the hospital to avoid being identified by criminal groups as health-care workers (González Antonio, 2012). Eventually, though, doctors and nurses in the cities of Tamaulipas did begin to protest in the streets and voice their concerns regarding the lack of infrastructure and the scarcity of prescription drugs. In doing so, they used the language of human rights.

Throughout the 1990s and 2000s, during the neoliberal state attack on collective labor and social rights, human rights language became part of the neoliberal public transcript. The Executive power created the National Commission for Human Rights in the early 1990s, a period characterized by the deepening of neoliberal policies such as privatization of public companies and communal land and the signing of the North American Free Trade Agreement (NAFTA). In 2000, national state authorities further appropriated the language of human rights when the right-wing party National Action Party (Partido Accion Nacional, or PAN) won the presidential elections after more than seventy years of PRI rule. The new presidential administration promised that the democratic transition would also feature a defense of human rights, which opened up Mexico's political system to the scrutiny of international human rights organizations such as the United Nations. The public transcript of human rights, however, also served to contain opposition parties and social movements (Manrique Giacomán 2018), as it focused on individual civil and political rights while state policies continued to undermine collective economic and social rights (López, 2017). Despite the new attention to human rights, then, human rights violations continued throughout the 1990s and 2000s. In the 1990s, the PRI presidential administration repressed several social movements and the suppression of dissent did not cease with the new PAN administration (Manrique Giacomán, 2018). In fact, human rights abuses intensified during the War on Drugs launched in 2006 by the PAN presidential administration of Felipe Calderón Hinojosa (2006–2012). Toward the end of the Calderón administration, the Mexican Congress passed a constitutional reform that placed human rights protected in the Mexican Constitution and those covered by international treaties on equal footing. This reform, with its emphasis on individual rights, displaced collective rights in Mexico. Labor reform followed, dismantling the legal framework guaranteeing labor rights. Mexico's 2017 Labor Law fulfilled the neoliberal mandate to make work contracts more flexible, permit trial periods for new employees, and reward workers for productivity rather than seniority (La Botz, 2016). In this neoliberal context, then, the new legal framework of human rights shifted attention away from collective economic and social rights toward limited civil and political rights.

Health-care workers in Tamaulipas imbued this public transcript regarding human rights with local meaning and redefined human rights as collective rights, including labor rights and the right to health (Goldstein, 2014: 112). Initially, it was the arrest of sixteen doctors that triggered this reframing nationally. A teenager died in 2014 in a hospital in central Mexico under the care of these doctors. In response, the #YoSoyMedico17 (IAmDoctor17) movement called attention to how doctors and nurses are demonized for wide-ranging social problems and decried the lack of investment in public health. Tens of thousands of doctors, nurses, and their supporters took to the streets in cities across the country in a protest against the criminalization of medical practice.

While protests and marches were not unusual in other parts of central and northern Mexico, they were rare in Tamaulipas because of the implosion of public life. Economic restructuring and insecurity limited the strategies that public health-care workers could use to bargain with state authorities. In the context of this national protest, though, health-care workers in Tamaulipas employed the language of human rights, focusing on the violence they experienced at their workplaces to address their harsh working conditions. Indirectly, they framed their workplace experiences as a human rights issue and berated state authorities for failing to protect their physical safety (Agencias, 2018; Reyez, 2018). Wider sectors of the population empathized with their vulnerability, and the health-care workers won broad support. By emphasizing the impact of violence on their professional lives, they also gained an entry point to address low wages, long working hours, and the lack of social benefits and job security. More specifically, the movement framed decent wages and working conditions as a human rights issue, and without openly confronting state officials, this mobilization of the public transcript placed pressure on local state authorities to follow their own rules.

Significantly, these workers linked their own precarious labor conditions to people's right to health care and access to health care as a human right. Using social media and public demonstrations, they called attention to widespread shortages of medicines and supplies, abusive work schedules, ill-treatment of patients, low salaries, and medical schooling problems (for an example, see Yosoy17Reynosa, 2017). They did not directly address the causes underlying these problems such as the private appropriation of public funds or the negative effects of neoliberalism on health services. Instead, they focused on how the lack of resources prevented them from doing their jobs. Their silence about the underlying causes protected the movement's members from being harassed or fired by local state officials in charge of the health infrastructure. The hidden transcript in this case maintained the impression of consent to stave off repression and meet collective goals (Scott, 1990: 17, 33). Workers could not openly confront the power of local capitalists, the PRI-dominated local state, or criminal groups, as they could lose their jobs and/or become victims of repression by state and non-state actors. Dissimulation thus became a strategy of resistance that indirectly challenged political and economic power (Scott, 1990: 106).

Workers also included a spatial dimension in their protests. They occupied public space to express their movement's demands, which was key for a social re-appropriation of the city in the context of violence. Doctors and nurses in Tamaulipas took to the streets every year in commemoration of the #YoSoy-Medico17 national movement. After 2014, they organized demonstrations outside hospitals in various urban centers as well as in front of the governor's office (González, 2016). This spatialized resistance, wielding the public transcript of human rights, delivered unmistakable political messages that state authorities could not easily dismiss. These protests also provided new ways of conceiving the urban landscape as an inclusive space of dissent and not as the exclusive space of state security forces and criminal groups. These protests contained a powerful critique of both neoliberalism and violence. The movement's demand for better working conditions identified the reasons for the lack of resources in the health sector: the privatization of health-care services, cuts in social spending, and the private appropriation of public funds facilitated by neoliberal decentralization. At the same time, the workers' emphasis on their vulnerability to violence at their workplaces presented an indirect critique of militarization in the War on Drugs and the violence it produced. While the movement of public health-care workers in Tamaulipas has not led to less violence in the region, it has led to wage increases, particularly for contract workers, with pay raises in 2019 ranging from 45 to 90 percent (El Mañana Staff, 2019).

The public health-care workers' movement in Tamaulipas illustrates how people mobilize to confront the neoliberal agenda in contexts of violence and repression. The movement used the public transcript of human rights to denounce the effects of neoliberal decentralization on public health care and violence in everyday life, particularly at the workplace and in the public space, while calling for city residents to appropriate the public space and reject privatized forms of health care, neoliberal economic segregation, and the implosion of public life caused by militarization, political repression, and criminal groups. Health-care workers in Tamaulipas inscribed collective rights into human rights legislation by appropriating the official neoliberal transcript of human rights and reinterpreting it in vernacular ways. In doing so, they developed novel strategies for connecting their labor demands to the wider needs of the community. As economic competition increases and violence breeds community distrust, these strategies become increasingly important. The workers' ability to connect their labor demands to issues of social reproduction in urban communities won wide social support for their movement (Manilla, 2016).

3   Structured Coherence, Collective Bargaining, and Transcripts of
       Labor

In January 2019, Mexico's left-center president, Andrés Manuel López Obrador (2018–2024), announced an increase to the minimum wage, and maquiladora workers in the border city of Matamoros called on their union leadership to make employers comply with a clause in the 2019 round of collective bargaining that would index their pay to this increase. López Obrador's minimum wage increase granted these workers a legal basis for demanding a 20-percent increase in their annual bonus (Cedillo, 2019a). In previous years, annual minimum wage increases had ranged from 4 to 6 percent, equivalent to an additional 142 to 192 U.S. dollars. In 2019, though, minimum wage increased to $1685 (Quintero, 2019). As a result, maquiladora workers demanded that their annual bonus rise to match the increase—an additional 32,000 pesos (approximately 1685 U.S. dollars) in their pockets. Employers refused to comply with the existing clause that would index wages and the annual bonus to such an increase, hence workers went on strike (Quintero Ramírez, 2019).

The strike was led by the most important union in Matamoros: Industrial Workers' Union. The Industrial Workers' Union represents 70 percent of the workers in the maquiladora sector in the border city of Matamoros—around forty thousand workers. Approximately thirty thousand members from this union, who work for forty-five maquiladoras, went on strike to demand these increases. Companies eventually granted the workers' demands, and the strike ended in February 2019 (Cedillc, 2019b). Thus, the maquiladoras ultimately relented—a victory the union won due to a combination of factors: compliance with the public transcript and the union's bargaining strength, partly acquired through its interactions with illegality and partly through its role in providing the structured coherence the maquiladoras rely on for production.

This struggle was located in the border city of Matamoros. Its urban landscape is dominated by export-processing zones, or maquiladoras, and the material space of the city, including roads, utilities, industrial parks, housing, and health and education services, is configured to meet the needs of maquiladora production. This development model allows companies to take advantage of cheap labor while receiving tax exemptions and incentives to produce goods, particularly exports. Private firms see the city of Matamoros as a hub of cheap labor and advantageous investment policies in global commodity chains, while state authorities see Matamoros as a territory for extracting tax revenues, promoting investment, and managing violence. Meanwhile, for residents, the lived experience of violence in the city included shootings, street blockades, and disappearances, as well as the growing presence of military and federal police forces during the period between 2010 and 2016.

While the strike in Matamoros took place outside the period under study in this book and under a left-center president who is critical of neoliberalism, I include this case study here to highlight the interplay between public transcript, illegality and legality and demonstrate how the interaction between the suspension of the law and legality between the 1960s to 1990s was central to labor gains in this city in the 2019 strike. This case study also provides a more nuanced analysis of union activism in Mexico, and particularly of labor organizations affiliated to the PRI. Many analyses portray Mexican labor unions as a legacy of Mexico's authoritarian regime under the PRI, and PRI unions are depicted as subordinate to the party's agenda, with detrimental consequences for workers' living conditions and wages (Bensusan and Middlebrook, 2013; Camp, 2013; Carrillo 1994; Roman and Velasco, 2006). However, as several authors point out, such generalizations can also overlook the heterogeneity of the Mexican labor movement and its activism, even within unions affiliated to the PRI via the Mexican Confederation of Workers (Confederacion de Trabajadores de Mexico or CTM) (Quintero Ramírez, 2003; De la O and Quintero Ramírez, 2002). This heterogeneity is shaped by the local contexts of organized labor—particularly each region's economic history and relationship with the local and national state. Historically, the union's activism and its affiliation to the PRI allowed the SJOIIM to make significant gains in its collective agreements with maquiladoras (Quintero Ramírez, 1997: 122–127). By the 1980s, the union had won a forty-hour work-week, extended health benefits, seniority rights, and investment in affordable housing and schools—conditions that were almost non-existent in other parts of the Mexican northern border region (Quintero Ramírez, 2004: 287–88). Despite the country's implementation of neoliberalism, the union was able to retain its role in collective bargaining with firms and it held on to most of the social benefits it had won throughout the 1990s (Quintero Ramírez, 2004).

SJOIIM's deference to the PRI's political and economic structures of power allowed the union to continue to play an active role in collective bargaining in Matamoros's export-processing zone. As we have seen with the Critical Mass bike rides and the health-care workers' movement, conformity is a tactical approach that subordinated social forces can use as a political resource (Scott 1990, 33). Indeed, the union's compliance with the public transcript maintained the impression of consent to meet collective ends (Scott, 1990: 17, 33). The SJOIIM fulfilled its PRI-assigned role by endorsing PRI candidacies and local and national state authorities, despite the agenda of austerity and labor flexibilization that local and national PRI authorities pushed through in the 1990s, which threatened to take away SJOIIM's right to collective bargaining. The union did not issue these endorsements because workers and union leaders blindly supported the dominant forces of the PRI, especially once economic and political attacks on the union became obvious (see Chapter 2). Rather, the workers accommodated these PRI demands in a context of economic compulsion and violence. The union could not openly confront the power of global companies and PRI state authorities because workers could lose their jobs and/or become victims of state repression. Dissimulation, in this context, was a strategy of resistance that was also compatible with challenging power. On the one hand, neoliberal austerity and precarious work on the rise at the local level threatened the right of the SJOIIM to collective bargaining as well as prior labor gains. On the other hand, local and national PRI politicians needed the support of union members for political strength. The latter made promises to workers to obtain their votes, which in turn allowed the SJOIIM to "call upon the elite to act according to its own public transcript" (Scott, 1990: 106). By asking politicians to follow their own rules and fulfill their promises, the union found leverage in its negotiations with politicians and firms in export-processing zones and used it to retain the right to the process of collective bargaining as well as the gains of previous rounds of collective bargaining.

Nonetheless, the 2007–2010 global financial crisis and the escalation of violence in the city starting in 2010 weakened the union's leverage. In Matamoros, the crisis led to layoffs, technical shutdowns, and a series of plant restructurings (CNIME, 2009). The union had to give in to private firms' demands in order to keep jobs in the city, agreeing to a longer workweek and wage cuts (Muñoz Martínez, 2010). The climate of violence in the city also led the union to self-censor, as protesting or criticizing the state government could lead to political repression, including a loss of support from national and local state authorities. Despite this dismal scenario though, the SJOIIM continued to support the PRI. This apparent deference to the PRI was a useful strategy for retaining the right to collective bargaining. In the context of neoliberalism—with precarious labor conditions and downward pressure on wages becoming the norm, particularly in export-processing zones in Mexico—this strategy was especially important. Indeed, in most export-processing zones in northern Mexico collective contracts were imposed from above by companies and/or the leadership of PRI-affiliated union confederation during the period of study. While the SJOIIM did not openly confront the neoliberal agenda of labor flexibilization and austerity endorsed locally by the PRI and the maquiladoras after the late 1990s, it did resist this agenda by retaining the right to negotiate collective agreements and defend some gains of previous rounds of collective bargaining.

The union's activism and its compliance with the public transcript is also related to the interaction between legal exception and legality between the 1950s and the 1980s. The union gained political strength from having participated in illegal activities in the past and successfully mobilizing workers to support the PRI. The leader of the Industrial Workers' Union mobilized members' support for the PRI to violate individual workers' right to a secret vote (see Chapter 2). This was central to strengthening state power during the PRI regime. At the same time, this ability of the leadership to mobilize workers' support gave the union strength to negotiate with both workers and state authorities at all levels, even though this strength did not derive from democratic internal elections. As such, the union leadership was able to retain a unique clause in the collective agreement for decades that linked salary increases and bonus rises to any percentage increase in the minimum wage. The union's compliance with the public transcript and the union leadership's involvement in past states of exception contributed to the success of the 2019 mass strike through the legal application of the collective agreement.

Also, the structured coherence of Matamoros lent bargaining leverage to the union. David Harvey defines structured coherence as the space where capital can circulate in a coordinated way through the geographical concentration of infrastructure, transport relations, housing, labor and consumer markets, and factories to ensure the availability of labor and the necessary conditions to accelerate the exchange of goods from plants to final markets (2001, 2006). This is particularly crucial in the context of international competition that makes firms—especially global manufacturing companies—more sensitive to small variations in investment location and the particular characteristics of local labor markets and infrastructures.

Several particularities of Matamoros' economic geography make it ideally suited to global firms, particularly in the auto sector. Matamoros is close to North American markets, which accelerates the pace of exchange between production and final markets. International bridges, binational railways, and highways connect the region to U.S. markets and deep-water port facilities at Brownsville and Corpus Christi for ocean cargo. American firms also have distribution facilities and administrative offices on the U.S. side and rely on the U.S. border for some legal, accounting, and financial services as well as industrial suppliers (Team NAFTA, 2010). Matamoros also boasts labor markets with extensive experience in the auto parts sector and complex manufacturing processes, boosted by the proximity of the auto parts industry in the United States (Quintero Ramírez, 1997: 60). This helps explain, for instance, why several plants that moved part of their operations from Matamoros to China in the early 2000s brought them back again in the mid 2000s. According to maquiladora managers, the learning curve in the late 2000s was steeper in China than it was in Matamoros as it took new companies less time to train their workers in Matamoros than in their Chinese operations (Castillo, 2010).

Furthermore, maquiladora investment in Matamoros relies not only on low production costs but also on the continuous restructuring and adaptation of production to changes in international demand (Quintero Ramírez, 1997). The existing physical and social infrastructure in the area is mostly oriented to maquiladora production, including roads, utilities, industrial parks, housing, and health-care and education services that support production. This infrastructure provides firms with the advantages of an available workforce and the capacity to speed up the delivery of products. The state, of course, played a hand in creating the local structured coherence in Matamoros upon which capital relies. The state and the municipal government provided tax incentives and subsidies for initial investment in the auto parts cluster in a bid to agglomerate large maquiladoras, local suppliers, and skilled labor in the same location. This need for structured coherence explains why companies did not automatically turn to capital flight when the strike was called in 2019; the capitalist organization of space—including material practices and representations—created its own contradictions, which provided room for labor to resist. As Jefferson Cowie notes, the "search for cheap labor has its own subversive logic" for firms because the required qualities of labor markets and workers' skills for complex manufacturing remain place-bound (1999, 6). This worked to the union's advantage in Matamoros, Tamaulipas. The union both benefited from and contributed to the area's structured coherence. The concentration of investment in the auto parts sector in Matamoros led to the expansion of union membership and provided workers with the skills and experience that firms required. This increasingly skilled workforce, in turn, formed part of the structured coherence the union then employed as leverage to retain collective bargaining during neoliberal reforms of the 1990s and 2000s and employers' threats to relocate to China during the same period.

There were limitations to how the union could take advantage of its contributions to the area's local structured coherence. Indeed, the characteristics of complex manufacturing make it less likely for firms to move all their operations to cheaper locations because this type of global production needs workers to consent to adapt their production experience and skills to changing global market demands (McKay, 2004; Burawoy, 1983). But restructuring in the existing location proved to be a viable alternative. When the 2007–2010 global financial crisis affected firms with investment in the maquiladoras, the firms looked to internal restructuring to reduce costs rather than relocate and forego the advantages of structured coherence in Matamoros. As a result, the union lost some of its previous accomplishments. While the previous collective agreement prior to the crisis stipulated a 40-hour workweek with payment equivalent to 56 hours per week, the new agreements after the crisis extended the workweek to 48 hours, meaning a wage reduction of close to 50 percent. In order to implement these new conditions, the SJOIIM negotiated with the firms to allow them to lay off workers and then rehire them under the new collective agreement (Muñoz Martínez, 2013). Though in a way this signified a loss for union activism in Matamoros, we can also interpret it as a form of resistance in the context of economic crisis; thanks to structured coherence and the strength of the union, firms could not lay off as many workers as they did in other maquiladora border cities. In Reynosa and Ciudad Juarez, for example, 24 and 26 percent of maquiladora jobs were lost, respectively, between 2007 and 2010. In contrast, Matamoros maquiladora jobs decreased by 19 percent during the same period (INEGI, 2010). The union also mitigated the effects of the crisis on workers by maintaining the fringe benefits in the collective agreement.

Thus spatial particularities of Matamoros, as part of the local structured coherence of global commodity chains in the auto sector, played an important role in the resolution of the mass strike of 2019. Most of the plants based in Matamoros form part of the thriving supply chain of the global automotive industry, and the firms ultimately granted concessions to workers on pay raises and the annual bonus because they already had prearranged supply contracts with global automakers. Work stoppages and relocation would be costly for global auto parts suppliers, thus they opted to stay put and settle with the union (Cruz Vargas, 2019). As expressed by Claudio X González, former president of the Mexican Business Council: "[l]osses are great because we're living in a world that is very integrated with supply chains that have to be very efficient and effective, and when you stop them, things foul up and costs rise" (Agren, 2019).

The SJOIIM's strategy of employing structured coherence as leverage also allowed it to appropriate social space. The union allocated money from union dues to build even entire working-class neighbourhoods, including schools and recreational spaces. These construction projects transformed space, enabling workers to give meaning to these spaces and use them in their own ways. Union investments in these projects also allowed the leadership to participate indirectly in planning workers' surroundings—a process often left to the market or the state in the (re)creation of structured coherence. While the union leadership controlled these decisions, its position in the organization still depended on membership support.

The union's position was one of logistical power (Webster et al., 2008). Global complex manufacturing processes rely on uninterrupted flows of production, particularly in more technologically complex sectors, and this reliance gives workers power to disrupt production in different assembly plants as a form of resistance to low wages, poor working conditions, and the 'race to the bottom' (Webster et al., 2008). The challenge for workers, however, is to ensure solidarity among several plants across different regions and countries to prevent the firm from targeting a single plant for closure. They must also strive to take "the matter out of the workplace and into the public domain where production is located" (Webster et al., 2008: 13). Strategies include community-union alliances that address the relationship between the current maquiladora development model and the limited political, social, and economic rights of

Mexico's vulnerable groups, expressed spatially through urban segregation and the implosion of public spaces.

4 Conclusion

The city is a key site for mobilization and resistance, where subordinated groups have the opportunity to shape everyday social, economic, legal, and political relations in a way that challenges spatial practices and representations of space imposed by neoliberal legality and criminal forms of urban governance. The three cases of social mobilization in Tamaulipas discussed here— the Critical Mass bike rides, the health-care workers' marches, and the maquiladora union strike—provide examples of how strategies of resistance in violent, unequal, and undemocratic contexts must maneuver the blurred boundaries between legality and illegality, comply with the public transcript, and use space as a political instrument to reappropriate the urban landscape.

The organizational flexibility behind the Critical Mass bike rides in Ciudad Victoria made it possible to navigate the ambiguities of the law to the cyclists' advantage; the movement used the individualized legal framework that established the right of freedom of movement to collectively and creatively reinvent the use of public space. Similarly, the health-care workers' movement employed the officially accepted language of individualized human rights to demand collective rights in the workplace and for the community. In doing so, the workers transformed abstract and universal individual rights into a basis for defending collective rights, which had been largely removed in the latest round of neoliberal legal reforms in the early 2010s. In the case of the Industrial Workers' Union, the union leadership's ongoing engagement with illegality from the 1950s to the 1980s and the workers' role legitimizing the state under the PRI strengthened the union and contributed to the success of the mass strike of 2019 in Matamoros. Legality and illegality, then, are not only instruments of domination; subordinated groups can also use them strategically in violent contexts for progressive ends. From this point of view, the law is not only the legal and institutional materialization of existing class relations; it also codifies the concessions subordinate classes procure from dominant forces (Poulantzas, 2014: 63, 81).

By engaging dominant social agents on their own terms—within the dominant legal orders and juridical institutional contexts—the three movements were able to mobilize the public transcript strategically to force state authorities to comply with their own rhetoric and rules. This strategic use of the law and its ambiguity is one way that movements can benefit from public transcripts. Similarly, all three movements showed deference and avoided openly confronting political and economic power in their bids to contest violence, economic exclusion and the implosion of public life. As Scott puts it, deference and conformity become strategies to ensure survival while "manipulating rituals of subordination" for collective advantage (1990: 33). At the same time, these movements imagined the workplace and the public space as inclusive and more democratic spaces of representation, inserting these meanings into the hidden transcript. These cases and their specificities remind us that struggles emerge locally through the experience of place (Bosco, 2012). Through this lens, social conflict acquires a spatial dimension and space becomes a site of political and social struggle (Butler, 2009: 322). The capitalist organization of space also produces its own contradictions, which is evident in the Industrial Workers' Union's strategic use of the local structured coherence that global production networks require. Global auto parts suppliers and automakers depended on the local particularities of Matamoros to guarantee continuity in the spatially fragmented process of production, and workers were able to use this dependency as leverage in the 2019 strike. The SJOIIM's involvement in constructing spaces in the city and the demands of the Critical Mass rides and the health-care workers' marches for safe and inclusive public spaces also called for a right to the city. According to Lefebvre (1996), the right to the city is not an individual right; it is, rather, a collective right to participate in decision-making on the creation, planning, and management of the urban landscape and to fully use and appropriate the spaces of the city. This is key in current processes of urbanization, particularly in cities with high levels of violence, as the effects of violence permeate the everyday experiences of city residents.

These three instances of everyday spatialized resistance commanded political attention and made it difficult for state authorities to dismiss their hidden political demands. The law in these cases constituted an instrument for spatialized resistance to the existing legal and spatial order. While these acts of resistance were not necessarily strategic moves to widely transform the economic and political structures of Mexican society, they show how everyday forms of resistance in urban contexts of violence and inequality, then, can be effective tools for avoiding repression while setting the ground for widespread collective political action and struggles for social inclusion against the neoliberal agenda. Most importantly, maquiladora and health care workers and the Critical Mass bike rides show how the desire for change might in fact re-shape and undermine the social structures that dominate peoples' lives.

CHAPTER 7

Conclusion: Geographies of State, Accumulation, and the Law

In March of 2017, my family and I heard more shootings than usual as well as helicopters flying over the capital city of Tamaulipas. We decided to wait in the living room for the gunfire to cease before we could leave the house to buy groceries. The reason for the shootings was the escape of 29 inmates from the state prison. Once the sound of gunfire stopped, we resumed our daily activities. Two months later, one of the fugitive inmates, a member of the criminal group Los Zetas, participated in the murder of Miriam Rodriguez Martinez, one of the leading activists for the families of the Disappeared in Tamaulipas. Rodriguez Martinez searched for her missing daughter after she was kidnapped in 2012. She found her daughter's remains in an unmarked grave and pressured state authorities to arrest those responsible for the murder, including one of the run-away inmates. The assassination of Rodriguez Martinez took place during Mother's Day in the municipality of San Fernando. This occurred after the right-center National Action Party (Partido Accion Nacional, or PAN) won the elections for governor in Tamaulipas, ending the state's more than 80-year domination by the Institutional Revolutionary Party (Partido Revolucionario Institucional, or PRI). During 2017, foreign direct investment in Tamaulipas reached one of its highest records in 19 years (Secretaria de Desarrollo Economico, 2019).

This personal experience illustrates how the normalization of violence in everyday life is connected to the reproduction of larger hierarchies of power and accumulation in Mexico. On the one hand, investment and partisan elections carry on as 'business as usual' without having to officially acknowledge the existing violence undertaken by state and non-state forces and its human cost. In this context, economic growth and changes in partisan politics did not guarantee a significant transformation towards a more peaceful and inclusive society. On the other hand, ordinary people have to deal with the reality of a *de facto* armed conflict while attempting to go on with their daily lives. In order to understand the connections between everyday practices of power in particular local contexts, the shifting relations of control and resistance, and larger political and economic structures of power and violence, the book argues that the *nexus of criminality, illegality and violence is a defining characteristic of neoliberal state formation in Mexico* after 2000.

The dismantling of existing mechanisms for managing capitalist contradictions and sustaining state power, namely the informal channels of compromise and negotiation with subordinate classes through the one-party rule, was
key to transforming Mexico's political economy in the 1980s and 1990s under
neoliberalism. The reconfiguration of state institutions no longer involved
consensus; instead, it employed punitive measures to enforce the implementation of the neoliberal agenda and weaken progressive resistance. At the center
of these punitive measures was the nexus between criminality, illegality and
violence. This nexus allowed for dispossession, in the form of forced displacement, extortion and private appropriation of public funds to take place in
Mexico after 2000 to assist accumulation as the previous 'rules' of the political
system were no longer in place. This facilitated dispossession due to the dismantling of local forms of (illegal) political negotiation and the rise of electoral competition among several political parties. While dispossession through
violence, criminality and illegality was underway, there was a parallel emphasis by state officials and proponents of neoliberalism on the rule of law to protect private property and contracts. This in turn redrew the boundaries between legality and illegality, which assisted in the veiling of the criminal and
violent origins of financial gain. Dispossession taking place in different parts of
the country illegally and violently became legal economic activity through its
integration to the global economy and the neoliberal version of the rule of law,
deeming dispossession legitimate behind the appearance of lawfulness.

The book unpacks the concepts of legality and illegality to understand the
underlying mechanisms that produce, perpetuate and spread violence in Mexico, yet many analyses of Mexico's contemporary violence take them for granted. I therefore problematize notions and practices related to legality and illegality, and I ask how and why the law reproduces exploitation and how subordinated
classes can employ it instead to resist and transform the state in a progressive
way (Chouinard, 1994: 415). I show how the constant reframing of the legal and
the illegal in the context of neoliberalism legitimizes state violence, reproduces
criminal forms of governance, promotes capital accumulation, and criminal-
izes dissent in Mexico at different political scales. Also lacking in the existing
literature on violence in Mexico is a geographical perspective that can eluci-
date the concrete and material practices that reproduce the coexistence of violence, neoliberalism, and state power locally, nationally, and globally. For that
reason, I ask how the politics of law and disorder are produced and reproduced in concrete spaces. Overall, the book employs a critical understanding
of the law and social space to address how the nexus of criminality, violence
and illegality became central to neoliberal state formation in Mexico after
2000, and focuses on the understudied northeastern region of Tamaulipas. This

case study sheds light on the interplay between criminality, violence and illegality prevailing in Mexico's neoliberal state as this region has been key to neoliberal economic development through export processing zones and oil and natural gas exploitation, the reproduction of the existing hierarchies of political power under the one-party rule of the PRI and during the rise of the right-center PAN in competitive elections after 2000. Also, this geographical region is the site where two powerful criminal organizations come from and where criminal innovation occurred in the 1990s, namely the creation of the enforcement arms with military training and counterinsurgency strategies by drug cartels.

In the preceding chapters, I illustrated the politics behind the framing of legality and illegality by addressing how rules and laws establish injunctions and prohibitions that create the framework for state and non-state violence according to the balance of forces prevailing in a particular historical and geographical context (Poulantzas, 2014: 65, 67). In Chapter 2, I examine the political and economic processes behind the connections between the state and the oil sector, the maquiladoras, and criminal activities in the case study of Tamaulipas. I show the transformation of legality and illegality prior and during the implementation of neoliberalism in the 1980s and 1990s through a local lens. Prior to the implementation and deepening of the neoliberal agenda, local leaders that were able to mobilize popular support constantly operated through the suspension of the law to reproduce the power of the PRI within the local and national state, particularly through votes and the control of dissent against the national agenda set by the PRI in exchange for concessions to subordinated classes. State institutions, facing difficulties managing the social pressures brought on by neoliberal restructuring during the 1980s and 1990s, shifted away from social compromise toward a more coercive form of neoliberalism. The imprisonment of local leaders in Tamaulipas as described in Chapter 2, who had previously been central to clientelistic arrangements, is a case in point. By the late 2000s, the coercive tendencies of the neoliberal agenda had become more obvious. Dominant groups in Mexico were no longer interested in appeasing resistance with social compromise; rather, they imposed neoliberal policies with legally created institutions and norms along with illegal forms of governance, sustained by a multiparty electoral system with limited democratic reach.

The latter occurred in two ways. On the one hand, the case of Tamaulipas depicts how the legal and the illegal became framed along neoliberal lines. For instance, the suspension of the law to transgress the law by companies and criminal groups became acceptable by state authorities in relation to labor, human and environmental rights and dispossession of land when investment by large companies was promoted, dissent was repressed and the power of the proponents of the neoliberal agenda was reproduced politically. This was illustrated in Chapter 2 with the increasing violation of environmental and labor rights in the Tamaulipas' northern border to favor maquiladoras and the energy sector, and the increasing role of criminal groups in forcing Tamaulipas residents to cast their vote for the PRI in local elections. Other examples are described in chapters 3 and 4, with dispossession resulting from forced displacement and extortion by criminal groups as well as disappearances of oil workers in the area. This allowed the exploitation of communal land for natural gas extraction and real estate development and discouraged opposition to neoliberal reforms in the energy sector and labor in the mid 2010s.

On the other hand, the increasing role of criminal groups in Mexico as governance mechanisms to repress dissent against neoliberalism and assist in the process of capital accumulation has been parallel to the rise of the neoliberal version of the rule of law—namely the selective use of the law to protect private property and enforce contracts. Neoliberal legality permitted the integration of the proceeds from criminal activities and the private appropriation of public funds into the formal national economy and global markets. This is illustrated in Chapter 3 in the role of contractual relations in the process of outsourcing and the legal transfer of title deeds in instances of dispossession. In both cases, the legal contractual and property transfer procedures assisted in the blurring of distinctions between illegal and legal economic activities carried out by private companies, state authorities and criminal groups. Chapter 4 shows how real estate development helped local capital and criminal groups to transform the criminal and illegal origins of their wealth into legal activities through contractual relations, particularly in the form of government debt and government contracts. Chapter 5 focuses on the ways in which criminal groups have participated in neoliberal state formation through their role in controlling migrant flows while benefiting economically from undocumented immigrants' illegal status. This problematization of law, disorder and corruption raises questions about who benefits from particular notions of legality and illegality, who can redraw these boundaries easily, and for what purpose do they do so. This in turn provides a more nuanced analysis which accounts for the historical transformation of the role of criminal groups in relation to the state, class power and capital accumulation in Mexico during the neoliberal era.

The book also emphasizes the links between (il)legality to social space with a particularly focus on uneven development and the politics behind geographical scales of accumulation and the law. In Mexico, processes of uneven development shaped the politics of law and lawlessness and vice versa. Chapter 2 describes how capitalist uneven development in Mexico between the 1950s and the 1980s, driven by import-substitution industrialization (ISI) and export-processing zones, shaped the selective institutional and juridical suspension of the law in Tamaulipas. Maquiladoras became zones of economic exception through tax exemptions codified into Mexican laws. In contrast, the ISI delineated zones where importing goods was prohibited. Transgressing these prohibitions to deliver contraband goods proved highly profitable and supported the development of one of Mexico's most powerful criminal groups. The ISI model also strengthened the oil sector, where the rising national oil union leadership operated in zones of exception in the form of illegal union practices. State authorities tolerated these transgressions as long as those involved continued to support the existing political configuration in Mexico, dominated by the PRI.

With the implementation of neoliberalism, the process of uneven development in Mexico became more connected to the global economy, further accentuating geographical differences and competition among localities both within and between countries. Chapter 3 and 4 show how processes of uneven development across borders were central to money laundering. That former Tamaulipas governors deposited laundered money in bank accounts in Texas and not in Mexico points to the role of uneven development across countries but also to intense competition among localities within the United States to attract financial resources, and this internal competition created legal frameworks for business that enabled money laundering. Competition among localities in Mexico to attract investment relied on infrastructural investment with local and national state funding in Tamaulipas. This provided the opportunity to local capitalists and criminal groups to participate in infrastructure construction to hide the illegal origin of their wealth. Chapter 5 shows how the neoliberal intensification of uneven development influenced the internalization of competition into everyday life in Mexico, shaping notions of the harmful and inferior Other. The latter manifested itself in discriminatory practices by ordinary citizens and state authorities against internal and Central American migrants. Indeed, migration helped to increase the labor reserve army that intensified competition, lowering costs for manufacturing industries and agricultural business in northeastern Mexico. At the same time, explanations that blamed the Other as the cause of unemployment and violence helped advocates of neoliberalism to divert away attention from the existing internal power structures within and outside the state that in fact perpetuate unequal and exclusionary relations.

The book also calls attention to the politics of geographical scales involved in the constitution of different legal systems operating in distinct jurisdictions.

The selection of a specific legal jurisdiction favors particular interests at the expense of others (Blomley, 1995: 46). I illustrate some of these dynamics in my discussions of stolen fuel exported into the U.S. economy and the money-laundering lawsuits against two former Tamaulipas governors in Texas. In the case of fuel theft, exporting and integrating the fuel into global commodity chains transformed the illegal into legal. The channeling of money into the international financial system either through money layering (see Chapter 3) or government debt with global banks involved in local construction projects (Chapter 4) as part of laundering activities show how the movement of money and capital across scales blurred the boundaries between legality and illegality.

Cities, too, are connected to larger political scales. Global economic dynamics and the national politics of violence have material effects, for example, on Ciudad Victoria, the capital city of Tamaulipas. As described in Chapter 4, urban spaces like Ciudad Victoria become the concrete physical manifestations of overlapping illegal and legal economies—all connected, in turn, to larger political scales of capital accumulation and neoliberal order. The chapter highlighted the role of criminal groups' extortion of small and medium business in opening spaces for large retail chains. The fear spread by the criminal groups as well as the connections of public officials to criminal activities set the conditions for the fragmentation of the city into poor and wealthy neighborhoods in the form of low-income housing and gated communities and the spatial isolation of material sites of local state decision-making from the rest of the population. The latter is illustrated through the design and construction of a new government building complex in the capital city of Tamaulipas. As such, the chapter shows that both local capital, informed by global standards of profitability and competition and operating between legality and illegality, can be key in urban decision-making and governance, sustaining neoliberal urban representations and material practices in the city.

The book also shows how these scalar politics are not isolated to one country, but rather permeates other countries, and their own processes of state-making. For that reason, the book acknowledges the connections of scalar politics and state-making occurring within Mexico with those of the United States. Chapter 2 shows how the politics of prohibition in the United States has not only strengthened criminal groups in Mexico but also state power in both the United States in Mexico. Prohibition then provides the basis for militarization in Mexico and punitive social policies in the United States. As depicted in Chapter 3, when the United States seized illegal funds, it directed them to U.S. law enforcement agencies and military aid for Mexico; that is, the illegal money then funded punitive legality in both the United States and Mexico. Chapter 5 shows how processes of uneven development and dispossession in Central America, Mexico and the United States force people to migrate without travel documents, and such migration provides cheap labor necessary to sustain accumulation in destination countries.

Law-making, illegality, criminality, violence and social space play key roles in processes of state formation. Legal and social interactions that constitute and shape the state also manifest in concrete, local ways in everyday life, which impact the rules of governing at larger scales and vice versa (Azuela and Meneses-Reyes, 2014; Chouinard, 1994: 432). Yet, these processes are shaped by relations of production, the social division of labor, and the history of political struggles (Poulantzas, 2014: 15). By understanding state power, law and space as processes resulting from class relations, the book uncovers how the local capitalist class, operating between legality and illegality, and the local scales of state power have become more important to the reproduction of accumulation and market discipline at larger political scales. The case study shows how the politics of fear supported by both criminal groups and local state authorities as well as the absorption of capital surpluses through money laundering in the form of real estate development and construction have become a central feature of Mexico's capitalism and neoliberal state formation. As Tina Hilgers and Laura Macdonald point out, "[w]ho engages in violence and gets away with it depends on subnational power structures and the connections among individuals with different types of resources" (2017, 4).

The spatial and legal dimensions of state power are not fixed but rely on everyday practices by different social actors, which are simultaneously shaped by the effects of state power (Radcliffe, 2001). This approach to everyday forms of state-making allows us to locate not only sites of state power in the quotidian but also sites of democratic and participatory transformation in everyday life. The law and its suspension can also provide a means for the democratic appropriation of social space (Chouinard, 1994: 430). This was illustrated in Chapter 5 with the mobilization of health workers, Critical Mass bike rides and the maquiladora strike of 2019 in Tamaulipas. The health workers' marches against precarious working conditions and the Critical Mass bike rides in Tamaulipas mobilized particular interpretations of the law. Whereas health workers employed official interpretations of human rights to defend their labor rights, the constitutional individual right to free movement in the country became the basis for the collective mobilization of bikers. In the case of the maquiladora strike, the local union's past illegal practices also strengthened its position and contributed to its success in making employers comply with the collective agreement during the 2019. The latter set an important precedent to further labor rights in Mexico.

These three movements in Tamaulipas used different representations of space in order to promote more participatory and inclusive public spaces and workplaces. The Critical Mass bike rides sought to appropriate public space at nighttime in the context of informal curfews, violence and militarization. Health care workers also employed public space to demand improvements in their labor conditions in order to also create more inclusive public health care facilities. The local maquiladora union leading the 2019 strike in the border city of Matamoros also extended their activities beyond the workplace to provide urban spaces to its members in a city landscape dominated by export processing plants. Still, the challenge for subordinated social forces is to expand these practices to larger scales while radically transforming the state in progressive ways to dismantle existing violent neoliberal institutional frameworks in Mexico.

These examples show how everyday processes of state formation and their intersection with the politics of (il)legality and space can therefore provide insights into forms of covert resistance in highly violent contexts. Such progressive social mobilizing in cities is central to contesting undemocratic forms of state intervention and exclusionary economic processes, as cities have become important sites of state legitimation and key to the social reproduction of capitalist social relations. My analysis of these movements also problematizes the reified concepts of legality, illegality, and corruption and raises questions regarding who benefits from transgressing the law, how social actors use the ambiguity of the law, and for what purpose. Subordinate actors employ the ambiguity of the law for survival purposes and to improve their living conditions in territories of fear and insecurity.

An analysis of the nexus of illegality, criminality and violence as a defining characteristic of neoliberal state formation in Mexico is central to understanding how the state becomes more coercive while sustaining limited forms of democracy. First, the actions of criminal groups justify punitive state interventions in social life in efforts to purportedly preserve national security and protect citizens. State authorities and large capital in Mexico also present this justification to criminalize dissent and the struggle for human rights in the country, while leaving party competition, elections, and political alternation intact. Second, and as the case study I have explored here shows, when state authorities and large capital tolerate the violence enacted by criminal groups, capital accumulation becomes more coercive and exploitative as well as more profitable. In fact, the governance that emanates from the violence of criminal groups in Mexico strengthens the state, as it distances state authorities from the politics of fear engendered by the criminal groups while facilitating social control and accumulation. And this intersection of different scales of accumulation with criminality and illegality is reproduced in everyday life.

The book opens two areas for further research on Mexico's violence. First, the study of everyday progressive resistance in the context of violence in different parts of the country can provide hints to the common forms of struggle that can be strategically linked to forge larger solidarity networks. Such networks could lead to a radical transformation outside and inside the state in order to turn Mexico's economics and politics into more inclusive and participatory processes. Second, the case study shows how the geographies of violence in Mexico are not uniform, but rather locally distinct according to the historically and socially specific articulation of the politics of (il)legality, processes of uneven development and the production of social space with the national state and the global economy. As such, the comparative study of these aspects of Mexico's political economy of violence at the local level in other parts of the country can offer insights into what kind of inclusive and democratic policy practices need to be elaborated according to a particular locality in order to deal with violence and its regional exclusionary effects in Mexico. This comparative study of processes of neoliberal state formation in Mexico through a local lens will also need to include the rural areas. Communities in these areas were first to experience the effects of neoliberalism and violence through the privatization of communal land, the withdrawal of state support for small agricultural producers and peasants, and the role of criminal groups as proxy governance mechanisms through forced displacement. Such analysis will also need to incorporate how quotidian practices of otherness imposed by state power enable residents to target gendered Others as part of the illegality, criminality and violence nexus in Mexico's neoliberal state formation.

While I hope this book makes a theoretical and empirical contribution to the study of politics of violence and illegality in Mexico's political economy, my initial drive to write this monograph was to understand the transformation of the place where I grew up. Through the approach presented in the book, I seek to understand why a city where my family, friends, neighbors and residents in general could walk freely at any time of the day became an urban landscape of fear and the site of disappearances, homicides, grenade explosions and car bombs within a few years. I hope that an approach to the concrete ways in which processes of domination and violence in everyday life relate to larger power structures, and the ways urban residents and workers resist militarization, violence and neoliberalism locally, can shed light on a different way of understanding violence in Mexico that leads to policies of economic and political inclusiveness from the local to the national level, particularly in relation to the democratic and participatory appropriation of public space and political institutions.

References

Abourahme, N. (2018) Of Monsters and Boomerangs: Colonial Returns in the Late Liberal City. *City* 22 (1):106–115.

Abrams, P. (2009) Notes on the Difficulty of Studying the State. In: Sharma A. and Gupta A. (eds) *The Anthropology of the State: A Reader.* New Jersey: John Wiley & Sons, 112–130.

Agamben, G. (1998) *Sovereign Power and Bare Life. Homo Sacer.* Stanford, California: Stanford University Press.

Agamben, G. (2005) *State of Exception* Chicago: University of Chicago Press.

Agencias (2018). Huyen médicos de Tamaulipas por inseguridad. *Zocalo*, 4 July. Available (consulted 8 August, 2018) at: http://www.zocalo.com.mx/new_site/articulo/huyen-medicos-de-tamaulipas-por-inseguridad.

Agren, D. (2019) We Won't Be Trampled On: Striking Mexican Workers Vow to Fight the Fight. *The Guardian*, 17 February. Available (consulted 20 February, 2019) at: https://www.theguardian.com/world/2019/feb/17/mexico-matamoros-strike-union-jobs.

Aguayo Quezada, S. (ed.). (2016) *En el desamparo. Los Zetas, el Estado, la Sociedad y las Víctimas de San Fernando, Tamaulipas y Allende, Coahuila.* Mexico City: COLMEX.

Aguilar Grimaldo, R. (2007) Por alta migración, gestionan oficina de migración en Reynosa. *El Universal*, 27 August. Available (consulted 15 August, 2015) at: http://archivo.eluniversal.com.mx/notas/622753.html.

Aguilera, R. and Castañeda, J. (2009) *El Narco: La Guerra Fallida.* Mexico City: Punto de Lectura.

Alanis Enciso, F. (2000) Las Autoridades Migratorias contra la Iglesia Católica. Un estudio de caso de los migrantes centroamericanos en la frontera nordeste de Mexico y Estados Unidos. *Revista del CELSA* 1:124–137.

Albo, G. (2005) Contesting the New Capitalism. In: Coates D. (ed.) *Varieties of Capitalism, Varieties of Approaches.* New York: Palgrave, 63–82.

Aldama, A.J. (2002) Borders, Violence and the Struggle for Chicana and Chicano Subjectivity. In: Aldama A.J. (ed.) *Violence and the Body: Race, Gender, and the State.* Bloomington, Indiana: Indiana University Press, 19–38.

Alejo Vazquez, D. (2018) Repensar la Pobreza y la Desigualdad en Mexico: El Espacio Urbano. *Nexos.* 10 August. Available (consulted 12 May, 2019) at: https://economia.nexos.com.mx/?p=1398.

Alfredo, C. (2014) Mexico Under Siege: Drugs Cartels or American Imperialism?, *Latin American Perspectives* 41 (2): 43–59

Alke, J. (2019) Authoritarian Neoliberal Rescaling in Latin America: Urban In/Security and Austerity in Oaxaca. *Globalizations* 16 (3): 304–319.

Alonso, A. (1994) The Politics of Space, Time and Substance: State formation, Nationalism and Ethnicity. *Annual Review of Anthropology* 23: 379–405.

Alonso, A. (2005) Sovereignty, the Spatial Politics of Security, and Gender: Looking North and South from the US–Mexico Border. In: Nustad K.G.and Krohn-Hansen C. (eds.) State Formation: Anthropological Perspectives. New York: Pluto Press, 27–52.

Alonso, A. and López, R. (1986) *El Sindicato de Trabajadores Petroleros y sus Relaciones con Pemex y el Estado 1970–1985*. Mexico City: El Colegio de Mexico.

Alonso Aranda, F. (2015) La historia de la política mexicana de drogas en el siglo XX. In: Labate B.C. and Rodrigues T. (eds.) *Drogas, Política y Sociedad en América Latina y el Caribe*. Mexico: CIDE, 53–73.

Alonso Pérez, P. (2014) Autoritarismos y Resistencia Social. Los Accidentados Cambios oliticos en la Historia Contemporánea de Tamaulipas (1947–1977). In: Hernandez Montemayor L., Certuche Llano M. and Anaya Merchant L. (eds.) *Lecturas Históricas de Tamaulipas. Política, Gobinero y Sociedad v. Ciudad Victoria*: UAT, 295–317.

Alsup, J. (2004) Protean Subjectivities: Qualitative Research and the Inclusion of the Personal. In Brown G. and Dobrin S.I. (eds.) *Ethnography Unbound. From Theory Shock to Critical Praxis*. Albany: SUNY Press, 219–240.

Althaus, D. (2018) Mexico's marines, sent to protect border city from cartel violence, now are implicated in disappearances. *Houston's Chronicle,* 29 September. Available (consulted 3 January 2019) at: https://www.houstonchronicle.com/news/article/Mexicos-marines-sent-to-protect-border-city-13268878.php.

Alvarez, L. (2017a) Tiene Victoria 6 colonias peligrosas. *En Linea Directa*. 1 November. Available (consulted 23 March, 2018) at: http://enlineadirecta.info/noticia.php?article=319159.

Alvarez, L. (2017b) Se burlo ETC de personal de Salud. *El Grafico*, 9 May. Available (consulted 17 August, 2017) at: https://elgraficotam.com.mx/2017/05/09/se-burlo-etc-de-personal-de-salud/ o.

Alvarez, R., Jr. (1995) The Mexico–US border: The Making of an Anthropology of Borderlands. *Annual Review of Anthropology* 24: 447– 470.

Alvarez, R.R. Jr. (2012) Reconceptualizing the Space of the US-Mexico Borderline. In: Wilson T.M. and Donnan H. (eds.) *A Companion to Border Studies*. John Wiley & Sons, Incorporated, 538–556.

Andrade Rubio, K.L. (2013) Identidad social negativa y exclusión social: Los jornaleros migratorios en Tamaulipas. *Revista de Ciencias Sociales* 19 (1): 81–91.

Andreas, P. (2009) *Border Games: Policing the U.S. -Mexico Divide*. Ithaca: Cornell University Press.

Andreas, P. and Wallman, J. (2009) Illicit Markets and Violence: What is the Relationship? *Crime, Law and Social Change* 52: 225–229.

Angel, A. (2019) Primer bimestre de 2019, el inicio de año más violento del que se tenga registro: 5,803 personas asesinadas. *Animal Politico*, 21 March. Available (consulted 30 March, 2019) at: https://www.animalpolitico.com/2019/03/homicidios-primer-bimestre-2019-violencia/.

Angles Hernández, M. (2017) La reforma en materia de hidrocarburos en Mexico como parte del proyecto neoliberal hegemonico violatorio de los derechos humanos. In: Angles Hernandez M., Rouox R. and Garcia Rivera E.A. (eds.) *Reforma en materia de hidrocarburos: Analisis juridicos, sociales y ambientales en prospectiva*. Mexico City: UNAM, UAT, 129–158.

Anguiano Tellez, M.E. (2005). Rumbo al norte: nuevos destinos de la emigración veracruzana. *Migraciones Internacionales* 3 (1): 82–110.

Anguiano Tellez, M.E. (1998) Migración a la frontera norte de México y su relación con el mercado de trabajo regional. *Papeles de Población* 4 (17): 63–79.

Aradau, C. (2007) Law Transformed: Guantanamo and the 'Other' Exception. *Third World Quarterly* 28 (3): 489–501.

Aretxaga, B. (2000) A Fictional Reality Paramilitary Death Squads and the Construction of State Terror in Spain. In: Sluka J.A. (ed.) *Death Squad: The Anthropology of State Terror*. Philadelphia: University of Pennsylvania Press, 46–69.

Arias, A. (2017) Realizaran Parada Civica en Matamoros por el Dia del Trabajo. *Hoy Tamaulipas*. April 20. Available (consulted 30 May, 2017) at: http://www.hoytamaulipas .net/.notas/291764/Realizaran-parada-civica-en-Matamoros-por-el-Dia-del-Traba jo.html.

Arias, E.D. (2017) *Criminal Enterprises and Governance in Latin America and the Caribbean*. New York: Cambridge University Press.

Arias, E.D., and Goldstein, D.M. (2010) Violent Pluralism: Understanding the New Democracies of Latin America. In: Arias E.D. and Goldstein D.M. (eds.) *Violent Democracies in Latin America*. Durham NC: Duke University Press, 1–34.

Arrona Palacios, A., Banda Cruz, D.A., Guevara López, C.A. and Villarreal Sotelo, K. (2011) El secuestro en Tamaulipas y sus repercusiones. *CienciaUAT*, 6 (2): 70–44.

Artículo 19 (2016) *Periodistas desaparecidos en México*. Mexico City: Artículo 19.

ASF (Auditoria Superior de la Federacion) (2010) *Recursos del Fondo de Aportaciones para el Fortalecimiento de las Entidades Federativas. Gobierno del Estado de Tamaulipas. Auditoría Financiera y de Cumplimiento: 10-A-28000-02-0285*. Mexico City.

Asmann, P. (2018) Mexico's Zetas: From Criminal Powerhouse to Fragmented Remnants. *Insight Crime*. 6 April. Available (consulted 29 October, 2018) at: https://www .insightcrime.org/news/analysis/mexico-zetas-criminal-powerhouse-fragmented-remnants/.

Astorga, L. (2003) *Drogas Sin Fronteras*. Mexico City: Grijalbo.

Astorga, L. (2005) *El Siglo de las Drogas*. Mexico City: Plaza y Janés.

Astorga, L. (2007) *El Poder y la Sombra: Seguridad, Traficantes y Militares*. Mexico City: Tusquets Editores.

Auchter, J. (2013) Border Monuments: Memory, Counter-memory, and (B)ordering Practices Along the U.S.-Mexico Border. *Review of International Studies* 39 (2): 291–311.

Azuela, A. (2009) Distancias y Disonancias del Ordenamiento Territorial en la Legisla-
cion Mexicana. In: Delgadillo J. (ed.) *Politica territorial en México. Hacia un modelo de
desarrollo basado en el territorio.* Mexico City: UNAM-SEDESOL, 467–492.

Azuela, A. and Meneses-Reyes, R. (2014) The Everyday Formation of the Urban Space.
Law and Poverty in Mexico City. In: Delaney D., Kedar A., Braverman I. and Blomley
N.K. (eds.) *The Expanding Spaces of Law: A Timely Legal Geography.* Stanford, Califor-
nia: Stanford Law Books, 167–189.

Bagley, W.D. (1994) The Limited Liability Company: A New Entity for the United States.
Commercial Law Bulletin 9 (22): 17.

Bailey, J. (2014) *The Politics of Crime in Mexico. Democratic Governance in a Security Trap.*
Boulder: FirstForum Press.

Bair, J., and Gereffi, G. (2002) NAFTA and the Apparel Commodity Chain: Corporate
Strategies, Interfirm Networks, and Industrial Upgrading. In: Bair J., and Gereffi G.
(eds.) *The North American Apparel Industry After NAFTA.* Pennsylvania: Temple University Press, 23–50.

Ballvé, T. (2012) Everyday State Formation: Territory, Decentralization, and the Narco
Landgrab in Colombia. *Environment and Planning D: Society and Space* 30 (4):
603–22.

Barkin, D. (1975) Mexico's Albatross: The United States Economy. *Latin American Perspectives* 2 (2): 64–80.

BBC (2015) Obama Pledges Mexico's Pena Nieto Drugs Support. *BBC News*, 6 January.
Available (consulted 13 August, 2017) at: https://www.bbc.com/news/world-us-
canada-30703229.

Beisner, N. (2009) *Gossip and the Everyday Production of Politics.* Honolulu: University of
Hawaii Press.

Beittel, J.S. (2011) Mexico's Drug Trafficking Organizations: Source and Scope of the
Rising Violence. *Congressional Research Service Report for Congress 7–5700,*
7 September.

Benjamin, W. (1986) *Reflections.* Trans. Edmund Jephcott. New York: Schocken Books.

Benson, E. (2015) Death and Twitter. *Texas Monthly*, February. Available (consulted 23
May, 2016) at: http://www.texasmonthly.com/the-culture/death-and-twitter/.

Bensusan, G. and Middlebrook, K. (2013). *Sindicatos y política en México: cambios, continuidades y contradicciones.* Mexico City: FLACSO, UAM, CLACSO.

Benton, L. (2010) *A Search for Sovereignty: Law and Geography in European Empires, 1400–
1900.* New York: Cambridge University Press.

Biebricher, T. (2018) The Rise of Juridical Neoliberalism. In: Golder B. and McLoughlin D.
(eds.) *The Politics of Legality in a Neoliberal Age.* New York: Routledge, 97–115.

Bieler, A. and Morton A.D. (2006) Globalization, the State and Class Struggle. A Critical
Economy engagement with Open Marxism. In: Morton A.D., Bieler A., Bonefeld W.
and Burham P. (eds.) *Global Restructuring, State, Capital and Labour.* New York: Palgrave, 155–175.

Bilak, A., Cardona-Fox, G., Ginnetti, J., Rushing, E.G., Scherer, I., Swain, M., Walicki, N. Yonetani, M. (2016.) *Global Report on Internal Displacement*. Geneva: Internal Displacement Monitoring Centre and Norwegian Refugee Council, May.

Birch, K. and Siemiatycki, M. (2015). Neoliberalism and the Geographies of Marketization: The Entangling of State and Markets. *Progress in Human Geography* 40 (2): 177–198.

Blomley, N.K. (1995) *Law, Space and the Geographies of Power*. New York: Guilford Press.

Boltvinik, J. and Hernández Laos, E. (1981) Origen de la Crisis Industrial, el Agotamiento del Modelo de Sustitución de Importaciones, un Análisis Preliminar. In Cordera R. (ed.) *Desarrollo y crisis de la Economía Mexicana*. Mexico City: FCE, 456–533.

Bonello, D. (2016) Criminal Groups Benefit from Mexico's Crackdown on Migrants. *Insight Crime*. Available (consulted 15 January, 2020) at: https://www.insightcrime.org/news/analysis/criminal-groups-and-corrupt-officials-beneficiaries-of-mexico-migrant-policy/.

Borger, J. (2018) Fleeing a hell the US helped create: why Central Americans journey north. *The Guardian*. 19 December, 2018. Available (consulted 19 January, 2020) at: https://www.theguardian.com/us-news/2018/dec/19/central-america-migrants-us-foreign-policy.

Bosco, F.J. (2012) Social Movements. Places, Spaces and Scales of Action. In: Jackiewicz E. and Bosco F.J. (eds.) *Placing Latin America*. London: Rowman and Littlefield, 129–173.

Bowden, C. (2010) *Murder City: Ciudad Juárez and the Global Economy's New Killing Fields*. New York: Nation Books.

Brabazon, H. (2017) Introduction. Understanding Neoliberal Legality. In: Brabazon H. (ed.) *Neoliberal Legality: Understanding the Role of Law in the Neoliberal Project*. New York: Routledge, 1–21.

Braticevic, S., Tommei C., Rascovan A. (eds.). 2017. *Bordes, límites, frentes e interfaces. Algunos aportes sobre la cuestión de las fronteras*. Tijuana: COLEF.

Braverman, I., Blomley, N.K., Delaney, D. and Kedar, A. (2014). "Introduction. Expanding Spaces of the Law." In: Braverman I., Blomley N.K., Delaney D. and Kedar A. (eds.) *The Expanding Spaces of Law: A Timely Legal Geography*. Stanford, California: Stanford Law Books, 1–29.

Brenner, N. (1997) Global, Fragmented, Hierarchical: Henri Lefebvre's Geographies of Globalization. *Public Culture* 10 (1): 135–167.

Brenner, N. (1998) Between Fixity and Motion: Accumulation, Territorial Organization and Historical Geography of Spatial Scales. *Environment and Planning D: Society and Space* 16 (4): 459–481.

Brenner, N. (1999) Globalisation as Reterritorialisation: The Re-scaling of Urban Governance in the European Union. *Urban Studies* 36 (3): 431–451.

Brenner, N. (2004) Urban governance and the production of new state spaces in western Europe, 1960–2000. *Review of International Political Economy* 11 (3): 447–488.

Brenner, N. and Elden, S. (2009) Henri Lefebvre on State, Space and Territory. *International Political Sociology* 3: 353–377.

Brenner, N., Peck, J. and Theodore, N. (2010) After Neoliberalization? *Globalizations* 7 (3): 327–45.

Brooks, D. (2018) Petroleras de EU quedan protegidas por el USMCA. *La Jornada*, 4 October. Available (consulted 4 November, 2018) at: https://www.jornada.com.mx/2018/10/04/economia/023n1eco.

Brown, S.G. and Dobrin, S. (2004) Introduction. New Writers of the Cultural Sage: From Postmodern Theory Shock to Critical Praxis. In: Brown S.G. Gilbert and Dobrin S.I (eds.) *Ethnography Unbound: From Theory Shock to Critical Praxis*. Albany: State University of New York Press, 1–12.

Bruff, I. (2014) The Rise of Authoritarian Neoliberalism. *Rethinking Marxism* 26 (1): 113–129.

Bruneau, T.C. (2011). Introduction. In: Bruneau T., Dammert L. and Skinner E. (eds.). *Maras: Gang Violence and Security in Central America*. Austin: University of Texas Press, 1–20.

Bruns, A. (2010) Two Realities in the Border Zone, Companies Look to Reconcile Risk and Rreward. *Site Selection Magazine,* July. Available (consulted 4 August, 2010) at: https://siteselection.com/issues/2010/jul/US-Mexico-Border.cfm.

Brussolo, R. (2017) Doctor Simi paga mejor a los médicos. *Expreso*, 21 March. Available (consulted 3 April, 2017) at: http://expreso.press/2017/03/21/doctor-simi-paga-mejor-los-medicos/.

Burawoy, M. (1983) Between the Labor Process and the State: The Changing Face of Factory Regimes Under Advanced Capitalism. *American Sociological Review* 48 (5): 587–605.

Burawoy, M. (2009) *The Extended Case Method: Four Countries, Four Decades, Four Great Transformations, and One Theoretical Tradition*. Berkeley: University of California Press.

Burnham, P. (1999). The Politics of Economic Management in the 1990s. *New Political Economy* 4 (1): 37–54.

Buscaglia, E. (2013) *Vacios de Poder en Mexico*. Mexico City: Debate.

Buscaglia, E. (2015) *Lavado de dinero y corrupción política*. Mexico City: Penguin Random House.

Butler, C. (2009) Critical Legal Studies and the Politics of Space. *Social and Legal Studies* 18 (3): 313–332.

Caldeira, T. (2000) *City of Walls: Crime, Segregation and Citizenship in Sao Paulo*. Berkeley: University of California Press.

Camp, R.A. (2013) *Politics in Mexico. Democratic Consolidation or Decline?* Oxford: Oxford University Press.

Canales Cerón, A.I. and Rojas Wiesner, M.L. (2018) *Panorama de la migración internacional en México y Centroamérica*. Santiago, Chile: CEPAL.

Cano, A. (1989) El caso 'La Quina' confirma la voluntad de Salinas para democratizar México. *El Pais*. 13 January. Available (consulted 3 June, 2015) at: https://elpais.com/diario/1989/01/13/internacional/600649213_850215.html.

Cantú Rivera, M.Á., Villarreal Sotelo, K. and Vargas Orozco, C.M. (2014) Violencia que sufre el migrante en su trayecto hacia la frontera de Reynosa, Tamaulipas. *Journal of Transborder Studies* 2 (2):1–15.

Cárdenas Gracia, J. (2016) *El modelo jurídico del neoliberalismo*. Mexico City: UNAM-Editorial Flores.

Carrillo, J. (1994) *Dos décadas de sindicalismo en la industria maquiladora de exportación*. Mexico City: Porrua.

Castañeda, J. (2001) La transición democrática en México. *El País*, 11 May. Available (consulted 12 August, 2013) at: http://elpais.com/diario/2001/05/11/internacional/989532015_850215.html.

Castillo, A. (2010) Expansión de 22 empresas generarán ocho mil empleos. *Hoy Tamaulipas*, 1 June. Available (consulted 30 January, 2013) at: https://www.hoytamaulipas.net/notas/520/Expansion-de-22-empresas-generaran-ocho-mil-empleos.html.

CCSPJ (2013) *Las 50 Ciudades Más Violentas del Mundo 2012*. Mexico City.

CCSPJ (2014) *Las 50 Ciudades Más Violentas del Mundo 2013*. Mexico City.

CCSPJ (2015) *Las 50 Ciudades Más Violentas del Mundo 2014*. Mexico City.

CCSPJ (2016) *Las 50 Ciudades Más Violentas del Mundo 2015*. Mexico City.

CCSPJ (2017) *Las 50 Ciudades Más Violentas del Mundo 2016*. Mexico City.

CCSPJP (Consejo Ciudadadano para la Seguridad Pública y Justicia Penal) (2012) *La violencia en los municipios de México 2012*. Mexico City.

Cedillo, J.A. (2014) En el noreste, en la mira transnacional, tierras abandonadas y secas. *Proceso*, 6 September. Available (consulted 4 September, 2016) at: https://www.proceso.com.mx/381477/en-el-noreste-en-la-mira-trasnacional-tierras-abandonadas-y-secas.

Cedillo, J.A. (2015) Secuestran a cirujano plástico en Nuevo Laredo. *Proceso*, 19 October, 2015. Available (consulted 21 December, 2015) at: https://www.proceso.com.mx/418536/secuestran-a-cirujano-plastico-en-nuevo-laredo.

Cedillo, J.A. (2017) Operador de Los Zetas era jefe de área en la Universidad Autónoma de Tamaulipas. *Revista Proceso*, 18 October. Available (consulted 5 May, 2018) at: https://www.proceso.com.mx/507941/operador-los-zetas-era-jefe-area-en-la-universidad-autonoma-tamaulipas.

Cedillo, J.A. (2019a) La abogada socialista que ampara a los obreros ante las armadoras en Matamoros. *Proceso*, 3 February, 2019. Available (consulted 20 February, 2019) at: https://www.proceso.com.mx/570307/la-abogada-socialista-que-ampara-a-los-obreros-ante-las-armadoras-en-matamoros.

Cedillo, J.A. (2019b) Avanzan acuerdos salariales para levantar huelga en Matamoros. *Proceso*, 28 January. Available (consulted 20 February, 2019) at: https://www.proceso.com.mx/569491/avanzan-acuerdos-salariales-para-levantar-huelga-en-matamoros.

Cervantes J. and Olmos, J.G. (2012) Caso Monex: Salen a la Luz mas Empresas Fachada. *Proceso*. 4 August. Available (consulted 13 December, 2014) at: https://www.proceso .com.mx/316068/316068-caso-monex-salen-a-la-luz-mas-empresas-fachada.

Chavez, L. (2008) *The Latino Threat: Constructing Immigrants, Citizens, and the Nation.* Stanford: Stanford University Press.

Chavez, L. (2009) Mexicans of Mass Destruction National Security and Mexican Immigration in a Pre and Post-9/11 World. In: Martinez S. (ed.) *International Migration and Human Rights*: The *Global Repercussions of U.S. Policy.* Berkeley: University of California Press, 82–97.

Chiodelli, F., Hall, T., Hudson, R. and Moroni, S. (2018) Grey Governance and the Development of Cities and Regions: The Variable Relationship Between (Il)legal and (Ill)licit. In: Chiodelli, F., Hall, T., Hudson, R. (eds.) *The Illicit and Illegal in Regional and Urban Governance and Development*, New York: Routledge. E-book collection.

Chouinard, V. (1994) Geography, Law and Legal Struggles: Which Ways Ahead. *Progress in Human Geography* 18 (4): 415–440.

CIDH (Comisión Interamericana de Derechos Humanos) (2013) *Derechos Humanos de los Migrantes y Otras Personas en el Contexto de la Movilidad Humana en México*, Washington: OEA, Doc 4813, OEA/Ser. L/V/II.

CNDH (Comisión Nacional de Derechos Humanos) (2009) *Informe especial sobre los casos de secuestro en contra de migrantes.* Mexico, June 15, 2009.

CNDH (2011) *Informe especial sobre secuestro de migrantes en México.* México, February 22, 2011.

CNDH (2016) *Informe especial sobre desplazamiento forzado interno en México.* Mexico City.

CNIME (Consejo Nacional de la Industria Maquiladora y Manufacturera de Exportación, A.C.) (2009) *Boletín de comunicación y difusión estadística entorno IMMEX*, 2 (2).

Comaroff, J.L. and Comaroff, J. (2006) Law and Disorder in the Postcolony: An Introduction. In: Comaroff J.L. and Comaroff J. (eds.) *Law and Disorder in the Postcolony.* Chicago: University of Chicago Press, 1–56.

Committee on Homeland Security (2011) *King McCaul Letter to Secretary Clinton on Mexican Drug Cartels.* 27 April. Available (consulted 20 April, 2013) at: http://homeland. house.gov/letter/mccaul-king-letter-secretary-clinton-mexican-drug-cartels.

Condon, B. (2016) Mexican Energy Reform and NAFTA Chapter 11. Article 20 and 21 of the Hydrocarbons Law and Access to Investment Arbitration. *The Journal of World Energy Law and Business* 9 (3): 203–219.

CONEVAL (Consejo Nacional de Evaluación de las Politicas Sociales) (2015a). *Evolución de las dimensiones de la pobreza 1990–2014.* CONEVAL: Mexico City. Available (consulted 4 October, 2017) at: https://www.coneval.org.mx/Medicion/EDP/Paginas/ Evolucion-de-las-dimensiones-de-la-pobreza-1990-2014-.aspx.

CONEVAL (2015b) *Anexo estadistico de la pobreza por ingreso*. CONEVAL: Mexico City. Available (consulted 4 October, 2017) at: https://www.coneval.org.mx/Medicion/ EDP/Documents/pobreza_evolucion_ingresos_1992_2014.zip.

CONEVAL (2016a) *Evolución de la Población en Pobreza y en Materia de Ingresos 1992– 2016*. CONEVAL: Mexico City. Available (consulted 3 January, 2017) at: https://www .coneval.org.mx/Medicion/Paginas/Evolucion-de-las-dimensiones-de-pobreza .aspx.

CONEVAL (2016b) *Evolución de la Pobreza por Ingresos Estatal y Muncipal 1990–2010*. CONEVAL: Mexico City. Available (consulted 3 January, 2017) at: https://www.coneval .org.mx/Medicion/Paginas/Evolucion-de-las-dimensiones-de-pobreza.aspx.

Congressional Research Services (2019) *Mexico: Background and U.S. Relations. CSR Report prepared for Members and Committees of Congress R42917*. Washington, May 2019.

Correa, E. (2006) Changing constraints on monetary policy. In: Randall, L. (ed.) *Changing Structure of Mexico: Political, Social and Economic Prospects*. New York: ME Sharpe, 159–175.

Correa-Cabrera, G. (2014) Violence on the 'Forgotten Border: Mexico's Drug War, the State, and the Paramilitarization of Organized Crime in Tamaulipas in a New Democratic Era? *Journal of Borderlands Studies* 29 (4): 419–433.

Correa-Cabrera, G. (2017) *Los Zetas Inc Criminal Corporations, Energy and Civil War in Mexico*. Austin: University of Texas Press.

Corrigan, P. (1994) State Formation. In: Joseph, M. and Nugent D. (eds.) *Everyday Forms of State Formation: Revolution and the Negotiation of Rule in Modern Mexico*. Durham: Duke University Press, xvii–xxi.

Corrigan, P. and Sayer, D. (1985) *The Great Arch: English State Formation as a Cultural Revolution*. Oxford: Basil Blackwell.

Cowie, J.R. (1999) *Capital Moves: RCA's 70-Year Quest for Cheap Labor*. Ithaca: Cornell University Press.

Coyle, P. (2001) *Nayari History, Politics and Violence: From Flowers to Ash*. Tucson: The University of Arizona Press.

Cruz, J.M. (2016) State and Criminal Violence in Latin America. *Crime, Law and Social Change* 66: 375–396.

Cruz, V. (2009) Nueva Asociación de Veracruzanos en Reynosa. *Hora Cero*, 2 January. Available (consulted 11 August, 2015) at: http://www.horacero.com.mx/reynosa/ nueva-asociacion-deveracruzanos-en-reynosa/.

Cruz Vargas, J.C. (2012) Cierran 169 mil empresas por narcoviolencia en 2011: Coparmex. *Proceso*, 3 April. Available (consulted 4 May, 2012) at: https://www.proceso.com .mx/303240/cierran-169-mil-empresas-por-narcoviolencia-en-2011-coparmex.

Cruz Vargas, J.C. (2019) Por huelga en maquiladoras peligran 40 mil empleos y se pierden 50 mmd diarios: Index. *Proceso*, 29 January. Available (consulted 20 February, 2019) at: https://www.proceso.com.mx/569658/por-huelga-en-maquiladoras-peligran-40- mil-empleos-y-se-pierden-50-mdd-diarios-index.

Das, V. and Poole, D. (2004) State and its Margins: Comparative Ethnographies. In: Das V. and Poole D. (eds.) *Anthropology in the Margins of the State*. Santa Fe: School of American Research Press, 3–34.

Davis, D. (2012) Policing and Regime Transition. From Postauthoritarianism to Populism to Neoliberalism. In: Pansters W.G. *Violence, Coercion, and State-making in Twentieth-century Mexico: The Other Half of the Centaur*. Stanford: Stanford University Press, 68–90.

DeChaine, R. (2012) For Rhetorical Border Studies. In DeChaine, R. (ed.) *Border Rhetorics: Citizenship and Identity on the US-Mexico Frontier*. Tuscaloosa: University of Alabama Press, 1–18.

De la Cruz, A. (2015) Obras hacen de colonias sectores 'VIP'. *Expreso*. 24 March. Available (consulted 4 March, 2017) at: http://expreso.press/2015/03/24/obras-hacen-de-colonias-sectores-vip/.

De la O, M.E. (2006) Geografía del trabajo femenino en las maquiladoras de México. *Papeles de Población* 12 (49): 91–126.

De la O, M.E. and Quintero Ramírez, C. (eds.) (2002) *Globalización, trabajo y maquilas*. Mexico City: Plaza y Valdes.

De la O, M.E. and Flores Ávila A.L. (2012) Violencia, Jóvenes y Vulnerabilidad en la Frontera Noreste de México. *Desacatos* 38: 11–28.

De Llano, P. (2013) El Poder del Crimen Anula a la Sociedad Civil en Tamaulipas. *El País*, 11 April. Available (consulted 20 May, 2013) at: http://internacional.elpais.com/internacional/2013/04/11/actualidad/1365703414_481661.html.

Delaney, D. (2010) *The Spatial, the Legal and the Pragmatics of World-Making: Nomospheric Investigations*. New York: Routledge.

Delgado Wise, R. (2013) The migration and labor question today: Imperialism, unequal development, and forced migration. *Monthly Review* 64 (9). Available (consulted 15 January, 2020) at: https://monthlyreview.org/2013/02/01/the-migration-and-labor-question-today-imperialism-unequal-development-and-forced-migration/.

Delgado Wise, R. (2014) A Critical Overview of Migration and Development: The Latin American Challenge. *Annual Review of Sociology* 40, 643–663.

Delgado Wise, R., Márquez Covarrubias, H. and Puentes, R. (2013) Reframing the Debate on Migration, Development and Human Rights. *Population, Space and Place* 19: 430–443.

Delgado Wise, R. and Márquez Covarrubias, H. (2013) In: Petras, J.F. and Veltmeyer H. (eds) *Imperialism and Capitalism in the Twenty-First Century: A System in Crisis. Globalization, Crises, and Change*. Farnham: Routledge.

Desmond Arias, E. and Goldstein, D.M. (2010) Violent Pluralism: Understanding the New Democracies of Latin America. In: Desmond Arias, E. and Goldstein, D.M. (eds.) *Violent Democracies in Latin America*. Durham and London: Duke University Press, 1–34.

Diamond, L. (2002) Elections Without Democracy: Thinking About Hybrid Regimes. *Journal of Democracy* 13 (2): 21–35.

Diaz, G.L. (2019) La CNDH condena que se ignoraran sus recomendaciones por se-cuestro de migrantes. *Proceso*. 18 March. Available (consulted 17 January, 2020) at: https://www.proceso.com.mx/575773/la-cndh-condena-que-se-ignoraran-sus-recomendaciones-por-secuestro-de-migrantes.

Díaz González, E. and Mendoza Sánchez, M.A. (2012) Crisis y recuperación económica en los estados de la frontera norte: Un análisis de los ciclos económicos. *Estudios fronter-izos* 13 (25): 89–130.

Dominguez Ruvalcaba, H. (2015) *Nación Criminal: Narrativas del Crimen Organizado y el Estado Mexicano*. Mexico: Ariel.

Duncan, G. (2013) Drug Trafficking and Political Power: Oligopolies of Coercion in Co-lombia and Mexico. *Latin American Perspectives* 41 (2): 18–42.

Durán Martínez, A. (2018) *The Politics of Drug Violence: Criminals, Cops and Politicians in Colombia and Mexico*. Oxford: Oxford University Press.

Düzenli, F.E. (2011) Introduction: Value, Commodity Fetishism, and Capital's Critique. *Rethinking Marxism* 23 (2): 172–79.

El Mañana Staff (2016) Arrastra Tamaulipas millonaria deuda pública: 13,691 mdp. *El Ma-ñana*. 8 May. Available (consulted 5 February, 2017) at: https://www.elmanana.com/arrastra-tamaulipas-millonaria-deuda-publica-13691-mdp/3282490.

El Mañana Staff (2019) Otorgan incremento salarial a trabajadores eventuales de Salud en Tamaulipas. *El Mañana*, 13 March. Available (consulted 14 March, 2019) at: https://www.elmanana.com/otorgan-incremento-salarial-a-trabajadores-eventuales-de-salud-en-tamaulipas-francisco-javier-garcia-cabeza-de-vaca-incremento-salarial-ceremonia-secretaria-de-salud/4775867.

El Pais (2013) Una reforma Crucial. *El Pais*, 15 August. Available (consulted 6 October, 2014) at: https://elpais.com/elpais/2013/08/15/opinion/1376594283_317522.html.

Erdi Lelandais, G. (2014) Lefbvre's Legacy: Understanding the City in the Globalisation Process. In: Erdi Lelandais, G. (ed.) *Understanding the City: Henri Lefebvre and Urban Studies*. Newcastle upon Tyne: Cambridge Scholars Publishing, 1–16.

Fabre, G. (2003) *Criminal Prosperity: Drug Trafficking, Money Laundering and Financial Crises After the Cold War*. London: Routledge.

Feldman, A. (1996). Ethnographic States of Emergency. In Nordstrom C. and Robben A CGM (eds.) *Fieldwork under Fire Contemporary Studies of Violence and Survival*. Berkeley and Los Angeles: University of California Press, 224–253.

Figueroa, O. (2018) Se van médicos de Tamaulipas por inseguridad. *Expreso*, 17 June. Available (consulted 20 July, 2018) at: https://expreso.press/2018/06/17/se-van-medicos-de-tamaulipas-por-inseguridad/.

Flores, L. (2018) Crimen organizado amenaza a notarios, alertan. *El Universal*. 26 January. Available (consulted 2 February, 2018) at: http://www.eluniversal.com.mx/cartera/economia/crimen-organizado-amenaza-notarios-alertan.

Flores Pérez, C. (2014a) Political Protection and the Origins of the Gulf Cartel. *Crime, Law and Social Change* 61 (5): 517–539.

Flores Pérez, C. (2014b) *Historias de polvo y sangre. Génesis y evolución del tráfico de drogas en el Estado de Tamaulipas, 1947–1987*. Mexico City: CIESAS.

Foster, J. (1990) Class. In: Eatwell J., Milgrate M, and Newman, P (eds.). *Marxian Economics*. New York: WW Norton, 79–84.

Franzblau, J. (2015) Why Is the US Still Spending Billions to Fund Mexico's Corrupt Drug War? *The Nation*, 27 February. Available (consulted 12 August, 2016) at: https://www.thenation.com/article/us-connection-mexicos-drug-war-corruption/.

Freedom House (2015) *Freedom on the Net. Mexico*. Washington D.C.: Freedom House.

Friedman, G. (2008) Mexico: On the Road to a Failed State? *Stratfor Geopolitical Weekly*, 13 May. Available (consulted 12 September, 2013) at: http://www.Stratfor.com/weekly/mexico_road_failed_state.

Galindo, M. (2005) El Capitalismo Criminal, Fase Superior del Imperialismo. *Mundo Siglo XXI* 2: 45–49.

Gallagher, C. (2016) Mexico, the Failed State Debate and the Merida Fix. *The Geographical Journal* 182 (4): 331–341.

Gallardo Cabiedes, E. (2015) En el Tamaulipas hundido en la guerra sin cuartel, médicos y enfermeras hacen de héroes. *SinEmbargo*, 3 February. Available (consulted 4 March, 2015) at: http://www.sinembargo.mx/03-02-2015/1237387.

Galvan, M. (2019) En el arranque de 2019, la violencia se recrudece en Tamaulipas. *ADN Politico*. 15 March. Available (consulted 28 March, 2019) at: https://adnpolitico.com/mexico/2019/01/15/en-el-arranque-de-2019-la-violencia-se-recrudece-en-tamaulipas.

GAO (Government Accountability Office) (1998) *Raul Salinas, Citibank, and Alleged Money Laundering*. Washington D.C., December 4.

García, A. (2015) Las colonias más peligrosas en Victoria. *Expreso*. 10 August. Available (consulted 23 March, 2018) at: http://expreso.press/2015/08/10/las-colonias-mas-peligrosas-en-victoria/.

García, A. (2016a) Hace negociazo con tierra ejidal. *Expreso*, 3 October. Available (consulted 5 February, 2017) at: http://expreso.press/2016/10/03/hace-negociazo-con-tierra-ejidal/.

García, A. (2016b) Paga gobierno 43 veces más que Pedro Luis. *Expreso*, 6 October. Available (consulted 5 February, 2017) at: http://expreso.press/2016/10/06/paga-gobierno-43-veces-mas-que-pedro-luis/.

García, A. (2016) Protestan enfermeras de Ciudad Victoria en demanda de bases. *La Silla Rota*, 16 March. Available (consulted 20 April, 2016) at: https://lasillarota.com/estados/protestan-enfermeras-de-ciudad-victoria-en-demanda-de-bases/107168.

García Fernández, F., Vaquera Salazar, R.A., and Serna Hinojosa, J.A. (2017) Tamaulipas: endeudamiento y gasto público (2003–2013). *Economia Informa* 403: 70–90.

Garduno, R. and Becerril, A. (2006) Gestionaron Gordillo y Cerisola apoyo a Calderón. *La Jornada*. 7 September. Available (consulted 4 November, 2008) at: http://www.jornada.unam.mx/2006/07/09/index.php?section=politica&article=004n1pol.

Gil Méndez, J. (2015) Neoliberalismo, Políticas Agrarias y Migración. Consecuencias de un Modelo Contra Los Productores. *Ra Ximhai*, 11 (2): 145–162.

Glendhill, J. (2013) Indigenous Autonomy, Delinquent States and the Limits of Resistance. *History and Anthropology* 25 (4): 507–529.

Glick-Schiller, N. (2010) A Global Perspective on Migration and Development. In: Glick-Schiller N. and Faist T. (eds.) *Migration, Development and Transnationalism: A Critical Stance*. New York, NY: Berghahn Books, 24–52.

Glick-Schiller, N. (2015). Explanatory Frameworks in Transnational Migration Studies: The Missing Multi-Scalar Global Perspective. *Ethnic and Racial Studies* 38 (13), 2275–2282.

Gobierno del Estado de Tamaulipas (2004) *Primer Informe de Gobierno*. Ciudad Victoria.

Gobierno del Estado de Tamaulipas (2009) *Quinto Informe de Gobierno*. Ciudad Victoria.

Gobierno del Estado de Tamaulipas (2010a) *Sexto informe de gobierno*. Ciudad Victoria. http://transparencia.tamaulipas.gob.mx/wp-content/uploads/2012/03/IV-6In forme2010.pdf.

Gobierno del Estado de Tamaulipas (2010b) *Plan estatal de desarrollo*. Ciudad Victoria, Tamaulipas.

Gobierno del Estado de Tamaulipas (2011) *Informes de Deuda Publica*. Ciudad Victoria, Tamaulipas. Available (consulted May 3, 2018) at: http://transparencia.tamau lipas.gob.mx/informacion-publica/por-fraccion/informacion-financiera/ deudapublica/.

Gobierno del Estado de Tamaulipas (2012) Programa municipal de ordenamiento territorial y desarrollo urbano de Ciudad Victoria. *Periodico Oficial*. 14 March. Available (consulted 3 March, 2017).

Gobierno del Estado de Tamaulipas (2014) *Informes de deuda pública*. Ciudad Victoria, Tamaulipas. Available (consulted 3 May, 2018) at: http://transparencia.tamau lipas.gob.mx/informacion-publica/por-fraccion/informacion-financiera/deuda publica/.

Gobierno del Estado de Tamaulipas (2015) *Quinto Informe de Gobierno*. Ciudad Victoria.

Gobierno del Estado de Tamaulipas (2016) Decreto 63–26 mediante el cual se aprueban los valores unitarios de suelo y construcciones, y coeficientes de incremento y de demérito, que servirán de base para la determinación del valor catastral de predios urbanos, suburbanos, centros de población de origen ejidal, congregaciones y demás localidades, así como de los predios rústicos del Municipio de Victoria, Tamaulipas, para el ejercicio fiscal del año 2017. *Periodico Oficial*. 10 November, 2016. Available (consulted 4 May, 2017) at: https://www.congresotamaulipas.gob.mx/Legislacio nEstatal/DisposicionesFiscales/TABLAS%20VALORES%20CATASTRALES%20 2017.pdf.

Gobierno del Estado de Tamaulipas (2018) Da Inicio Campaña de Seguridad y Prosperidad en el Area de los 2 Laredos. *Comunicado Gobierno del Estado de Tamaulipas*, 10 September. Available (consulted 29 October, 2018) at: https://www.tamaulipas.gob

.mx/2018/09/da-inicio-campana-de-seguridad-y-prosperidad-en-el-area-de-los-2-laredos.

Goldstein, D.M. (2014) Whose Vernacular? Translating Human Rights in Local Contexts. In: Goodale, M. (ed). *Human Rights at the Crossroads*. New York: Oxford University Press 111–121.

Gómez, C. (2017) Una decada sin medicinas. *Periodico Milenio*, 17 July: 10–11.

González, V. (2016) Médicos se unen en protesta por bases laborales en Victoria, *Milenio*, 28 March. Available (consulted 30 May, 2016) at: http://www.milenio.com/region/Hospital_Civil_Victoria_protesta_0_709129298.html.

González Antonio, H. (2012) Médicos en Tamaulipas cambian horario por violencia. *Excelsior*, 14 February. Available (consulted 20 March, 2012) at: http://www.excelsior.com.mx/2012/02/14/nacional/810279.

González Antonio, H. (2017) Por estafadores, dos Notarios de Tamaulipas van a Prision. *Excelsior*, 28 February. Available (consulted 7 October, 2017) at: https://www.excelsior.com.mx/nacional/2017/02/28/1149207.

González Arévalo, A.L. (2015) La contaminación de la Cuenca de Burgos en México ocasionada por la extracción de gas. *Revista Internacional de Ciencias Sociales Interdisciplinares* 4 (1): 105–115.

González Rodarte, J. (2002) Crisis y Reajuste Del Control Corporativo en el Sindicalismo Petrolero Mexicano, 1989–2000. *PhD Thesis, History*. Mexico: UAM-Iztapalapa.

Gradin, G. (2006) *Empire's Workshop: Latin America, the United States, and the Rise of the New Imperialism*. New York: Metropolitan Books.

Grandoni, D. (2018) Big Oil and Gas Companies are Winners in Trump's New Trade Deal. *Los Angeles Times, 3* October. Available (consulted 4 November, 2018) at: http://www.latimes.com/business/la-fi-oil-gas-nafta-usmca-20181003-story.html.

Grayson, G.W. (2010) *Mexico: Narco-Violence and a Failed State?* New Brunswick, NJ: Transaction Publishers.

Grayson, G.W. (2014) *The evolution of Los Zetas in Mexico and Central America: Sadism as an Instrument of Cartel Warfare*. Carlisle Barracks, PA: Strategic Studies Institute and U.S. Army War College Press.

Green, L. (1996) Living in a State of Fear. In: Nordstrom C. and Robben A. (eds.) *Fieldwork under Fire. Contemporary Studies of Violence and Survival*. Berkeley and Los Angeles: University of California Press, 105–128.

Guillén Romo, H. (2013) México: de la sustitución de importaciones al nuevo modelo-económico. *Revista de Comercio Exterior* 63 (4): 34–60.

Hanson, S. (2004) Critical Auto/Ethnography: A Constructive Approach to Research in the Composition Classroom. In: Brown S.G. and Dobrin S.I. (eds.) *Ethnography Unbound: From Theory Shock to Critical Praxis*. Albany: State University of New York Press, 183–200.

Harris, O. (1996) Introduction. Inside and Outside the Law. In: Harris O. and European Association of Social Anthropologists (eds.) *Inside and Outside the Law: Anthropological Studies of Authority and Ambiguity*. London: Routledge, 1–18.

Harvey, D. (1989) *The Urban Experience*. Baltimore: John Hopkins University Press.

Harvey, D. (1999) *The Limits to Capital* London: Verso.

Harvey, D. (2001) *Spaces of Capital: Towards a Critical Geography*. New York: Routledge.

Harvey, D. (2005) *The New Imperialism*. Oxford: Oxford University Press.

Harvey, D. (2006) *Spaces of Global Capitalism: A Theory of Uneven Geographical Development*. New York: Verso.

Harvey, D. (2007) *A Brief History of Neoliberalism*. Oxford: Oxford University Press.

Harvey, D. (2010) *A Companion to Marx's Capital*. London: Verso.

Harvey, D. (2012) *Rebel Cities*. New York: Verso.

Harvey, D. (2014) *Seventeen Contradictions and the End of Capitalism*. Oxford: Oxford University Press.

Hellman, J. (1994) Mexican Popular Movements, Clientelism and the Process of Democratization. *Latin American Perspectives* 81 (21): 124–142.

Hernández, O.M. (2017) Dangerous Ethnography: Unraveling the Smuggling of Migrants in the Border. *Practicing Anthropology* 39 (4): 35–38.

Herrera Ledesma, P.A., Sanchez Limon, M. and Sanchez Rocha, V.M. (2016) Racismo entre Mexicanos y Lucha entre Imaginarios. Consecuencias del Mercado Laboral Oligopsónico en las Maquilas. *Aldea Mundo* 21(41).

Herrigel, G. (2004) Emerging Strategies and Forms of Governance in High-Wage Component Manufacturing Regions. *Industry and Innovation* 11 (1/2): 45–79.

Hiernaux, D. (1991) En la Búsqueda de un Nuevo Paradigma Regional. In: Ramírez B. (ed.) *Nuevas Tendencias en el Análisis Regional*. Mexico: UAM, 33–48.

Hilgers, T. and Macdonald, L. (2017) How Violence Varies: Subnational Place, Identity and Embeddedness. In: Hilgers T. and Macdonald L. *Violence in Latin America and the Caribbean: Subnational Structures, Institutions and Clientelistic Networks*. New York: Cambridge University Press, 1–35.

Homedes, N. and Ugalde, A. (2011) Descentralización de los servicios de salud: Estudios de caso en seis estados mexicanos. *Salud Pública de México*, 53 (6): 493–503.

HT Agencia (2017) Exigen basificación y mejores salarios enfermeras de Tamaulipas. *Hoy Tamaulipas*, 30 November. Available (consulted 4 December, 2017) at: http://www.hoytamaulipas.net/notas/321597/Exigen-basificacion-y-mejores-salarios-enfermeras-de-Tamaulipas .html.

Human Rights Watch (2013) *Mexico's Disappeared. The Enduring Cost of a Crisis Ignored*. Washington D.C.

IACHR (2018) *Internal displacement in the Northern Triangle of Central America*. Washington: OAS, 27 July.

ICHR (Inter-American Commission of Human Rights) (2017). *Situation of Human Rights in Mexico*. Washington D.C.: OAS.

IMSS (Instituto Mexicano del Seguro Social) (2014) *Base de datos con información estadística mensual de asegurados registrados en el IMSS, patrones y salario asociado 2014*. October 31, 2014. Mexico City. Accessed September 5, 2018. https://datos.gob.mx/busca/dataset/informacion-estadistica-mensual-de-asegurados-registrados-en-el-imss-de-imss/resource/f28oc35b-cdee-4bff-b2be-6bf0d21c71a9.

IMF (International Monetary Fund) (2018) *IMF and Good Governance*. Accessed September 5, 2018. https://www.imf.org/en/About/Factsheets/The-IMF-and-Good-Governance.

INEGI (Instituto Nacional the Geografia y Estadistica) (1990) *XI Censo General de Poblacion y Vivienda*. Aguascalientes: INEGI.

INEGI (2000) *XII Censo General de Poblacion y Vivienda*. Aguascalientes: INEGI.

INEGI (2001) *Sistema de Cuentas Nacionales de México. La Producción, Salarios, Empleo y Productividad de la Industria Maquiladora de Exportación. 1990–2000. Por Región Geográfica y Entidad Federativa*. Aguascalientes: INEGI.

INEGI (2007) *Estadísticas Económicas. Industria Maquiladora de Exportación*, Aguascalientes: INEGI.

INEGI (2010) *Estadística mensual del programa de la industria manufacturera, maquiladora y de servicios de exportación*. Aguascalientes.

INEGI (2013) *Encuesta Nacional de Victimización y Percepción sobre Seguridad Pública, Resultados Tamaulipas*. Aguascalientes.

INEGI (2014) *Encuesta Nacional de la Dinámica Demográfica 2014*. Aguascalientes.

INEGI (2018a) PIB por entidad federativa. Base 2013. *Sistemas de cuentas nacionales*. Aguascalientes.

INEGI (2018b) *Censos economicos. Sistema automatizado de informacion censal*. Aguascalientes.

INEGI (2018c) *Total de Viviendas e Inversion en Vivendas*. Aguascalientes.

Izcara Palacios, S.P. (2012a) Violencia contra inmigrantes en Tamaulipas. *European Review of Latin American and Caribbean Studies* 93: 3–24.

Izcara Palacios, S.P. (2012b) Coyotaje y Grupos Delictivos en Tamaulipas. *Latin American Research Review* 47 (3): 41–61.

Izcara Palacios, S.P. (2014) Exclusion Social y Aislamiento Social. Los Migrantes Asentados en la Comarca Citricola de Tamaulipas. In: Villarreal Sotelo K. and Alvarado Vazquez R.I. (eds.) *La discriminación y exclusión de los jóvenes en América Latina*. Cualiacan: Universidad Autonoma de Sinaloa, 109–121.

Izcara Palacios, S.P. (2015) Los Transmigrantes Centroamericanos en Mexico. *Latin American Research Review*. 50 (4): 49–68.

Izcara Palacios, S.P. (2019) Corruption at the Border: Intersections between US Labour Demands, Border Control, and Human Smuggling Economies. *Antipode* 51 (4): 1210–1230.

Izcara Palacios, S.P. and Andrade Rubio, K.L. (2012) Capital Social vs. Aislamiento Social. Los Jornaleros Migratorios de Tamaulipas. *Revista de Geografía Norte* 52: 109–125.

Izcara Palacios, S.P. and Andrade Rubio, K.L. (2019) Violencia y Migracion en Tamaulipas. *Coloquio Politicas Sociales Sectoriales, Universidad Autonoma de Nuevo Leon* 6 (6): 260–275.

Jessop, B. (2016) *The State. Past, Present and Future.* Cambridge: Polity.

Jones, N.P. (2016) *Mexico's Illicit Drug Networks and the State Reaction.* Washington D.C.: Georgetown University Press.

Joseph, G.M. and Nugent, D. (1994) Popular culture and State formation in Revolutionary Mexico. In: Joseph, G.M. and Nugent, D. (eds.) *Everyday Forms of State Formation. Revolution and the Negotiation of Rule in Modern Mexico.* Durham: Duke University Press, 3–23.

Joseph, G. and Buchenau, J. (2013) *Mexico's Once and Future Revolution.* Durham: Duke University Press.

Juárez, C.M. (2017) Asesinan a Madre de Joven Desaparecida y Activista de San Fernando, Tamaulipas. *Animal Politico.* 11 May. Available (consulted 12 August, 2017) at: https://www.animalpolitico.com/2017/05/integrante-grupo-desaparecidos-asesinada-san-fernando/.

Judd, D. (1998) The Case of Missing Scales: A Commentary on Cox, *Political Geography* 17 (1): 29–34.

Katz, A. and Campbell, D. (2015) Inside the Money Laundering Scheme That Citi Overlooked for Years. *Bloomberg Markets Magazine.* 20 November. Available (consulted 5 Septermber, 2018) at: https://www.bloomberg.com/news/articles/2015-11-20/inside-the-money-laundering-scheme-that-citi-overlooked-for-years.

Kirsch, S. (2002) Rumour and Other Narratives of Political Violence in West Papua. *Critique of Anthropology* 22, (1): 53–79.

Knight, A. (1999) Political Violence in Post-Revolutionary Mexico. In: Koonings K. and Kruijt D. (eds.) *Societies of Fear: The Legacy of Civil War, Violence and Terror in Latin America.* New York: Zed Books, 105–124.

Knight, A. and Pansters, W. (eds.). (2005). *Caciquismo in twentieth-century Mexico.* London: Institute for the Study of the Americas.

Krohn-Hansen, C. and Nustad, K.G. (2005). Introduction. In: Krohn-Hansen C. and Nustad K.G. (eds.) *State Formation: Anthropological Perspectives.* London: Pluto Press, 3–26.

Kubik, J. (2009) Ethnography of Politics: Foundations, Applications, Prospects. In: Schatz, E. (ed.) *Political Ethnography: What Immersion Contributes to the Study of Power.* Chicago: University of Chicago Press, 25–52.

Kulish, N. (2018) What It Costs to Be Smuggled Across the U.S. Border. *New York Times*, June 30. Available (consulted 20 December, 2019) at: https://www.nytimes.com/interactive/2018/06/30/world/smuggling-illegal-immigration-costs.html.

Kyeger, M. (2018) Transformations of the Rule of Law: Legal, Liberal, and Neo. In: Golder B. and McLoughlin D. (eds.) *The Politics of Legality in a Neoliberal Age*. New York: Routledge, 19–43.

La Botz, D. (2016) Mexico's Labor Movement After the Elections: A House Still Divided. *NACLA Report on the Americas* 45 (4): 34–37.

Lacarriere Lezama, N. (2010) Temples que Cambiaron a Matamoros. *Contralinea*. June https://www.contralinea.com.mx/archivo-revista/2010/06/01/temples-que-cambiaron-a-matamoros/.

Lapavitsas, C. (2009) Financialised Capitalism: Crisis and Financial Expropriation. *Historical Materialism* 17: 114–148.

Layton, L. (2010). Irrational exuberance: Neoliberal subjectivity and the perversion of truth. *Subjectivity, 3*, 303–322.

Lee, A.E. (2018) US-Mexico Border Militarization and Violence: Dispossession of Undocumented Laboring Classes from Puebla, Mexico. *Migraciones Internacionales*, 9 (4): 211–238.

Lee, B., Renwick, D. and Cara Labrador, R. (2019) Mexico's Drug War. *Council on Foreign Relations Backgrounder*. 22 October. Available (consulted 15 May, 2020) at: https://www.cfr.org/backgrounder/mexicos-drug-war.

Lefebvre, H. (1991) *Critique of Everyday Life Vol. I: Introduction*. London: Verso.

Lefebvre, H. (1996) The Right to the City. In: Kofman E. and Lebas E (eds.). *Writings on Cities*. Cambridge: Blackwell: Cambridge.

Lefebvre, H. (2001) *The Production of Space*. Malden Massachusetts: Blackwell.

Lefebvre, H. (2003) Space and the State. In: Brenner N., Jessop B. and Jones M. (eds.) *State/ Space. A reader*. Oxford: Blackwell, 84–100.

Leon, F. (2018) "Lidera Reynosa en casas nuevas solas. Reporta la Comisión Nacional de Vivienda." *El Mañana*, 17 March. Available (consulted 18 April, 2018) at: https://www.elmanana.com/lidera-reynosa-casas-nuevas...solas-reporta-comision-nacional-vivienda-reynosa-vivienda-abandono-fraccionamientos/4351229.

Leutert, S. (2018) *Organized Crime and Central American Migration in Mexico*. Austin: Lyndon B. Johnson School of Public Affairs Policy Research Project Report, 198.

Levine, D. (2017) Who Pays Taxes in Texas? *Center for Public Policy Priorities Brief*. Austin, March. Available (consulted 7 December, 2017) at: http://forabettertexas.org/images/IT_2017_03_WhoPaysTxTaxes.pdf.

Ley de Inversión Extranjera (1993) Mexico.

Ley Reglamentaria del Artículo 27 Constitucional (1995) Mexico.

Ley de Hidrocarburos (2014) Mexico.

Linares, R. and Montalvo, T. (2016) Pemex perdió 300 millones de dólares en juicios por robo de combustible en Estados Unidos. *Animal Politico*, 17 November. Available (consulted15September,2017)at:https://www.animalpolitico.com/2016/11/pemex-robo-combustible-narcotrafico/.

López, A.J. (2017) ONG de derechos humanos y violencia en México. Institucionalización, fragmentación y dinámicas contenciosas. In: Estévez A. and Vázquez D. (eds.) *Nueve razones para (des)confiar de la luchas por los derechos humanos.* Mexico City: FLACSO, UNAM, 31–54.

López García, R. (2015) Pagan caro por vivir en Zona Dorada. *Expreso.* 14 October. Available (consulted 3 October, 2018) at: http://expreso.press/2015/10/14/pagan-caro-por-vivir-en-zona-dorada/.

López García, R. (2017) Ganan terreno las viviendas amuralladas. *Expreso.* 30 January. Available (consulted 3 October, 2018) at: http://expreso.press/2017/01/30/ganan-terreno-las-viviendas-amuralladas/.

López García, R. (2018) Victoria: Tierra de nadie y de casas vacías. *Expreso.* 27 May. Available (consulted 3 October, 2018) at: https://expreso.press/2018/05/27/victoria-tierra-de-nadie-y-de-casas-vacias/.

López Jiménez, J.J. (2010) Crisis económica mundial e inversión extranjera directa en México y Jalisco. *México y la Cuenca del Pacífico* 13 (38): 37–60.

López León, A. (2014) Conclusiones sobre la Participacion Ciudadana y el Capital Social. In: Lopez Leon A. (ed.) *Matamoros Violento I. Participacion Ciudadana y Capital Social.* Tijuana: COLEF, 13–30.

López Medellín, M.O. (2015) *Tamaulipas: La construccion del silencio.* Washington D.C.: Freedom House.

López Obrador, A.M. (2018) *Versión estenográfica de la conferencia de prensa matutina del presidente Andrés Manuel López Obrador.* Mexico City, 27 December. Available (consulted 28 December, 2018) at: https://lopezobrador.org.mx/2018/12/27/version-estenografica-de-la-conferencia-de-prensa-matutina-del-presidente-andres-manuel-lopez-obrador-12/.

Lorey, D.E. (1999) *The US-Mexico Border into the Twentieth Century.* Willmington: SR Books.

Macías, T. (2014) Tamaulipas va por 1000 mdd en inversión extranjera. *El Financiero,* 6 May. Available (consulted 30 May, 2014) at: http://www.elfinanciero.com.mx/monterrey/tamaulipas-va-por-000-mdd-en-inversion-extranjera.

Maldonado, S. (2010) *Los Margenes del Estado Mexicano. Territorios Ilegales, Desarrollo y Violencia en Michoacan.* La Piedad: El Colegio de Michoacan.

Mandel, E. (1975) *Late Capitalism.* London: New Left Books.

Manilla, E. (2016) Califica alcalde a médicos como 'sicarios con licencia'. *El Mañana,* 9 November. Available (consulted 30 November, 2016) at: https://www.elmanana.com/califica-alcalde-medicos-como-sicarios-licencia-jose-rios-silva-negligencia-medica/3482272.

Manrique Giacomán, G.A. (2018) Violence, Neoliberal Legality, and Human Rights as Politics of Contestation in Mexico. *MA Thesis in Political Science*, University of New Brunswick, Saint John, NB.

Maquiladora Solidarity Network and El Equipo de Investigaciones Laborales (2016) *Las trabajadoras(es)de la industria maquiladora en Centroamérica*, El Salvador and Toronto. June. Available (consulted 20 November, 2019) at: https://www.maquilasoli darity.org/sites/default/files/attachment/Trabajadores_de_la_maquila_C.A_2016. pdf.

Maquiladora Solidarity Network and Equipo de Investigaciones Laborales (2018). *Salarios de Maquila en Centro América 2018 e Iniciativas internacionales por un Salario Digno.* Toronto and El Salvador, September. Available (consulted 20 November, 2019) at: https://www.maquilasolidarity.org/sites/default/files/attachment/Salarios_maqui la_centroam%C3%A9rica_EIL_RSM-Oct2018.pdf.

Marichel, Y. (2015) Fomentan en Facebook odio racial entre veracruzanos y tamaulipecos. *Versiones*, 10 April. Available (consulted 12 August, 2015) at: http://www.versiones. com.mx/fomentan-en-facebook-odio-racial-entre-veracruzanos-y-tamaulipecos/.

Marois, T. (2008) The 1982 Mexican Bank Statization and Unintended Consequences for the Emergence of Neoliberalism. *Canadian Journal of Political Science / Revue Canadienne De Science Politique* 41 (1): 143–67.

Marois, T. (2011) "Emerging Market Bank Rescues in an Era of Finance-led Neoliberalism: A Comparison of Mexico and Turkey." *Review of International Political Economy* 18: 168–196.

Marois, T. (2012) *States, Banks and Crisis: Emerging Finance Capitalism in Mexico and Turkey.* Cheltenham, Glos: Edward Elgar.

Marois, T. and Muñoz Martínez, H. (2016). Navigating the Aftermath of Crisis and Risk in Mexico and Turkey. *Research in Political Economy* 31: 165–96.

Marosi, R. (2012) Deportees to Mexico's Tamaulipas preyed upon by gangs. *Los Angeles Times*, 8 September. Available (consulted 10 August, 2015) at: http://articles.latimes. com/2012/sep/08/local/la-me-deportee-danger-20120909.

Martin, P. (2007) Mexico's Neoliberal Transition: Authoritarian Shadows in an Era of Neoliberalism. In: Leitner H., Peck J. and Sheppard E.S. (eds.) *Contesting Neoliberalism: Urban Frontiers.* New York: Guilford Press, 51–70.

Marx, K. (1976) *Capital I. A Critique of Political Economy*, translated by Ben Fowkes. New York: Penguin Books.

Mbembe, A. (2003) Necropolitics. *Public Culture* 15 (1): 11–40.

McGirr, L. (2016) *The War on Alcohol: Prohibition and the Rise of the American State.* New York: W.W. Norton and Company.

McIntyre, M. and Nast, H.J. (2011) Bio(necro)polis: Marx, Surplus Populations, and the Spatial Dialectics of Reproduction and Race. *Antipode* 43 (5): 1465–1488.

McKay, S.C. (2004) Zones of Regulation: Restructuring Labor Control in Privatized Export Zones. *Politics and Society* 32: 171–202.

McKenzie Stevens, S. (2004) Debating Ecology: Ethnography Writing that Makes a Difference. In: Brown S.G. and Dobrin S.I. (eds.) *Ethnography Unbound: From Theory Shock to Critical Praxis.* Albany: State University of New York Press, 157–181.

McMichael, P. (1990) Incorporating Comparison Within a World-Historical Perspective: An Alternative Comparative Method. *American Sociological Review* 55 (3): 385–397.

McMichael, P. (2000) World-Systems Analysis, Globalization, and Incorporated Comparison. *Journal of World Systems Research* 6 (3): 668–690.

Medina-Zárate, J., Uchôa de Oliveira, F.M. (2019). Why should we be interested in the specificity of subjectivity and neoliberalism in Latin America?. *Subjectivity* 12, 281–287.

Medrano Herrera, D.V. (2017) Reabriran expedientes del Parque Bicentenario. *El Mercurio de Ciudad Victoria.* 26 October: A1.

Mendoza, R. (2016a) Desarrollo urbano, una calamidad para los habitantes del Ejido Guadalupe Victoria. *La Luz de Tamaulipas.* 12 October. Available (consulted 5 May, 2017) at: http://laluzdetamaulipas.mx/2016/10/12/desarrollo-urbano-una-calamidad-para-los-habitantes-del-ej-guadalupe-victoria/.

Merkel, W. (2004). Embedded and Defective Democracies. *Democratization* 11 (5): 33–58.

Mexico's President Gets Tough (1989) *New York Times,* 20 January. Available (consulted 27 March 2018) at: https://www.nytimes.com/1989/01/20/opinion/mexico-s-president-gets-tough.html.

Meza, J.M. (2010) Cuenca de Burgos: Riqueza abajo, miseria arriba. *Contralinea,* 1 June. Available (consulted 12 March, 2015) at: https://www.contralinea.com.mx/archivo-revista/2010/06/01/cuenca-de-burgos-riqueza-abajo-miseria-arriba/.

Middlebrook, K.J. and Zepeda, E. (2003) *Confronting Development: Assessing Mexico's Economic and Social Policy Challenges.* Stanford, Calif.: Stanford University Press.

Moctezuma, A. (2017) De éste tamaño es la miseria laboral en Tamaulipas. *Posta,* 15 November. Available (consulted 5 February, 2018) at: http://www.posta.com.mx/perspectivas/de-este-tamano-es-la-miseria-laboral-en-tamaulipas.

Molina, H. (2019) Tamaulipas, Una Historia de Desapariciones. *El Economista,* 12 March, 2019. Available (consulted 12 March, 2019) at: https://www.eleconomista.com.mx/politica/Tamaulipas-una-historia-de-desapariciones-20190312-0009.html.

Monárrez Fragoso, J.E. (2009) *Trama de una injusticia. Feminicidio sexual sistémico en Ciudad Juárez.* Tijuana: El Colegio de la Frontera Norte/Miguel Angel Porrúa.

Monárrez Fragoso, J.E. (2010) Death in a Transnational Metropolitan Region. In: Staudt K., Fuentes C.M. and Monárrez Fragoso J.E. (eds.) *Cities and Citizenship at the U.S.-Mexico Border: The Paso del Norte Metropolitan Region.* New York: Palgrave, 23–42.

Monárrez Fragoso, J.E. and Bejarano, C. (2010) The Disarticulation of Justice: Precarious Life and Cross-Border Feminicides in the Paso del Norte Region. In: Staudt K., Fuentes C.M. and Monárrez Fragoso J.E. (eds.) *Cities and Citizenship at the U.S.-Mexico Border: The Paso del Norte Metropolitan Region.* New York: Palgrave, 43–70.

Montalvo, T. (2017) Empresa ligada a Yarrington recibió contratos del gobierno pese a ser demandada en EU por fraude. *Animal Politico*, 12 April. Available (consulted 13 January, 2018) at: https://www.animalpolitico.com/2017/04/empresa-yarrington-contratos-irregulares/.

Montes, J. (2019) Strikes at Low-Wage Plants Signal Revival of Labor Demands in Mexico; Workers Want Higher Pay as Country Prepares to Overhaul Labor Laws. *Wall Street Journal*, 13 February. Available (consulted 20 February, 2019) at: https://www.wsj.com/articles/strikes-at-low-wage-plants-signal-revival-of-labor-demands-in-mexico-11550087620.

Montoya, A. (2018) *The Violence of Democracy: Political Life in Postwar El Salvador*. Cham, Switzerland: Palgrave-MacMillan.

Moore, J. and Perez Rocha, M. (2019) *Extraction Casino: Mining companies gambling with Latin American lives and sovereignty*. Ottawa: Mining Watch Canada, Institute for Policy Studies and Center for International Environmental Law.

Morales, A. (2017) De genistas los fraccionamientos patito. *El Cinco*, 27 March. Available (consulted 4 June, 2017) at: https://www.elcinco.mx/cd-victoria/genistas-los-fraccionamientos-patito.

Morett-Sánchez, J.C. and Cosío-Ruiz, C. (2017) Panorama de los ejidos y comunidades agrarias en México. *Agricultura, sociedad y desarrollo* 14 (1): 125–152.

Morris, S.D. (2009) *Political Corruption in Mexico: The Impact of Democratization*. Boulder: Lynne Rienner Publishers.

Morton, A.D. (2012). The War on Drugs in Mexico: A Failed State? *Third World Quarterly* 33 (9): 1631–1645.

Morton, A.D. (2013). *Revolution and State in Modern Mexico. The Political Economy of Uneven Development*. Lanham, Maryland: Rowman and Littlefield.

Müller, M.M. (2016) Penalizing Democracy: Punitive Politics in Neoliberal Mexico. *Crime, Law and Social Change* 65: 227–249.

Munguia, V. (1993) Matamoros-Sur de Texas: El Tránsito de los Migrantes de América Central para la Frontera México-Estados Unidos. *Estudios Sociológicos* 11 (31): 183–207.

Municipio de Ciudad Victoria (2005) *Plan de desarrollo municipal*. Ciudad Victoria, Tamaulipas.

Municipio de Ciudad Victoria (2013a) *Plan de desarrollo municipal*. Ciudad Victoria, Tamaulipas.

Municipio de Ciudad Victoria (2013b). *Tercer informe de gobierno*. Ciudad Victoria, Tamaulipas.

Municipio de Ciudad Victoria (2014a) Décimo octava sesión ordinaria de Cabildo. *City Council Minutes*. Ciudad Victoria, Tamaulipas. September 9, 2014. Accessed May 7, 2017. http://www.ciudadvictoria.gob.mx/transparencia/docs/orden-del-dia/actas/09-09-14.pdf.

Municipio de Ciudad Victoria (2014b) *Primer informe de gobierno*. Ciudad Victoria, Tamaulipas.

Municipio de Ciudad Victoria (2017) *Plan de desarrollo municipal*. Ciudad Victoria, Tamaulipas.

Muñoz Martínez, H. (2008) The Global Crisis and Mexico: The End of Mexico's Development Model? *Relay* 24: 18–20.

Muñoz Martínez, H. (2010) The Double Burden on Maquila Workers: Violence and Crisis in Northern Mexico. *Global Labour University Conference*, Berlin, Germany, September 14–16.

Muñoz Martínez, H. (2013) The Political Scales of Market and Violence in Mexico. *Paper presented at the conference Dimension of Corruption*, St. Thomas University, Fredericton, NB, March 22, 2013.

Munoz Martinez, H. (2016) Hedging neoliberalism: Derivatives as state policy in Mexico. *New Political Economy*, 21(3): 291–314.

Nacar, J. (2015) Operan en México casi 50 escisiones de cárteles de la droga. *Vanguardia*, 28 August. Available (consulted 12 May, 2016) at: http://www.vanguardia.com.mx/operanenmexicocasi50escisionesdecartelesdeladroga-2369429.html.

Naim, M. (2006) *Illicit. How Smugglers, Traffickers and Copycats are Hijacking the Global Economy*. New York: Penguin Random House.

Nordstrom, C. (2000) Shadows and Sovereigns. *Theory, Culture and Society* 17 (4): 35–54.

Nordstrom C. and Robben, A.C.G.M. (1996) The Anthropology and Ethnography of Violence and Sociopolitical Conflict. In: Nordstrom C. and Robben A.C.G.M. (eds.) *Fieldwork under Fire. Contemporary Studies of Violence and Survival*, Berkeley and Los Angeles: University of California Press.

Nuijten, M. (2003) *Power, Community and the State. The Political Anthropology of Organisation in Mexico*. London: Pluto Press.

Nuijten, M. and Anders, G. (2008). Corruption and the Secret of the Law. An Introduction. In: Nuijten M. and Anders G. (eds.) *Corruption and the Secret of Law: A Legal Anthropological Perspective*. Aldershot, Hants, England: Ashgate, 1–24.

O'Connor, M. (2010) Analysis: A PR Department for Mexico's Narcos. *Global Post*, November 5. Available (consulted 12 March 2013) at: https://www.pri.org/stories/2010-11-05/analysis-pr-department-mexicos-narcos.

O'Donnell, G. (1994) Delegative Democracy. *Journal of Democracy*. 5 (1): 55–69.

Olivera, G. (2001). Trayectoria de las reservas territoriales en México: Irregularidad, desarrollo urbano y administración municipal tras la reforma constitucional de 1992. *EURE* 27 (81): 61–84.

Olvera, J. (2016) The State, Unauthorized Mexican Migration, and Vulnerability in the Workplace. *Sociology Compass* 10 (2): 132–142.

Osorio Machado, L. (2013). Ambiguedad en lo legal y lo ilegal. Redes de tráfico ilícitas y territorio. In: Chavez Bries M. and Checa Artasu M. (eds.) *El Espacio en las Ciencias Sociales*. Zamora: El Colegio de Michoacan, 315–330.

Oszlak, O. (1981) The Historical Formation of the State in Latin America: Some Theoretical and Methodological Guidelines for Its Study. *Latin American Research Review* 16 (2): 3–32.

Otero, G. (2004) *Mexico in Transition: Neoliberal Globalism, the State and Civil Society*. Black Point, N.S.: Fernwood.

Padgett, H. (2016) *Tamaulipas la casta de los narcogobernadores*. Mexico City: Urano.

Paley, D. (2014) *Drug War Capitalism*. Chico, California: A K Press.

Panitch, L., and Konings, M. (eds.) (2008) *American Empire and the Political Economy of Global Finance*. New York: Palgrave.

Pansters, Will G. (2012). Zones of State-Making: Violence, Coercion, and Hegemony in Twentieth-Century Mexico. In Pansters W.G. (ed.) *Violence, Coercion, and State-Making in Twentieth-Century Mexico: The Other Half of the Centaur*. Stanford, Calif.: Stanford University Press, 3–41.

Pansters, W.G. (2018) Drug trafficking, the informal order, and caciques. Reflections on the crime-governance nexus in Mexico. *Global Crime*, 19 (3–4): 315–338.

PEP (Pemex Exploracion y Produccion) v. BASF Corporation et al., No. 4:2010cv01997 (S.D. Tex. 2014).

Pérez, A.L. (2011) *El cartel negro*. Mexico City: Grijalbo.

Pérez, A.L. (2012). Ordena de gas condensado en la Cuenca de Burgos. *Contralinea*, 8 May. Available (consulted 4 October, 2014) at: https://www.contralinea.com.mx/archivo-revista/2012/05/08/ordena-de-gas-condensado-en-la-cuenca-de-burgos/.

Pérez, A.L. (2017) *PEMEX RIP. Vida y asesinato de la principal empresa mexicana*. Mexico City: Grijalbo.

Perrone, N. (2017) Neoliberalism and Economic Sovereignty: Property, Contracts, and Foreign Investment Relations. In Brabazon H. (ed.) *Neoliberal Legality: Understanding the Role of Law in the Neoliberal Project*. New York: Routledge, 43–60.

Pinson, G. and Journel C.M. (2016). The Neoliberal City – Theory, Evidence, Debates. *Special Issue. Territory, Politics, Governance* 4, (2): 137–153.

Pizzo, B. and Altavilla, E. (2017) Embedding Illegality, or When the Illegal Becomes Illicit: Planning Cases and Urban Transformations in Rome. In: Chiodelli F., Hall T. and Hudson R. (eds.) *The Illicit and Illegal in Regional and Urban Governance and Development*. New York: Routledge. E-book collection.

Poole, D. (2004) Between Threat and Guarantee: Justice and Community in the Margins of the Peruvian State. In: Das V. and Poole D. (eds.) *Anthropology in the Margins of the State,* Santa Fe: School of American Research Press, 25–66.

Portugal, K. (2010). Lavan notarios narcoextorsiones. *Reforma*, 8 February. Available (consulted 3 April, 2014). https://busquedas.grupoureforma.com/reforma/Documento/Impresa.aspx?id=3687978|InfodexTextos&url=https://hemerotecalibre.reforma

.com/20100208/interactiva/RPRI20100208-001.JPG&text=Notarios+lavan+narcoext orsiones&tit=Lavan%20notarios%20narcoextorsiones.

Poulantzas, N. (1974) *Classes in Contemporary Capitalism*. London: New Left Books.

Poulantzas, N. (2014). *State, Power and Socialism*. London: Verso.

Powell, K. (2012). Political Practice, Everyday Political Violence, and Electoral Processes During the Neoliberal Period in Mexico. In: Pansters W.G. (ed.) *Violence, Coercion, and State-Making in Twentieth-Century Mexico: The Other Half of the Centaur*. Stanford, California: Stanford University Press, 212–232.

Presidencia de la República (2013). 10 puntos claves de la reforma energética. *Blog Presidencia de la República*, 22 December. Available (consulted 4 October, 2014) at: https://www.gob.mx/presidencia/articulos/10-puntos-clave-de-la-reforma-energetica.

Presidencia de la República (2014) *Presidente de los Estados Unidos Mexicanos, licenciado Enrique Peña Nieto, en la Sesión de Preguntas y Respuestas durante la Conferencia Magistral: Transformando México: Sociedad, Política, Economía*. 23 January. Available (consulted 9 May, 2014) at: http://www.presidencia.gob.mx/articulos-prensa/presidente-de-los-estados-unidos-mexicanos-licenciado-enrique-pena-nieto-en-la-sesion-de-preguntas-y-respuestas-durante-la-conferencia-magistral-transfor mando-mexico-sociedad-politica-economia/.

Public Citizen (2018) *NAFTA's Legacy: Expanding Corporate Power to Attack Public Interests Laws*. Washington D.C., 22 January. Available (consulted 5 May, 2018) at: https://www.citizen.org/sites/default/files/nafta_factsheet_isds_january.pdf.

Quintero, L. (2019). Empresarios de Matamoros, en jaque: cláusula los obliga a subir el sueldo a 60,000 trabajadores. *EconomiaHoy*, 24 January. Available (consulted 20 February, 2019) at: https://www.economiahoy.mx/economia-eAm-mexico/noticias/9654472/01/19/Empresarios-de-Matamoros-en-jaque-clausula-los-obliga-a-subir-el-sueldo-a-60000-trabajadores.html.

Quintero Ramírez, C. (1997) *Restructuración Sindical en la Frontera Norte. El Caso de la Industria Maquiladora*. Tijuana: El Colegio de la Frontera Norte.

Quintero Ramírez, C. (2001). La maquila en Matamoros. Cambios y continuidades. In: de la O M.E. and Quintero Ramírez C. (eds.) *Globalización, trabajo y maquilas: las nuevas y viejas fronteras en México*. Mexico City: CIESAS-Plaza y Valdez, 73–110.

Quintero Ramírez, C. (2003). El sindicalismo actual en la industria maquiladora. *Paper presented at the 4th Congress of the Mexican Association of Labor Studies*, Hermosillo, April 9–11, 2003.

Quintero Ramírez, C. (2004a). Union and Social Benefits in the Maquiladoras. In: Kopinak K. (ed.) *The Social Costs of Industrial Growth in Northern Mexico*. San Diego: Center for US-Mexican Studies-UCSD, 283–308.

Quintero Ramírez, C. (2004b) Cuarenta años de maquila en el Norte de México. Los avances y retrocesos de un proyecto industrial fallido. *Presentation for the Second Congress on Economic History,* Universidad Nacional Autónoma de México, Mexico City, October 27–29.

Quintero Ramírez, C. (2019) Las movilizaciones obreras en Matamoros Tamaulipas. *Correo Fronterizo*, 7 February. Available (consulted 20 February, 2019) at: https://www. colef.mx/opinion/las-movilizaciones-obreras-en-matamoros-tamaulipas/?e= correo-fronterizo.

Quintero Ramírez, C. and Romo Aguilar, M.L. (2001) Riesgos Laborales en la Maquiladora. El Caso Tamaulipeco. *Frontera Norte* 13 (2): 11–46.

Radcliffe, S.A. (2001) Imagining the State as a Space: Territoriality and the Formation of the State in Ecuador. In: Hansen T.M. and Stepputat F. (eds.) *States of Imagination: Ethnographic Explorations of the Postcolonial State*. Durham, N.C.: Duke University Press, 123–148.

Ravelo, R. (2018) *Los incómodos. Los gobernadores que amenazan el futuro político del PRI*. Mexico City: Temas de Hoy.

Read, J. (2003) *The Micropolitics of Capital: Marx and the Prehistory of the Present*, Albany: SUNY Press.

Redacción (1978) Sólo sus chicharrones truenan. *Proceso*, 14 January. Available (consulted 6 March, 2016) at: https://www.proceso.com.mx/122184/solo-sus-chicharrones-truenan.

Redacción (1990) Junto con Fidel Empiezan a Cambiar Líderes. *Proceso,* 22 September. Available (consulted 3 February, 2013) at: http://www.proceso.com.mx/155729/ junto-con-fidel-empiezan-a-cambiar-lideres.

Redacción (1991) A los 77 años y en Silla de Ruedas. *Proceso*, 26 October. Available (consulted 10 March 2012) at: http://www.proceso.com.mx/158061/a-los-77-anos-y-en-silla-de-ruedas.

Redacción (1992) Nada que Estorbe la Negociación del TLC. *Proceso*, 8 February. Available (consulted 3 February, 2013) at: http://www.proceso.com.mx/158721/nada-que-estorbe-la-negociacion-del-tlc.

Redacción (1995) Los sacadólares Martínez Manautou y Aramburuzavala ganaron el juicio al inversor Roberto Polo. *Proceso*, 26 June 26. Available (consulted 4 October, 2016) at: https://www.proceso.com.mx/169442/los-sacadolares-martinez-manautou-y-aramburuzavala-ganaron-el-juicio-al-inversor-roberto-polo.

Redacción (2004) Tamaulipas, Operación Cuerno de Chivo. *Proceso*, 21 November. Available (consulted 3 February, 2013) at: https://www.proceso.com.mx/193561/tamaulipas-la-operacion-cuerno-de-chivo.

Redacción (2007a) Presenta Calderón plan para combatir la delincuencia organizada. *Proceso*. 23 January. Available (consulted 24 August, 2015) at: https://www.proceso .com.mx/205027/presenta-calderon-plan-para-combatir-la-delincuencia-organizada.

Redacción (2007b) Por eso lo Mataron. *Proceso*, 9 December. Available (consulted 3 February, 2013) at: https://www.proceso.com.mx/90353/por-eso-lo-mataron.

Redacción (2007c) Tamaulipas: Berlanga Bolado, el constructor consentido. *Proceso*, 12 February. Available (consulted 14 October, 2010) at: https://www.proceso.com. mx/205519/tamaulipas-berlanga-bolado-el-constructor-consentido.

Redacción (2007d) Líder veracruzano contendrá por alcaldía en Reynosa, Tamaulipas. *Proceso*, 4 August. Available (15 August, 2015) at: http://www.proceso.com.mx/?p= 210197.

Redacción (2009) Autorizan a gobernador de Tamaulipas mega deuda por 6 MMDP. *Proceso*, 3 June. Available (consulted 14 October, 2010) at: https://www.proceso. com.mx/115774/autorizan-a-gobernador-de-tamaulipas-mega-deuda-por-6-mmdp.

Redacción (2010) Águila bicentenaria refleja el temple tamaulipeco, afirma gobernador. *Hora Cero*, 14 September. Available (consulted 3 September, 2016) at: https:// www.horacero.com.mx/tamaulipas/aguila-bicentenaria-refleja-el-temple-tamaulipeco-afirma-gobernador/.

Redacción (2011) Suman casi 5 millones de casas abandonadas en el país. *Animal Politico*, 12 August. Available (consulted 3 July, 2015) at: https://www.animalpolitico.com/ 2011/08/suman-casi-5-millones-de-casas-abandonadas-en-el-pais/.

Redacción (2012a) Empresa que lavó dinero del Cartel del Golfo era contratista de la SCT. *Aristegui Noticias*, 25 May. Available (consulted 4 November, 2018) at: https://ariste guinoticias.com/2505/mexico/empresa-que-lavo-dinero-de-yarrington-era-contratista-de-sct/.

Redacción (2012b) El gran narcolavadero de Yarrington. *Proceso*, 29 May. Available (consulted 13 June, 2013) at: https://www.proceso.com.mx/481666/gran-narcolavadero-yarrington.

Redacción (2013) Gobierno y narco, unidos contra Valor por Tamaulipas. *Proceso*, 30 April. Available (consulted 30 July, 2014) at: https://www.proceso.com.mx/340554/ gobierno-y-narco-unidos-contra-valor-por-tamaulipas-2.

Redacción (2015) Rompe records Tamaulipas en inversión extranjera. *Excelsior*, 16 November. Available (consulted 14 April, 2016) at: https://www.excelsior.com.mx/ nacional/2015/11/16/1057657.

Redacción (2017a) Romero Deschamps se reelige: será líder sindical de Pemex 31 años consecutivos, hasta 2024. *SinEmbargo*, 11 December. Available (consulted 12 December, 2017) at: http://www.sinembargo.mx/11-12-2017/3361874.

Redacción (2017b) Yarrington dio contratos a Eugenio y a Egidio. *Milenio*, 30 November. Available (consulted Accessed October 4, 2018) at: http://www.pressreader.com/ mexico/milenio-tamaulipas/20171130/281612420722229.

Redacción (2017c) Investigan a seis notarios públicos por presunto despojo de terrenos en Tamaulipas. *Proceso*, 17 August. Available (consulted 4 October, 2018) at: https:// www.proceso.com.mx/499407/investigan-a-seis-notarios-publicos-presunto-despojo-terrenos-en-tamaulipas.

Redacción (2018) Gobierno de Tamaulipas Arranca Operative Binacional con Texas. *El Universal*, 7 June. Available (consulted 29 October, 2018) at: http://www.eluniversal. com.mx/estados/gobierno-de-tamaulipas-arranca-operativo-binacional-con-texas.

Redacción/SinEmbargo (2015) Tamaulipas usó software de Hacking Team para prevenir infiltraciones en seguridad. *SinEmbargo*, 9 September. Available (consulted 10 September, 2015) at: http://www.sinembargo.mx/09-09-2015/1474892.

Red de Periodistas de a Pie (2015) Masacre San Fernando: 5 Años de Impunidad. *El Universal*, 24 August. Available (consulted 24 August, 2015) at: http://www.elunive rsal.com.mx/articulo/periodismo-de-investigacion/2015/08/24/masacre-san-fernando-5-anos-de-impunidad.

Red de Solidaridad de la Maquiladora (2001) Trabajadores de Custom Trim Testifican Sobre Violaciones de Salud y Seguridad Ocupacional. *El Boletín* 6 (1): 4–5.

Reed, T. (2014) Amid Mexico's Energy Reform, Fuel Theft Poses Risks. *Starter Worldview Stratfor*, 4 December. Available (consulted 7 October, 2016) at: https://worldview .stratfor.com/article/amid-mexicos-energy-reform-fuel-theft-poses-risks.

Reina, E. (2018) Matan a balazos a una familia y tres civiles más en un tiroteo entre narcos y militares en Tamaulipas. *El Pais*, 13 April. Available (consulted 27 May, 2018) at: https://elpais.com/internacional/2018/04/13/mexico/1523577466_597391.html.

Rendón, I. (2016) Sin Desfile del Dia de Trabajo en Matamoros. *Hoy Tamaulipas*, 25 March. Available (consulted 4 June, 2016) at: http://www.hoytamaulipas.net/notas/218722/ Sin-desfile-del-Dia-del-Trabajo-en-Matamoros.html.

Reporte Indigo (2012) Fox los exonera, Calderón los persigue. *Zocalo*, 18 February. Available (consulted 20 March, 2013) at: http://www.zocalo.com.mx/seccion/articulo/ fox-los-exonera-calderon-los-persigue.

Reyez, J. (2018) Crimen organizado reina en Tamaulipas. *Contralinea*, 10 July. Available (consulted 11 July, 2018) at: https://www.contralinea.com.mx/archivo-revista/2018/ 07/10/crimen-organizado-reina-en-tamaulipas/.

Reyna, H. (2010) Veracruzanos enfrentan estigma y rechazo en Reynosa. *En Línea Directa*, 1 April. Available (consulted 11 August, 2015) at: http://enlineadirecta.info/? option=view&article=122774#sthash.VeDcA7q7.dpuf.

Ribando Seelke, C. and Finklea, K. (2017) US/Mexican Security Cooperation: The Merida Initiative and Beyond. *Congressional Research Service Report*, 7–5700, June 29, Washington, D.C.

Robinson, W.I. (2000) Polyarchy: Coercion's New Face in Latin America. *NACLA Report on the Americas* 34 (3): 42.

Rodríguez, T., Montané, D. and Pulitzer, L. (2007) *Las hijas de Juárez*. Mexico City: Atria Books.

Rodríguez Padilla, V. (2010) Contratos de servicios multiples en Pemex: Eficacia, eficiencia y rentabilidad. *Revista Problemas del Desarrollo*, 163 (41): 119–140.

Roitman, J.L. (2005) *Fiscal Disobedience: An Anthropology of Economic Regulation in Central Africa*. Princeton, N.J.: Princeton University Press.

Roman, R. and Velasco, E. (2006). State, Bourgeoisie and the Unions. The Recycling of Mexico's System of Labor Control. *Latin American Perspectives* 33 (2): 95–103.

Rosagel, S. (2014). La corrupción hunde a Pemex pero usan la pérdida récord para justificar la reforma energética: PRD y Morena. *SinEmbargo*, 1 May 1. Available (consulted 13 March, 2016) at: http://www.sinembargo.mx/01-05-2014/978139.

Rose, N. (2001) The Politics of Life Itself. *Theory, Culture and Society*, 18(6):1–30.

Rousseau, I. (2017) *Tribulaciones de dos Empresas Petroleras Estatales*. Mexico City: El Colegio de Mexico.

Ruiz Duran, C. (1981) La Petrolización de Mexico. *Nexos*, January. Available (consulted 20 November, 2013) at: https://www.nexos.com.mx/?p=3778.

Ruiz Marrujo, O. (2009) Women, Migration and Sexual Violence: Lessons from Mexico's Borders. In: Staudt K., Payan T. and Kruszewski Z.A. (eds.) *Human Rights Along the U.S.-Mexico Border: Gendered Violence and Insecurity*. Tucson: The University of Arizona Press, 31–47.

Saez, A. (2019) En Reynosa, enclave del narco, nace otro negocio: cobrar cuota a migrantes para cruzar hacia EU. *Sin Embargo*, 20 December. Available (consulted 4 January, 2020) at: https://www.sinembargo.mx/20-12-2019/3699797.

Said, E. (1978) *Orientalism*. New York: Pantheon Books.

Salazar, C. and Velázquez, I. (2017) Acusan corrupción en robo de combustible. *Reforma*. 9 May. Available (consulted 7 October, 2018) at: https://www.reforma.com/aplicacioneslibre/articulo/default.aspx?id=1109672&md5=b8c683e444bc7567c29efb64ce6117aa&ta=0dfdbac11765226904c16cb9ad1b2efe.

Salinas de Gortari, C. (1988) *Discurso de toma de posesión de Carlos Salinas de Gortari como presidente constitucional de los Estados Unidos Mexicanos*. 1 December. Mexico City.

Salter, M. (2006) The Global Visa Regime and the Political Technologies of the International Self: Borders, Bodies, Biopolitics. *Alternatives* 31: 167–89.

Salyer, J.C. (2009) The Treatment of Noncitizens after September 11 in Historical Context. In: Martinez S. (ed.) *International Migration and Human Rights: The Global Repercussions of U.S. Policy*. Berkeley: University of California Press, 63–81.

Sánchez Munguía, V. (2014) La Transgresion como Costumbre. Una Mirada a la Cultura de la Legalidad en Matamoros. In: Zarate Ruiz A. (ed.) *Matamoros Violento II. La Legalidad en su Cultura y la Debilidad en sus Instituticones*. Tijuana: COLEF, 157–186.

Sánchez Treviño, M. (2007) Renuncia primo de mandatario de Tamaulipas a la Secretaría Técnica. *La Jornada*, 21 September. Available (consulted 23 August, 2017) at: http://www.jornada.com.mx/2007/09/21/index.php?section=estados&article=038n2est.

Sandoval, F. (2016) Tamaulipas: La raíz del miedo de la prensa en México. In: Artículo 19 (ed.) *Informe MIEDO*. Mexico City: Artículo 19.

Sandoval Alarcón, F. (2017) Empresa investigada en EU y ligada a Yarrington recibió 1,473 mdp en contratos públicos. *Animal Politico*, 14 February. Available (consulted 4 October, 2018) at: https://www.animalpolitico.com/2017/02/empresas-yarrington-lavado/.

Sassen, S. (1998) *Globalization and Its Discontent*. New York: New Press.

Sassen, S. (2011) When Cities Become Strategic. *Architectural Design* 81 (3): 124–27.

Saviano, R. (2013) *ZeroZeroZero*. New York: Penguin Random House.

Schedler, A. (2005) From Electoral Authoritarianism to Democratic Consolidation. In: Crandall R., Paz G. and Roett R. (eds.) *Mexico's Democracy at Work: Political and Economic Dynamics*. Boulder: Lynne Rienner, 9–38.

Schedler, A. (ed.) (2006). *Electoral Authoritarianism: The Dynamics of Unfree Competition*. Boulder: Lynne Rienner Publishers.

Scheper-Hughes, N. (1995) *Death without Weeping: The Violence of Everyday Life in Brazil*. Berkeley, California: University of California Press.

Scheper-Hughes, N. (2003) Bodies, Death and Silence. In: Scheper-Hughes N. and Bourgois Philippe I. (eds.) *Violence in War and Peace: An Anthology*. London: Blackwell Publishers, 175–185.

Scheper-Hughes, N. and Bourgois, P. (2004). *Violence in War and Peace*. Malden, MA: Blackwell.

Schmid, C. (2008) Henri Lefebvre's Theory of the Production of Space: Towards a Three-Dimensional Dialectic. In: Goonewardena K., Kipfer S., Milgrom R. and Schmid C. (eds.) *Space, Difference, Everyday Life: Reading Henri Lefebvre*. London: Routledge, 27–45.

Scott, J.C. (1985) *Weapons of the weak: everyday forms of resistance*. New Haven and London, Yale University Press.

Scott, J.C. (1990) *Domination and the Arts of Resistance: Hidden Transcripts*. New Haven: Yale University Press.

Scott, J.C. (1998) *Seeing Like a State: How Certain Schemes to Improve the Human Condition Have Failed*. New Haven: Yale University Press.

SEC (Securities and Exchange Commission) (2007) *Continental Fuel Inc. Quarterly* Report. Commission file number 33-33042-NY, Washington, DC.

Secretaria de Desarrollo Economico (2019) Tamaulipas dentro del Top Ten De Inversión Extranjera a Nivel Nacional. *Prensa Gobierno del Estado de Tamaulipas* Available (consulted 12 May, 2019) at: https://www.tamaulipas.gob.mx/desarrolloeconomico/2019/11/conquista-tamaulipas-resultados-historicos-en-inversiones-extranjeras/.

Senado de la República (2015) La desaparicion forzada de personas. *Mirada Legislativa* 75 (March). Available (consulted 20 September, 2016) at: http://bibliodigitalibd.senado.gob.mx/bitstream/handle/123456789/2017/ML75.pdf?sequence=1&isAllowed=y.

Serna, A. (2017) Seis colonias más peligrosas. *El Grafico de Tamaulipas*, 7 March. Available (consulted 23 March, 2018) at: https://elgraficotam.com.mx/2017/03/07/seis-colonias-son-las-mas-peligrosas/.

Serrano, M. (2012) States of Violence: State-Crime Relations in Mexico. In: Pansters W.G. *Violence, Coercion, and State-making in Twentieth-century Mexico: The Other Half of the Centaur*. Stanford: Stanford University Press, 135–158.

SESNSP (Secretariado Ejecutivos del Sistema Nacional de Seguridad Pública) (2015) *Informe de víctimas de homicidio, secuestro y extorsión 2014*. Mexico City, June.

Sheppard, E. (2011) Geographical Political Economy. *Journal of Economic Geography* 11: 319–331.

Simons, A. (1996) The Beginning of the End. In: Nordstrom C. and Robben A.C.G.M. (eds.) *Fieldwork Under Fire. Contemporary Studies of Violence and Survival*. Berkeley and Los Angeles: University of California Press, 42–60.

SJOIIM (Sindicato de Jornaleros y Obreros Industriales de la Industria Maquiladora) (2012) *Libro Ilustrado del SJOIIM, 1932–2012*. Matamoros: SJOIIM.

SJP (Seguridad, Justicia y Paz) (2018) *Metodología del ranking de las 50 ciudades más violentas del mundo*. Mexico City.

Snyder, J.G. (2013) The Structure and Operations of the Department of Justice Assets Forfeiture Fund. *Money Laundering and Forfeiture*, 61 (5): 67–72.

Soederberg, S. (2015) Subprime Housing Goes South: Constructing Securitized Mortgages for the Poor in Mexico. *Antipode* 47 (2): 481–499.

Solís, L. (1997) *Evolución del Sistema Mexicano Financiero*. Mexico City: Siglo XXI.

Solís González, J.L. (2013) Neoliberalismo y crimen organizado en México: El surgimiento del Estado narco. *Frontera Norte* 25 (50): 7–34.

Soto, D. (2016) Acosa crimen a médicos en Tamaulipas. *Reforma*, 26 June. Available (consulted 21 July, 2016) at: https://www.reforma.com/aplicacioneslibre/preacceso/articulo/default.aspx?id=878881&urlredirect=https://www.reforma.com/aplicaciones/articulo/default.aspx?id=878881.

Spivak, G.C. (1985) The Rani of Sirmur: An Essay in Reading the Archives. *History and Theory* 24: 247–272.

Springer, S. (2012) Neoliberalising Violence: of the Exceptional and the Exemplary in Coalescing Moments. *Area*, 44 (2): 136–143.

Staff (2018) Cae notario por nexos al crimen. *El Norte*, 24 September 24. Available (consulted 4 October, 2018) at: https //www.reforma.com/aplicacioneslibre/preacceso/articulo/default.aspx?id=1499263&fuente=md&urlredirect=https://www.reforma.com/aplicaciones/articulo/default.aspx?Id=1499263&Fuente=MD.

Stanek, L. (2011) *Henri Lefebvre on Space: Architecture, Urban Research, and the Production of Theory*. Minneapolis Minn.: University of Minnesota Press.

Staudt, K. (2009) Violence at the Border: Broadening the Discourse to Include Feminism, Human Security and Deeper Democracy. In: Staudt K., Payan T. and Kruszewski Z.A.

(eds.) *Human Rights Along the U.S.-Mexico Border: Gendered Violence and Insecurity.* Tucson: The University of Arizona Press, 1–28.

Staudt, K. and R. Robles Ortega (2010) Surviving Domestic Violence in the Paso del Norte Border Region. In: Staudt, K., Fuentes, C.M. and Monarrez Fragoso J.E. (eds.) *Cities and Citizenship at the U.S.-Mexico Border: The Paso del Norte Metropolitan Region.* New York: Palgrave, 71–89.

Stewart, P.J. and Strathern, A. (2004) *Witchcraft, Sorcery, Rumours, and Gossip.* Cambridge: Cambridge University Press.

Stewart, S. (2018) Tracking Mexico's Cartels in 2018. *Stratfor Worldview,* 1 February. Available (consulted 29 October, 2018) at: https://worldview.stratfor.com/article/tracking-mexicos-cartels-2018.

Swyngedouw, E. (1997) Excluding the Other: The Production of Scale and Scaled Politics. In: Lee R. and Willis J. (eds.) *Geographies of Economies.* London: Arnold, 167–176.

Swyngedouw, E. (2004) Globalisation or 'Glocalisation'? Networks, territories and rescaling. *Cambridge Review of International Affairs* 17(1): 25–48.

Syal, R. (2009) Drug Money Saved Banks in Global Crisis, Claims UN Advisor. *The Guardian,* December 13, 2009. Accessed December 5, 2016. https://www.theguardian.com/global/2009/dec/13/drug-money-banks-saved-un-cfief-claims.

Tagle Gómez, S. (2008) Elections in Mexico: What's the Use? *NACLA Report on the Americas* 41 (5): 12–16.

Team NAFTA (2010) *Matamoros Industrial Profile.* Available (consulted 10 June, 2010) at: http://www.teamnafta.com/index.php/Market-Profiles/matamoros-manufacturing-industrial-maquiladora-mexico.html.

Texans for Public Justice (2011a) *The Rick Perry Primer.* Austin. Available (consulted 14 February, 2018) at: http://info.tpj.org/reports/pdf/perryprimer.fin.pdf.

Texans for Public Justice (2011b) *Con Job: Most Enterprise Fund Grantees Failed to Deliver in 2010.* Austin. Available (consulted 23 March, 2017) at: http://info.tpj.org/watchyourassets/enterprise4/ConJob.pdf.

Texas Secretary of State (2018) *Selecting a Business Structure.* Available (consulted 3 May, 2018) at: https://www.sos.state.tx.us/corp/businessstructure.shtml.

Thacker, E. (2011) Necrologies or the Death of the Body Politic. In: Clough, P.T. and Wilse C. (eds.) *Beyond Biopolitics.* Durham: Duke University Press, 139–162.

The State of Texas Governor (2016) *Texas business Incentives and Programs Overview.* Available (consulted 23 March, 2017) at: https://gov.texas.gov/uploads/files/business/incentivessummary.pdf.

Thomas, D.A. (2011) *Exceptional Violence: Embodied Citizenship in Transnational Jamaica.* Durham, NC: Duke University Press.

Torre Cantalapiedra, E. (2017). Las respuestas mexicanas frente a la Ley Arizona y la función de los estados en la gestión inmigratoria estadounidense. *Revista mexicana de ciencias políticas y sociales,* 62 (229): 17–43.

Torres, A. (2012) Sabiamos que Pasaba, pero Nadie Hablaba. *El Universal*, 20 February. Available (consulted 11 August, 2015) at: http://archivo.eluniversal.com.mx/nacion/194114.html.

Torres, L. (2011) Torre Bicentenario: No se hunde, solo atrapa gente en el elevador. *Hoy Tamaulipas*, 2 February. Available (consulted 6 June, 2016) at: http://hoytamaulipas.net/notas/26558/Torre-bicentenario-No-se-hunde-Solo-atrapa-gente-en-el-elevador.html.

Torres, L. (2018) Se incremento un 20c% desapariciones en Tamaulipas. *Hoy Tamaulipas*, 27 August. Available (consulted 3 March 3, 2019) at: http://www.hoytamaulipas.net/notas/353901/Se-incremento-un-200-desapariciones-en-Tamaulipas.html.

Tovar, S. (2018) Siete Notarios Públicos de Tamaulipas en la Mira. *El Universal*, 28 September. Available (consulted 4 October, 2018) at: http://www.eluniversal.com.mx/estados/siete-notarios-de-tamaulipas-en-la-mira-tres-han-ido-detenidos.

Tsoukalas, K. (1999) Globalisation and the Executive Committee: Reflections on the Contemporary Capitalist State. In: Panitch L. and Leys C. (eds.) *Socialist Register 1999: Global Capitalism vs. Democracy*. London: Merlin Press, 56–75.

Tuckman, J. (2010) Leading Politician Rodolfo Torre Cantú Murdered in Mexico. *The Guardian*, 29 June. Available (consulted 10 August, 2011) at: http://www.guardian.co.uk/world/2010/jun/29/leading-politician-rodolfo-torre-cantu-murdered-mexico.

Uhlig, M.A. (1991) Behind a Mexican Prison Uprising: Two Warring Drug Lords and Corrupt Police on Either Side. *New York Times*, 6 October, Sunday Magazine, SM40.

United States Consulate in Matamoros (2009) *Dark Security Cloud Hovers Over Matamoros Business Community*. Cable, Canonical ID: 09MATAMOROS188_1. Available (consulted 13 August, 2013) at: https://wikileaks.org/plusd/cables/09MATAMOROS188_a.html.

United States Embassy in Mexico (2011) *A Perilous Road through Mexico for Migrants*, cable, sensitive, 6 pp. 31 January 31.

United States, Mexico and Canada Free Trade Agreement. Signed on 30 November 2018. *Canada Treaty series*. Available (consulted 5 January, 2019) at: https://international.gc.ca/trade-commerce/trade-agreements-accords-commerciaux/agr-acc/cusma-aceum/text-texte/toc-tdm.aspx?lang=eng.

United States of America Attorney's Office (2014) Investment Account of Former Mexican Governor's Political Appointee Seized by United States. *Press Release*. 24 December Available (consulted 5 May, 2018) at: https://www.justice.gov/usao-sdtx/pr/us-seizes-investment-account-former-mexican-governor-s-political-appointee.

United States of America Congress. Senate Caucus on International Narcotics Control (2010). *Drug Trafficking Violence in Mexico: Implications for the U.S: Hearing Before the Senate Caucus on International Narcotics Control*, 111th Cong. 5 May.

United States of America v. Antonio Pena-Arguelles, No. 5:12-mj-00120-NSN (W.D. Tex. 2012).

United States of America v. Fernando Cano-Martinez, No. B-12-435 (S.D. Tex. 2012).

United States of America v. Real Property Known As 334 Padre Boulevard Condominium Unit 1401 Cameron County South Padre Island, Tx 78597, No. 12-CV-00167 (S.D. Tex. 2012).

United States of America v. Tomas Yarrington-Ruvalcaba and Fernando Cano Martinez, No. B-12-435-Sl (S.D. Tex. 2013).

United States of America v. Pablo Zarate-Juarez, No. 2:15-cr-216 (S.D. Tex 2015).

United States of America v. Luis Carlos Castillo Cervantes, No. 16-CR-00802, (S.D. Tex. 2017).

United States of America v. All Property and Assets On Deposit Or Held In The UBS Financial Services, Inc. Account Number Om 05095, Case 2:14-Cv-00484 (S.D. Texas 2014).

United States Treasury. *Treasury Forfeiture Fund Accountability Report.* (2004–2015) Washington DC.

Uresti, J. (2013) Suspenden desfile del Día del Trabajo en Matamoros. *Hoy Tamaulipas, 13* April 13. Available (consulted 20 November, 2013) at: http://www.hoytamaulipas.net/moviles/?v1=notas&v2=77121.

Valadez, S. (2017) En Victoria el suelo es más caro. *Expresso*, 9 March. Available (consulted 16 January, 2018) at: http://expreso.press/2017/03/09/victoria-suelo-mas-caro/.

Valdes Castellanos, G. (2013) *Historia del Narcotrafico en Mexico*. Mexico City: Random House.

Valencia, S. (2016) *Capitalismo gore. Control económico, violencia y narcopoder*. Mexico City: Paidos.

Valenzuela Aguilera, A. and Monroy Ortiz, R. (2014) Formal/informal/ilegal: Los tres circuitos de la economía espacial en América Latina. *Journal of Latin American Geography* 13 (1): 117–135.

van Houtum, H. and van Naerssen, T. (2002) Bordering, Ordering and Othering. *Tijdschrift Voor Economische En Sociale Geografie (Journal of Economic & Social Geography)* 93 (2): 125–136.

Vaughan, V. (2011) Valero named in case. *MySA*, 25 January. Available (consulted 5 December 5, 2016) at: https://www.mysanantonio.com/business/article/Valero-named-in-case-977320.php.

Velasco, J.L. (2005) *Insurgency, Authoritarianism and Drug Trafficking in Mexico's Democratization*. New York: Routledge.

Velazquez, C. (2011) Invaden veracruzanos frontera tamaulipeca, *RN Noticias*, 23 June. Available (consulted 12 August, 2015) at: http://www.rnnoticias.com.mx/nuevo-laredo/invaden-veracruzanos-frontera-tamaulipeca.

Vidal, G. (1984) *La Inflación en México*. Mexico: Editorial Nuestro Tiempo.

Villarreal, R. (2005) *Industrialización, Deuda y Desequilibrio Externo en México: Un en-foque macroindustrial y financiero*. Mexico: FCE.

Viswanatha, A. and Wolf, B. (2012) HSBC to Pay 1.9 Billion U.S. Fine in Money Laundering Case. *Reuters*, 10 December. Available (consulted 5 December, 2016) at: https://www .reuters.com/article/us-hsbc-probe/hsbc-to-pay-1-9-billion-u-s-fine-in-money-laundering-case-idUSBRE8BA05M20121211.

Vogt, W.A. (2013) Crossing Mexico: Structural Violence and the Commodification of Un-documented Central American Immigrants. *American Ethnologist*. 40 (4): 764–780.

von Benda-Beckmann, F., von Benda-Beckmann, K. and Griffiths, A.M.O. (2009) Space and Legal Pluralism: An Introduction. In: von Benda-Beckmann, F., von Benda-Beck-mann, K. and Griffiths, A.M.O. (eds.) *Spatializing Law: An Anthropological Geography of Law in Society*. Surrey, England: Ashgate, 1–30.

Vulliamy, E. (2012) Global Banks are the Financial Services Wing of the Drug Cartels. *The Guardian*, 21 July 21. Available (consulted 5 December, 2016) at: https://www.the guardian.com/world/2012/jul/21/drug-cartels-banks-hsbc-money-laundering.

Vulliamy, E. (2015) HSBC Has Form: Remember Mexico and Laundered Drug Money. *The Guardian*, 15 February. Available (consulted 5 December, 2016) at: https://www .theguardian.com/commentisfree/2015/feb/15/hsbc-has-form-mexico-laundered -drug-money.

Wacquant, L. (2009) *Punishing the Poor: The Neoliberal Government of Social Insecurity*. Durham NC: Duke University Press.

Wainwright, T. (2016) *Narconomics. How to Run a Drug Cartel*. New York: Public Affairs.

Watt, P. and Zepeda, R. (2013) *Drug War Mexico. Politics, Neoliberalism and Violence in the New Narcoeconomy*. London: Zed Books.

Webster, E., Lambert, R. and Bezuidenhout, A. (2008) *Grounding Globalization: Labor in the Age of Insecurity*. Malden, MA: Wiley-Blackwell.

Whalen, J. (2018) Trump's USMCA delivers Big Wins to Drugmakers, Oil Companies and Tech Firms. *The Washington Post*, 2 October. Available (consulted 4 November, 2018) at: https://www.washingtonpost.com/business/economy/trumps-usmca-delivers-big-wins-to-drugmakers-oil-companies-and-tech-firms/2018/10/02/ 2d68ad10-c66f-11e8-b1ed-1d2d65b86doc_story.html?noredirect=on&utm _term=.59b065bfb0d4.

White, R. (1992) *State, Class and the Nationalization of the Mexican Banks*. New York: Tay-lor and Francis.

WOLA (Washington Office for Latin America) Amnesty International; Centro de Derechos Humanos Miguel Agustín Pro Juárez (Centro Prodh); Centro de Derechos Humanos de la Montaña Tlachinollan; Ciudadanos en Apoyo de Derechos Humanos (CADHAC); Comisión Mexicana de Defensa y Promoción de los Derechos Humanos (CMDPDH); Fundar, Centro de Análisis e Investigación; Latin America Working Group (LAWG). 2018. *Civil Society Assessment of the Human Rights Situation in*

Mexico. Executive Summary of a Memo to the U.S. Department Of State Regarding Conditions On U.S. Assistance. Washington, July. Available (consulted 30 July, 2019) at: https://www.wola.org/wp-content/uploads/2018/07/EXECUTIVE-SUMMARY-2018-Merida-Memo.pdf.

Wolf, S. (2011) La Guerra de Mexico contra el Narcotrafico y la Iniciativa Merida: Piedras Angulares en la Búsqueda de Legitimidad. *Foro Internacional* 51 (4): 669–714.

World Bank (2019) Databank. Poblacion Urbana. Available (consulted 23 May, 2019) at: https://datos.bancomundial.org/indicador/SP.URB.TOTL.IN.ZS?end=2018&locations=MX&name_desc=false&start=1960&view=chart.

YoSoy17Reynosa (2017) *YoSoy17Reynosa Facebook page.* Facebook, 12 October. Available (consulted 13 September 2019) at: https://www.facebook.com/groups/1502356129996065/permalink/1802308030000872/.

Zárate Ruiz, A. (2014) Las Instancias de Justicia, la Impunidad y el Miedo. In: Zárate Ruiz A. (ed.) *Matamoros Violento II. La Legalidad en su Cultura y la Debilidad en sus Instituticones.* Tijuana: COLEF, 187–228.

Index

www.ingramcontent.com/pod-product-compliance
Lightning Source LLC
Chambersburg PA
CBHW070930030426
42336CB00014BA/2608